MURPHY'S LAW: LAWYERS

Wronging the Rights in the Legal Profession!

Arthur Bloch

Illustrated by Tom Glass

PSS!

PRICE STERN SLOAN
a member of Penguin Putnam Inc.
New York

Published by Price Stern Sloan
a member of Penguin Putnam Inc.
375 Hudson Street
New York, NY 10014

Library of Congress Cataloging-in-Publication Data

Bloch, Arthur, date.
Murphy's law: lawyers: wronging the rights in the legal
profession! / Arthur Bloch.
p. cm.
ISBN 0-8431-7580-X
1. Lawyers—Humor. 2. Law—Humor. I. Title.
PN6231.L4B59 2000   00-028288
818'.5402—dc 21
Printed in the United States of America
1 3 5 7 9 10 8 6 4 2

ACKNOWLEDGMENTS

Special thanks to the following for
their knowledgeable input and ideas:

Bill Egan
Paul Fogel
David Headley
Peter Hinton
Steven Mendelson
Claudia Shafer

CONTENTS

MURPHY'S LAW: LAWYERS

Introduction

In preparing material for the present volume I had occasion to interview a number of attorneys of various stripes and colors. One of these, a life-long public defender with 20 years of thankless experience, is now assigned to defend only those accused of the most serious criminal acts. He told me this story.

One of his clients, a confirmed recidivist, was charged with a violent and senseless murder. During the course of their first meeting the client asked repeatedly whether he (the attorney) believed that he (the client) was guilty of the crime.

After avoiding the question as long as he could, the defender said, "Look, it doesn't matter whether I believe you're guilty or innocent. My job is to get you the best deal possible; either to get you off, or to get you the shortest possible sentence."

"You mean you would defend me even if you thought I did it?" asked the defendant.

"Yes, I would."

"Gee," the criminal said, "I could never do that."

It is said that the trouble with lawyer jokes is that lawyers don't think they are funny, and others don't think they are jokes. It's hard to feel sorry for lawyers as a group—or individually for that matter—but they are certainly the most maligned of all professions earning more than $120,000 per year.

Like doctors (whose companion volume is being published simultaneously with this one), we are not pleased when we have to see one, but we are glad they are there when we need them.

This book contains laws for clients, for lawyers, for their secretaries, for clerks, for judges, in fact for anyone who has anything to do with the legal profession. That is, for all of us.

A.B., Oakland, January 2000

GENERAL MURPHOLOGY

MURPHY'S LAW:

If anything can go wrong, it will.

Corollaries:

1. Nothing is as easy as it looks.
2. Everything takes longer than you think it will.
3. If there is a possibility of several things going wrong, the one that will cause the most damage will be the one to go wrong.
4. If you perceive that there are four possible ways in which a procedure can go wrong, and circumvent these, then a fifth way will promptly develop.
5. Left to themselves, things tend to go from bad to worse.
6. Whenever you set out to do something, something else must be done first.
7. Every solution breeds new problems.
8. It is impossible to make anything foolproof because fools are so ingenious.
9. Mother nature is a bitch.

FARNSDICK'S COROLLARY TO THE FIFTH COROLLARY:

After things have gone from bad to worse, the cycle will repeat itself.

BENEDICT'S PRINCIPLE:

Nature always sides with the hidden flaw.

CHISHOLM'S FIRST LAW:

When things are going well, something will go wrong.

Corollaries:

1. When things just can't get any worse, they will.
2. Any time things appear to be going better, you have overlooked something.

CHISHOLM'S SECOND LAW:

Proposals, as understood by the proposer, will be judged otherwise by others.

GUMPERSON'S LAW:

The probability of anything happening is in inverse ratio to its desirability.

SODD'S FIRST LAW:

An entity attempting a task will be thwarted in that task by the unconscious intervention of some other presence, animate or inanimate. Nevertheless, some tasks are completed, since the intervening presence is itself attempting a task and is, of course, subject to interference.

SODD'S SECOND LAW:

Sooner or later, the worst possible set
of circumstances is bound to occur.

Corollary:

Any system must be designed to with-
stand the worst possible set of
circumstances.

SIMON'S LAW:

Everything put together falls
apart sooner or later.

LOFTA'S LAMENT:

Nobody can leave
well enough alone.

ALLEN'S LAW:

Almost anything is easier to
get into than to get out of.

FROTHINGHAM'S LAW:

Urgency varies inversely
with importance.

RUDIN'S LAW:

In crises that force people to choose among alternative courses of action, most people will choose the worst one possible.

GINSBERG'S THEOREMS:

1. You can't win.
2. You can't break even.
3. You can't even quit the game.

MURPHY'S LAW OF THERMODYNAMICS:

Things get worse under pressure.

PUDDER'S LAWS:

1. Anything that begins well, ends badly.
2. Anything that begins badly, ends worse.

SCHNATTERLY'S SUMMING UP OF THE COROLLARIES:

If anything can't go wrong, it will.

SILVERMAN'S PARADOX:

If Murphy's Law can go wrong, it will.

THE EXTENDED MURPHY'S LAW:

If a series of events goes wrong, it will do so in the worst possible sequence.

GATTUSO'S EXTENSION OF MURPHY'S LAW:

Nothing is ever so bad that it can't get worse.

NAGLER'S COMMENT ON THE ORIGIN OF MURPHY'S LAW:

Murphy's Law was not propounded by Murphy, but by another man of the same name.

**KOHN'S COROLLARY
TO MURPHY'S LAW:**

Two wrongs are only
the beginning.

**O'TOOLE'S COMMENTARY
ON MURPHY'S LAW:**

Murphy was an optimist.

MAAHS' LAW:

Things go right so they
can go wrong.

MURPHY'S UNCERTAINTY PRINCIPLE:

You can know something has gone wrong only when you make an odd number of mistakes.

TUSSMAN'S LAW:

Nothing is as inevitable as a mistake whose time has come.

LAW OF PROBABLE DISPERSAL:

Whatever hits the fan will not be evenly distributed.

GROSSMAN'S MISQUOTE OF H. L. MENCKEN:

Complex problems have simple, easy-to-understand wrong answers.

DUCHARME'S PRECEPT:

Opportunity always knocks at the least opportune moment.

HUNT'S LAW:

Every great idea has a disadvantage equal to or exceeding the greatness of the idea.

MURPHY'S TIME/ACTION QUANDARY:

You never know how soon it will be too late.

HANE'S LAW:

There is no limit to how bad
things can get.

PERRUSSEL'S LAW:

There is no job so simple that it
cannot be done wrong.

MAE WEST'S OBSERVATION:

To err is human, but it feels divine.

MESKIMEN'S LAW:

There's never time to do it right, but there's always time to do it over.

LAW OF SELECTIVE GRAVITY:

An object will fall so as to do the most damage.

Jennings' Corollary:

The chance of the bread falling with the buttered side down is directly proportional to the cost of the carpet.

O'BRIEN'S LAW:

Nothing is ever done for the right reasons.

MEYER'S LAW:

It is a simple task to make things complex, but a complex task to make them simple.

HLADE'S LAW:

If you have a difficult task, give it to a lazy man—he will find an easier way to do it.

JOSE'S AXIOM:

Nothing is as temporary as that which is called permanent.

Corollary:

Nothing is as permanent as that which is called temporary.

THE ROMAN RULE:

The one who says it cannot be done should never interrupt the one who is doing it.

BLAIR'S OBSERVATION:

The best laid plans of mice and men are usually about equal.

SEAY'S LAW:

Nothing ever comes out
as planned.

PATRY'S LAW:

If you know something can go
wrong, and you take due pre-
cautions against it, something
else will go wrong.

SCHRANK'S FIRST LAW:

If it doesn't work, expand it.

Corollary:
The greater the magnitude,
the less notice will be taken
that it does not work.

ROYSTER'S REFINEMENT OF MURPHY'S LAW:

When things go wrong somewhere, they are apt to go wrong everywhere.

LEAHY'S LAW:

If a thing is done wrong often enough, it becomes right.

ROTHMAN'S RULE:

When things go wrong, don't go with them.

TUDISCO'S ASYMMETRY PRINCIPLE:

Things go wrong all at once, but things go right gradually.

Corollary:

It takes no time at all to break something, but it takes forever to have something repaired.

MCNULTY'S RULE:

First things first, but not necessarily in that order.

KELLEY'S LAW:

Nothing is ever as simple as it first seems.

JONES' LAW OF EXPERIENCE:

Experience enables you to recognize a mistake when you make it again.

LEE'S LAW:

It takes less time to do something right than it takes to explain why you did it wrong.

IRENE'S LAW:

There is no right way to do the wrong thing.

FRESCO'S DISCOVERY:

If you knew what you were doing, you'd probably be bored.

Corollary:
Just because you're bored doesn't mean you know what you're doing.

CANNON'S CANON:

Experience is what causes you to make new mistakes instead of old ones.

MENCKEN'S MAXIM:

There's always an easy solution to every human problem—neat, plausible, and wrong.

LEGAL MURPHOLOGY

JEFFERSON'S PRESCIENT PRINCIPLE:

It is the trade of lawyers to question everything, to yield nothing, and to talk by the hour.

OPPENHEIMER'S PRECEPT:

Ignorance of the law does not prevent a losing lawyer from collecting his bill.

PARSONS' LAW:

In a town where one lawyer can't survive, two lawyers will thrive.

DALTON'S LAW:

A bad lawyer can let a case drag out for several years. A good lawyer can make it last even longer.

THE LAWYER-JOKE LAW:

The problem with lawyer jokes is that lawyers don't think they're funny, and nobody else thinks they're jokes.

DAVIS' DICTUM:

If half the lawyers would become plumbers, two of man's biggest problems would be solved.

GRIFFIN'S LAW:

If it weren't for lawyers, we wouldn't need them.

NAESER'S LAW:

You can make it foolproof, but you can't make it client-proof.

CHISHOLM'S DISTINCTION:

A contingency fee means that a lawyer who doesn't win your suit gets nothing. If the lawyer does win it, you get nothing.

DREW'S LAW OF PROFESSIONAL PRACTICE:

The client who pays the least complains the most.

MATSUI'S LAW OF BUSINESS CALLS:

The most persistent callers have the least important business.

MR. MENDELSON'S LAW:

Ten percent of your clients give you ninety percent of your grief.

OLSEN'S RULE OF MISSED OPPORTUNITY:

Your biggest case arrives right after you have committed your time to a smaller case.

G. DAVID'S LAW:

It doesn't matter if you win or lose . . . until you lose.

SID'S LAW:

You can't win them all if you don't win the first one.

SPENCER'S LAWS OF LAW:

1. Any lawyer can present a case given enough facts.
2. A good lawyer can present a case without enough facts.
3. A perfect lawyer can operate in perfect ignorance.

TRUMAN'S LAW:

If you cannot convince them, confuse them.

SWIPPLE'S RULE OF ORDER:

He who shouts loudest has the floor.

BALDRIDGE'S LAW:

If we knew what we were getting into we would never get into anything.

PHILO'S LAW:

To learn from your mistakes, you must first realize that you are making mistakes.

MAXIMS OF JURISPRUDENCE
(c. 1872):

1. When the reason for a rule ceases, so should the rule itself.

2. Anyone may waive the advantage of a law intended solely for his benefit. But a law established for a public reason cannot be contravened by a private agreement.

3. He who consents to an act is not wronged by it.

4. Acquiescence in error takes away the right of objecting to it.

5. No one can take advantage of his own wrong.

6. He who has fraudulently dispossessed himself of a thing may be treated as if he still had possession.

7. No one should suffer by an act of another.

8. He who can and does not forbid that which is done on his behalf, is deemed to have bidden it.

9. For every wrong there is a remedy.

10. The law never requires impossibilities.

MAXIMS OF JURISPRUDENCE
(c. 2000):

1. A proliferation of new laws creates a proliferation of new loopholes.

2. Nothing is illegal if a hundred business-men decide to do it.

3. You cannot sign away your right to sue.

4. Never admit your own part in anything that doesn't work.

5. The man who can smile when something goes wrong has thought of someone to blame it on.

6. Possession is nine-tenths of the law.

7. To err is human. To blame it on someone else is even more human.

8. Give all orders verbally. Never write down anything that might go into a "Pearl Harbor" file.

9. For every wrong, there is a lawyer.

10. Anything is possible if you don't know what you're talking about.

BOREN'S LAWS:

1. When in doubt, mumble.
2. When in trouble, delegate.
3. When in charge, ponder.

FUTILITY FACTOR:

No case is ever a complete failure—it can always serve as a negative example.

RUDNICK'S RULE:

Cases billed by the hour always last longer than contingency cases.

Compliments of
the author

FOGEL'S LAW OF APPEALS:

The landmark case, which is the basis of your appeal, will be overturned the day before your appeal.

Corollary:

You will not learn it has been overturned until the day after you present your case.

HINTON'S PRINCIPLE OF CLOSING ARGUMENTS:

If you clear time to prepare your closing argument, something will come up to occupy that time.

EVANS' AND BJORN'S LAW:

No matter what goes wrong,
there is always somebody who
knew that it would.

Legal Restatement:
No matter what goes wrong,
there is always an attorney
willing to sue.

HUMPHREY'S DISTINCTION:

The right to be heard does not
automatically include the right
to be taken seriously.

IRON LAW OF LIABILITY:

The degree of negligence varies directly with the depth of the pocket.

SCHAFFER'S TRUST LAWS:

1. The page missing from the trust will contain the dispositive clause.
2. If you put off your estate planning long enough, you won't need it.

KLIPPSTEIN'S FIRST LAW:

A patent application will be preceded by a similar application submitted one week earlier by an independent worker.

THE AWFUL TRUTH:

Estate planning is not intended to protect your heirs if you die. It is intended to protect your heirs *when* you die.

LAW OF PRODUCT LIABILITY:

Paranoia is healthy.
Cynicism is mandatory.

LANNING'S LAW:

Murphy's Law always hits at the worst time.

MAYNE'S LAW:

Nobody notices
the big errors.

MERCADO'S LAW:

After getting a client off on a grand theft auto charge, he will steal your car.

FIRST LAW OF DEBATE:

Never argue with a fool—people might not know the difference.

DE NEVERS' LAW OF LEGAL DEBATE:

Two monologues do not make a dialogue.

LAW OF LEGAL PRECEDENT:

Established precedent tends to persist in spite of new precedent.

CAESAR'S CODICIL:

All bad precedents began as justifiable measures.

BERYL'S SECOND LAW:

It's always easy to see both sides of an issue we are not particularly concerned about.

SCHROEDER'S LAW:

Indecision is the basis for flexibility.

WETHERN'S LAW OF SUSPENDED JUDGMENT:

Assumption is the mother of all screw-ups.

HUTCHINSON'S LAW:

If a situation requires undivided attention, it will occur simultaneously with a compelling distraction.

HORACE'S WARNING:

Beware of the superficially profound.

GARDENER'S PHILOSOPHY:

Brilliant opportunities are
cleverly disguised as insolvable problems.

Corollary:
The reverse is also true.

HERMAN'S LAW:

A good scapegoat is almost as good as a
solution.

THE KIBBITZER'S RULE:

It is much easier to suggest solutions when
you know nothing about the problem.

BIG AL'S LAW:

A good solution can be successfully applied to almost any problem.

BALZAC'S AXIOM:

Behind every great fortune, there is a crime.

LARSON'S LAW:

A lot of people mistake a short memory for a clear conscience.

DANNY'S RULE:

The best way to tell a lie is to cozy up to the truth.

THURBER'S LAW:

There is no safety in numbers,
or in anything else.

LA ROCHEFOUCAULD'S RULE:

We all have the strength to endure
the misfortune of others.

BIERCE'S DEFINITION:

A boor is a person who talks
when you wish him to listen.

LEVY'S FIRST LAW:

No amount of genius can overcome a preoccupation with detail.

LEVY'S SECOND LAW:

Only God can make a random selection.

GREEN'S LAW OF DEBATE:

Anything is possible if you don't know what you're talking about.

MCGUFFIN'S LAW:

It's easy to see the bright side of other people's problems.

LORD ELLENBOROUGH'S RULE:

The greater the truth, the greater the libel.

H. W. SHAW'S RULE:

A slander is like a hornet. If you cannot
kill it dead with the first blow,
better not strike at it.

A TWAIN OBSERVATION:

Good breeding consists of concealing
how much we think of ourselves and
how little we think of the other person.

PAINE'S POSTULATE:

A man may write himself out of
reputation when nobody else can do it.

DANISH PROVERB:

Lawyers and painters can soon
change white to black.

ABE LINCOLN'S ADVICE:

Discourage litigation. Persuade
your neighbor to compromise
whenever you can. There will still
be business enough.

RULE OF JOURNALISM:

"Off the record" comments aren't.

SPARK'S RULES FOR LAWYERS:

1. Strive to look tremendously important.

2. Speak with authority; however, only expound on the obvious and proven facts.

3. Listen intently while others are arguing the problem. Pounce on a trite statement and bury them with it.

4. If a subordinate asks you a pertinent question, look at him as if he has lost his sense. When he looks down, paraphrase the question back at him.

5. Walk at a fast pace when in the office—this keeps questions from subordinates and superiors at a minimum.

6. Always keep the office door closed. This puts visitors on the defensive and also makes it look as if you are always in an important conference.

RULE OF THE GREAT:
When the eminent attorney
you greatly admire and respect
appears to be thinking deep
thoughts, he is probably
thinking about lunch.

RULE OF LEGAL
ISO-MURPHISM:
No two legal situations
are identical.

THE SHOEMAKER'S
CHILDREN PRINCIPLE:
Law firms' corporate papers
are never in order.

LAW OF THE BUSINESS LUNCH:

A clean tie attracts
the soup of the day.

MURRAY'S LAW:

Don't believe everything you hear
or anything you say.

THE LIPPMAN LEMMA:

People specialize in their area
of greatest weakness.

JEROME'S RULE:

It is always the best policy to speak
the truth—unless of course you are
an exceptionally good liar.

GOLDSTICK'S RULE:

Be kind to everyone you talk
with. You never know who's
going to be on the jury.

ANDREW'S LAW:

Honesty is almost
the best policy.

LAW OFFICE LAWS

Slous' law:

If you do a job too well,
you will get stuck with it.

Clyde's law:

If you have something to
do and put it off long enough, chances are
that someone else will do it for you.

OWENS' LAW:

If you are good, you will be assigned all
the work. If you are really good, you will
get out of it.

SHAND'S LAW:

The more efficiently a project is done,
the greater the chance it will have to be
undone.

GROSSMAN'S LEMMA:

Any task worth doing was worth doing yesterday.

ADVANCED LAW OF THE SEARCH:

The first place to look for anything is the last place you would expect to find it.

BOOB'S LAW:

You always find something in the last place you look.

HAMPTON'S HOMILY:

The trouble with doing something right the first time is that nobody appreciates how difficult it was.

OIEN'S OBSERVATION:

The quickest way to find something is to start looking for something else.

MARYANN'S LAW:

You can always find what you're not looking for.

MCGEE'S FIRST LAW:

It's amazing how long it takes to complete something you are not working on.

OESER'S LAW:

There is a tendency for the person in the most powerful position in a law firm to spend all of his time serving on committees and signing letters.

PINTO'S LAW:

Do someone a favor and
it becomes your job.

LAWS OF PROCRASTINATION:

1. Procrastination shortens the job and places the responsibility for its termination on someone else (the authority who imposed the deadline).

2. It reduces anxiety by reducing the expected quality of the project from the best of all possible efforts to the best that can be expected given the limited time.

3. Status is gained in the eyes of others and in one's own eyes, because it is assumed that the importance of the work justifies the stress.

4. Avoidance of interruptions including the assignment of other duties usually can be achieved so that the obviously stressed worker can concentrate on the single effort.

5. Procrastination avoids boredom; one never has the feeling that there is nothing important to do.

6. It may eliminate the job if the need passes before the job can be done.

SIX LAWS OF
OFFICE MURPHOLOGY:

1. Important letters that contain no errors will develop errors in the mail.

2. Office machines that function perfectly during normal business hours will break down when you return to the office at night to use them for personal business.

3. Machines that have broken down will work perfectly when the person who repairs them arrives.

4. Envelopes and stamps that don't stick when you lick them will stick to other things when you don't want them to.

5. Vital papers will demonstrate their vitality by spontaneously moving from where you left them to where you can't find them.

6. The last person who quit or was fired will be held responsible for everything that goes wrong—until the next person quits or is fired.

JEROME'S LAW OF BUSINESS LETTERS:

If there are two possible ways to spell a person's name, you will pick the wrong spelling.

RULE OF THE INTERNAL CLOCK:

No document can be read clearly after 4:40 P.M. on Friday.

TILLIS' ORGANIZATIONAL PRINCIPLE:

If you file it, you'll know where it is, but you will never need it.

If you don't file it, you'll need it, but you will never know where it is.

TABLE OF
HANDY OFFICE EXCUSES:

1. That's the way we've always done it.
2. I didn't know you were in a hurry for it.
3. No one told me to go ahead.
4. I'm waiting for an OK.
5. How did I know this was different?
6. That's her job, not mine.
7. Wait 'til the boss comes back and ask her.
8. We don't make many mistakes.
9. I didn't think it was very important.
10. I'm so busy, I just can't get around to it.
11. I thought I told you.
12. I wasn't hired to do that.

SANDILAND'S LAW:

Free time that unexpectedly becomes available will be wasted.

ROSA'S LAW OFFICE LAWS:

1. Clients calling for appointments never have their appointment books in front of them.
2. The phone never rings until you've just dialed a number on the other line.

ROGERS' RULE OF THE BUSINESS LETTER:

Never ask two questions in a business letter. The reply will discuss the one you are least interested in and will say nothing about the other.

THE OFFICE MAXIM:

The phone never rings when you have nothing to do.

THE VOICE-MAIL PRINCIPLE:

Those whom the gods wish to destroy, they first put on hold.

GILLETTE'S LAW OF TELEPHONE DYNAMICS:

The phone call you've been waiting for comes the minute you leave the office.

RICHARD'S COMPLEMENTARY RULES OF OFFICE UTILITY:

1. If you keep anything long enough, you can throw it away.
2. If you throw anything away, you will need it as soon as it is no longer accessible.

BLOCH'S REBUTTAL TO BOOB'S LAW:

You always find something in the first place you look, but you never find it the first time you look there.

HEISENBERG'S UNCERTAINTY PRINCIPLE:

The location of all objects cannot be known simultaneously.

Corollary:
If a lost thing is found, something else will disappear.

LAW OF APPLIED CONFUSION:

After adding two weeks to the schedule for unexpected delays, add two more for the unexpected, unexpected delays.

JOHNSON'S LAW:

The number of minor illnesses among the employees is inversely proportional to the health of the firm.

PARKINSON'S FIRST LAW:

Work expands to fill the time available for its completion; the thing to be done swells in perceived importance and complexity in a direct ratio with the time to be spent on its completion.

THE EINSTEIN EXTENSION OF PARKINSON'S LAW:

A work project expands to fill
the space available.

Corollary:

No matter how large the workspace, if two
projects must be done at the same time,
they will require the use of the same part
of the workspace.

SCOTT'S LAW OF BUSINESS:

Never walk down a hallway without
a piece of paper in your hand.

CONNOR'S LAW:

If something is confidential, it
will be left in the copier
machine.

RINGWALD'S LAW OF OFFICE GEOMETRY:

Any horizontal surface
is soon piled up.

LAW OF UNRELIABILITY:

To err is human, but to really foul things up requires a computer.

GREER'S LAW:

A computer program does what you tell it to do, not what you want it to do.

BEISER'S COMPUTER AXIOM:

When putting it into memory, remember where you put it.

DeVRIES' DILEMMA:

If you hit two keys on the keyboard, the one you don't want appears on the screen.

GILB'S LAWS OF UNRELIABILITY:

1. Computers are unreliable, but humans are even more unreliable.

2. Any system that depends on human reliability is unreliable.

3. Undetectable errors are infinite in variety, in contrast to detectable errors, which by definition are limited.

4. Investment in reliability will increase until it exceeds the probable cost of errors, or until someone insists on getting some useful work done.

RECTOR'S LAW OF E-MAIL:

Typos are not noticed until after the "Send" button has been hit.

MURPHY'S COMPUTER SYSTEM DEFINITIONS:

Hardware: The parts of a computer system that can be kicked.

Software: The parts of a computer system that don't work.

Hard disk: The part of a computer system that freezes up at the worst possible time.

Peripherals: The parts that are incompatible with your computer system.

Printer: The part of the computer system that jams when you're not looking.

Cable: The part of the computer system that is too short.

Mouse: See *Cursing*.

Backup: An operation that is never performed on time.

Restore: A procedure that works perfectly until it is needed.

Memory: The part of a computer system that is insufficient.

Error message: A request to OK the destruction of your own data.

File: The part of the computer system that cannot be found.

Processor: The part of a computer system that is obsolete.

Manual: The element of your computer system that is incomprehensible.

BELINDA'S LAW:

The chance of a computer crash is directly proportional to the importance of the document that you are working on.

ROBBINS' RULE:

One good reason why computers can do more work than people is that they never have to stop and answer the phone.

CRAYNE'S LAW:

All computers wait at the same speed.

HOROWITZ'S RULE:

A computer makes as many mistakes in two seconds as twenty men in twenty years.

LAW OF REPAIR:

You can't fix it if it ain't broke.

THE PRINCIPLE CONCERNING MULTIFUNCTIONAL DEVICES:

The fewer functions a device is required to perform, the more perfectly it can perform those functions.

Applied to Contractual Agreements:

The fewer areas covered by the agreement, the more adequately those areas are covered.

SULLIVAN'S LEMMA:

Artificial intelligence is no match
for natural stupidity.

FIRST RULE OF
SUPERIOR INFERIORITY:

Don't let your superiors know
you're better than they are.

WHISTLER'S LAW:

You never know who's right, but you
always know who's in charge.

WEILER'S LAW:

Nothing is impossible for the one
who doesn't have to do it himself.

HARRISON'S
POSTULATE:

For every action, there is an equal
and opposite criticism.

CONWAY'S LAW:

In any organization there will always be one person who knows what is going on. This person must be fired.

STEWART'S LAW OF RETROACTION:

It is easier to get forgiveness than permission.

VAIL'S AXIOM:

In any human enterprise, work seeks the lowest hierarchical level.

LAW CLERK'S DILEMMA:

1. No matter how much you do, you'll never do enough.
2. What you don't do is always more important than what you do do.

LAW OF SOCIO-ECONOMICS:

In a hierarchical system, the rate of pay for a given task increases in inverse ratio to the unpleasantness and difficulty of the task.

EVAN'S LAW:

If you can keep your head when those around you are losing theirs, then you just don't understand the problem.

WILBERT'S LAW:

It's easier to criticize than to correct.

LAUNEGAYER'S OBSERVATION:

Asking dumb questions is easier than correcting dumb mistakes.

BRINTNALL'S LAW:

If you are given two contradictory orders, obey them both.

LANGSAM'S ORNITHOLOGICAL AXIOM:

It's difficult to soar with eagles when you work with turkeys.

GRANDE'S LAW:

Always do exactly what your boss would do if he knew what he was talking about.

THE FIRST PITFALL OF GENIUS:

No boss will keep an employee who is right all the time.

THEORY OF SELECTIVE SUPERVISION:

The one time in the day that you lean back and relax is the one time the boss walks through the office.

STRANO'S LAW:

When all else fails, try the boss's suggestion.

CHAPMAN'S LAW:

Don't be irreplaceable. If you can't be replaced, you can't be promoted.

THAL'S LAW:

For every vision, there is an equal and opposite revision.

FINAGLE'S RULE:

Teamwork is essential. It allows you to blame someone else.

TRUTHS OF MANAGEMENT:

1. Think before you act; it's not your money.
2. All good management is the expression of one great idea.
3. No executive devotes effort to proving himself wrong.
4. If sophisticated calculations are needed to justify an action, don't do it.

GOTTLIEB'S RULE:

The boss who attempts to impress employees with knowledge of intricate details has lost sight of the final objective.

**RUBENSTEIN'S
LAW OF PUNCTUALITY:**

> Being punctual means only
> that your mistake will be
> made on time.

BOGOVICH'S LAW:

> He who hesitates is probably right.

KUSHNER'S LAW:

The chances of anybody doing anything
are inversely proportional to the number
of other people who are in a position
to do it instead.

HECHT'S LAW:

There's no time like the present for
postponing what you don't want to do.

HARDIN'S LAW:

You can never do
just one thing.

DEHAY'S AXIOM:

Simple jobs always get put
off because there will be
time to do them later.

LAWS
OF CONTRACTS
AND
NEGOTIATION

KLINE'S RULE OF CONTRACT LAW:

The one document that is missing will contain the information upon which all other documents depend.

GRELB'S LAW OF ERRORS:

In any document, errors tend to occur at the opposite end from which you begin checking.

FINAGLE'S THIRD LAW:

In any document, the clause most obviously correct, beyond all need of checking, is the mistake.

Corollaries:

1. No one you ask for help will see it.
2. Everyone who stops by with unsought advice will see it immediately.

FINAGLE'S FOURTH LAW:

Once a job is fouled up, anything done to improve it only makes it worse.

GREEN'S RULE:

What the large print giveth,
the small print taketh away.

Corollaries:

1. Anything in bold can be ignored.

2. The smaller the print, the more
   carefully one should read a clause.

ROONEY'S RULE:

Nothing in fine print is ever good news.

FIRST LAW OF CONTRACT WRITING:

Never write that which you can cut and paste.

MORRIS' LAW OF EXPEDIENCE:

The easier an agreement is to reach, the harder it is to change.

EDDIE'S LAW OF BUSINESS:

Never conduct negotiations before 10:00 A.M. or after 4:00 P.M. Before ten you appear too anxious, and after four they think you're desperate.

UNIVERSAL LAWS
FOR NAIVE ENGINEERS
(ADAPTED FOR ATTORNEYS):

1. In any document, any error that can creep in will do so.

2. Any error in any document will be in the direction of most harm.

3. The best anticipation of future contingencies will not begin to meet those contingencies encountered in the real world.

4. The most vital element in any contract stands the greatest chance of being omitted.

5. If only one company can provide a necessary service, the price will be unreasonable.

6. All delivery promises must be multiplied by a factor of 2.0.

7. Major contract changes will always be requested after the negotiation is nearly completed.

8. If more than one person is responsible for an error, no one will be at fault.

KIM'S LAW OF CONTRACTS:

After an hour has been spent amending a sentence, someone will suggest deleting the paragraph.

HOLDEN'S LAW:

Many small, insignificant changes in a contract will be perceived as one large, unacceptable change.

CUNNINGHAM'S LAW OF CONTRACTS:

The party for whom proposed changes are unacceptable will be the last party to review the document.

MOORE'S DOCUMENT DICTUM:

In any document, the most egregious error will go unnoticed.

CULBERT'S CONTRACT PRINCIPLE:

The fatal omission will not be noticed until all parties have signed off.

LOOMIS' LAW OF DIVORCE:

Vindictiveness is not grounds for custody.

FOGEL'S RULE OF VERSION CONTROL:

If there are several versions of a document, the next-to-last draft will be the one that is submitted.

Corollary:
The submitted draft contains notes such as "How are we ever going to support this?"

FIRST LAW OF CONTRACT REVISION:

Information necessitating a change will be conveyed to the writer after—and only after—the contract is complete. (Often called the "Now they tell us!" Law.)

Corollary:
In simple cases, presenting one obvious right way versus one obvious wrong way, it is often wiser to choose the wrong way, so as to expedite subsequent revision.

SECOND LAW OF CONTRACT REVISION:

The more innocuous the modification appears to be, the further its influence will extend and the more the contract will have to be rewritten.

POLLARD'S RULE OF NEGOTIATION:

The perfect compromise language becomes apparent after both sides have generated such animosity that compromise is impossible.

REICH'S LAW OF CONTRACTS:

Anything that can be changed will be changed until there is no time left to change anything.

MILLER'S COMMENT:

This contract is so one-sided that I am astonished to find it written on both sides of the paper.

GOLDWYN'S RULE OF LAW:

A verbal contract isn't worth the paper it's written on.

GUALTIERI'S LAW OF INERTIA:

Where there's a will, there's a won't.

SANDERSON'S LAW:

Where there's a will, there's a lawyer.

MADISON'S RULE OF DIVORCE:

The briefer the courtship, the more contentious the divorce.

LAWS OF CONTRACT NEGOTIATIONS:

1. Each unacceptable offer has an equal and opposite unreasonable demand.
2. Any concession won is offset by a concession granted.

FIRST LAW OF NEGOTIATION:

A negotiation shall be considered successful if all parties walk away feeling screwed.

SCOTT'S FIRST LAW:

No matter what goes wrong, it will probably look right.

SCOTT'S SECOND LAW:

When an error has been detected and corrected, it will be found to have been correct in the first place.

Corollary:

After the correction has been found to be in error, it will be impossible to return the document to its original form.

HELGA'S RULE:

Say no, then negotiate.

COURTROOM
MURPHOLOGY

NELSON'S RULE OF JURISPRUDENCE:

In an adversarial proceeding, it is no one's job to argue the truth.

THUMB'S SECOND POSTULATE:

An easily understood, workable falsehood is more useful than a complex, incomprehensible truth.

DE BEAUMARCHAIS' MOTTO:

It is not necessary to understand things in order to argue about them.

WEBER'S MAXIM:

A single fact can spoil a good argument.

HANLON'S RAZOR:

Never attribute to malice that which is adequately explained by stupidity.

SPENCER'S POSTULATE:

A jury is a group of twelve people of average ignorance.

FIRST RULE OF ACTING
(AND OF LAW):

Whatever happens, look as if
it were intended.

HERTZBERG'S LAW
OF WING WALKING:

Never lose hold of what you've
got until you've got hold of
something else.

Legal Corollary:
Never abandon a line of
inquiry until you have a more
fruitful line of inquiry.

THE COURTROOM RULE:

People will believe anything
if you whisper it.

TWAIN ON FACTS:

Get your facts first, and then you can distort them as much as you please.

FIRST RULE OF CROSS EXAMINATION:

Never ask a question to which you don't know the answer.

SYRUS' AXIOM:

Not every question deserves an answer.

VOLTAIRE'S MAXIM:

A witty saying proves nothing.

**HALGREN'S
COURTROOM SOLUTION:**

When in trouble, obfuscate.

**GLYME'S FORMULA
FOR COURTROOM SUCCESS:**

The secret of success is sincerity. Once
you can fake that, you've got it made.

GILBERT'S LAW OF CROSS EXAMINATION:

One stupid question can ruin a good hour of interrogatory.

POWERS' PRINCIPLE:

If the law is on your side, pound on the law. If the facts are on your side, pound on the facts. If neither is on your side, pound on the table.

GROSS' RULE FOR ATTORNEYS:

If you have bad facts, argue the law; if you have a bad case on the law, argue the facts; and if your case has bad facts and bad law, get a big retainer!

MORTON'S LAW:

When it's time for oral arguments, you will lose your voice.

PEARS' POSTULATE:

A lawyer who begins a sentence with
"Frankly" is:
a) about to lie; or
b) about to accuse you of lying.

SOLOMON'S SOLUTION:

Always provide your adversary two
options, one of which is much worse than
the one you are seeking.

POTTER'S PARKING PRINCIPLE:

The person you beat out of a prime park-
ing spot will be the judge in your first case
of the day.

Corollary:
The driver you insulted will be foreman
of the jury.

DAVID'S TIMING TRUISM:

The judge you need a favor from went out on a limb in the case just prior to yours.

FISCHER'S LAW:

The judge in your most important case will be the one-night stand you don't remember.

BLOOMFIELD'S LAW:

The most far-reaching judicial decisions are written by the least senior law clerk.

GROSS' COURTROOM LAWS:

1. If you are early for a court appearance, the judge will be late; if you are late for a court appearance, the judge will be on time.
2. Even if your case is the first case on a long court calendar, it will be the last one heard—unless you are late.

TEMPLETON'S THEOREM:

Even the strongest of arguments can be nullified by an unfriendly jury instruction.

Corollary:
When the jury instruction favors your side, the jury will disregard the instruction.

BLOOM'S LAW:

The judge's jokes are always funny.

COURTNEY'S COURTHOUSE CODICIL:

The degree of attentiveness paid by the jury is inversely proportional to the importance of the evidence.

FROST ON THE COURTS:

Jury: Twelve people who determine which client has the better lawyer.

LAW OF JURY SELECTION:

Lessons learned in prior jury selection are useless for future jury selection.

Corollaries:
1. The only juror you are sure you don't want is a wealthy professional man.
2. High IQ in a juror is never in your defendant's interest.

LAW OF THE LIE:

No matter how often a lie is shown to be false, there will remain a percentage of people who believe it to be true.

Corollary:
That percentage will be represented on the jury.

LAW OF
THE COURTROOM:
You don't realize your fly is
open until you are standing
in front of the jury.

YOU KNOW YOU'RE IN TROUBLE WHEN:

a) The judge begins a sentence with "Do you really expect us to believe ..."

b) The jury applauds your opponent's opening argument.

c) The court reporter tells you to shut up.

d) The judge and your opponent call each other by their childhood nicknames.

PROOF TECHNIQUES:

1. Proof by referral to nonexistent authorities

2. Reduction ad nauseam

3. Proof by assignment

4. Method of least astonishment

5. Proof by hand-waving

6. Proof by intimidation

7. Method of deferral until later in the trial

8. Proof by reduction to a sequence of unrelated lemmas

9. Method of convergent irrelevancies

BLACKBURN'S RULE OF EMBARRASSMENT:

Your opponent's errors are always off the record. Your own errors are always in front of the jury.

TERRY'S TRIAL PRINCIPLE:

Your opponent's witnesses are always more credible than your witnesses.

JUDGE FANIN'S LAW:

Liability follows damages.

MENDELSON'S LAWS:

1. No case settles before it is fully billed.
2. There is no such thing as "our" attorney.

THE PROXIMITY PRINCIPLE:

Relations with your opposition are
frequently more cordial than relations
with your colleagues.

LAW OF DEFEAT:

Your worst defeat will be against
an attorney who learned law by
correspondence course.

SAX'S LAW:

If you own two briefcases,
you will take the wrong
one to court.

THE DEPOSITION DILEMMA:

The critical piece of information will not have been covered in the deposition.

PRATT'S POSTULATE:

The more effort you put into trial preparation, the greater the chance of a last-minute out-of-court settlement.

STEVEN'S LAW OF PERSONAL INJURY LAW:

If you can't see it on an X ray, it doesn't exist.

Corollary:

1. A broken bone that heals in six weeks is worth more than a permanent, inoperable neck injury.
2. Plaintiffs always forget their major complaint at the deposition.

TRUTHS OF COURTROOM DEMONSTRATIONS:

1. Realistic models aren't.
2. Medical illustrations don't.
3. Fail-proof demos do.

RULE OF COURTROOM PERVERSITY:

Mechanical demonstrations that worked perfectly in preparation for the trial will fail during the trial.

GROSS' TRIAL PREPARATION PRINCIPLE:

The more thoroughly you prepare for a trial, the greater the chance of a continuance.

MENDELSON'S TRIAL PRINCIPLES:

1. If you have two trials to prepare for and you prepare for only one, the other one goes to trial.

2. Your strongest witness won't be available at the time of trial.

Corollary:
If the witness is available, he will change his testimony at the last minute.

DIAMOND'S LAW OF MISTRIALS:

Mistrials only occur when you are winning your case.

ROTHMAN'S RULE OF EVIDENCE:

Admissibility of evidence varies inversely with its relevance.

STORRY'S PRINCIPLE OF CRIMINAL INDICTMENT:

The degree of guilt is directly proportional to the intensity of the denial.

MURPHY'S FIRST LAW FOR DEFENSE ATTORNEYS:

If a client asks you three times whether you believe he's innocent, he's guilty.

C. I. MORSE'S LAW:

There's a fifty/fifty chance that the one who found the body did the deed.

UNEQUAL RIGHTS LAW:

The worse the crime, the more the state will spend on defense.

Corollary:

A client wrongfully accused of shoplifting will receive no defense at all.

BIERCE'S DEFINITION:

Accuse: To affirm another's guilt or unworth; most commonly as a justification of ourselves for having wronged them.

AESCHYLUS' LOST PRINCIPLE:

Wrong must not win by technicalities.

VOLTAIRE'S COMMENT:

It is much more prudent to acquit two persons, though actually guilty, than to pass sentence of condemnation on one who is virtuous and innocent.

MURPHY'S SECOND LAW FOR DEFENSE ATTORNEYS:

The juror you fought hardest to retain will be the one hold out for conviction.

HEADLEY'S LAWS FOR PUBLIC DEFENDERS:

1. The better the deal offered to your guilty client, the more convinced he becomes of his own innocence.

2. The innocent client has the worst tattoos.

3. The one time you manage to seat a racially balanced jury, then:
   a) They are all Republicans;
   b) The case settles out of court; or
   c) Your client has a swastika tattooed on his forehead.

4. When you have an opportunity to let the jury know your client loves his dog, the dog will be a pit bull.

   Corollary:
   You didn't know it was a pit bull until the judge asks your client what kind of dog "Fluffy" is.

5. The more petty the crime, the more obnoxious the client.

6. Nice defendants do the most time.

MURPHY'S LAWS FOR DISTRICT ATTORNEYS:

1. Your most compelling evidence will be disallowed.

2. No matter how unambiguous the evidence, the defense will find an expert to refute it.

   Corollary:
   There will always be one juror who believes the expert.

3. If the police search was conducted legally, the evidence was compromised.

4. Your strongest evidence will be in areas that are not in dispute.

TRIAL LAWYER'S LAMENT:

The agony of defeat
lasts longer than the
flush of victory.

LAW OF SUPERCESSION:

In court, Murphy's
Law supercedes local,
state, and federal law.

LAWS
FOR CLIENTS

MURPHY'S LAW FOR CLIENTS:

No matter what goes wrong, there is always someone willing to sue.

GOLDENSTERN'S RULES:

1. Always hire a rich attorney.
2. Never buy from a rich salesman.

BERSANI'S LAW:

If a lawyer says, "I'm expensive," believe him.

GIBB'S LAW:

Infinity is one lawyer
waiting for another.

WILLIS' RULE FOR SUCCESS:

No successful attorney ever takes a phone call.

THE PRIME PRINCIPLE:

The quality of the attorney is more important than he quality of the case.

RODRIGUEZ'S RULE:

There is nothing as cynical in law as the expectation of good faith by the attorneys involved.

J.T.'S REMINDER:

It's seldom in your lawyer's interest
to settle.

MCKEVITT'S RULE:

The jury summons comes the one week
you have no excuse to get out of it.

MILLER'S LAW OF INSURANCE:

Insurance covers everything except
what happens.

BRALEK'S RULE FOR SUCCESS:

Trust only those who stand to lose as much as you when things go wrong.

VAN HERPEN'S LAW:

The solving of a problem lies in finding the solvers.

SUPREME COURT RULING:

A defendant is entitled to a fair trial but not a perfect one.

RUCKERT'S LAW:

There is nothing so small that it can't be blown out of proportion.

FOX ON PROBLEMATICS:

When a problem goes away, the people working to solve it do not.

SMITH'S LAW:

No real problem has a solution.

DRAZEN'S LAW OF RESTITUTION:

The time it takes to rectify a situation is inversely proportional to the time it took to do the damage.

BIG AL'S LAW:

A good solution can be successfully applied to almost any problem.

HOARE'S LAW OF LARGE PROBLEMS:

Inside every large problem is a small problem struggling to get out.

THE SCHAINKER CONVERSE TO HOARE'S LAW OF LARGE PROBLEMS:

Inside every small problem is a larger problem struggling to get out.

JONES' LAW:

The man who can smile when
something goes wrong has thought
of someone to blame it on.

JACOB'S LAW:

To err is human—to blame
it on someone else is even
more human.

MALEK'S LAW:

Any simple legal notion will be worded
in the most complicated way.

MASON'S RULE
OF CONTRACTS:

Always have your own attorney
write the first draft.

Corollary:

Never sign a contract written by the
other party's attorney.

LUPOSCHAINSKY'S HURRY-UP-AND-WAIT PRINCIPLES:

1. If you're early for your appointment, it will be canceled.
2. If you knock yourself out to be on time, you will have to wait.
3. If you're late, you will be too late.

MISHLOVE'S LAW:

Never trust a lawyer who says he just slapped something together.

GROSS' LAW FOR CLIENTS:

The more times a client changes attorneys, the worse the case.

MCDOWELL'S
LAW OF CAPITAL
PRESERVATION:
Never let your attorney know how
much money you have.

LAWS OF LAWMAKING AND GOVERNMENT

RODHAM'S RULE:

Having lawyers make laws
is like having doctors make
diseases.

POLIS' LAW:

Any law enacted with more
than fifty words contains at
least one loophole.

COOPER'S METALAW:

A proliferation of new laws
creates a proliferation of new
loopholes.

SWIFT'S LAW:

Laws are like cobwebs: They may catch small flies, but the wasps and hornets break through.

DE MONTESQUIEU'S RULE:

The wording of laws should mean the same thing to all men.

DEFOE'S DICTUM:

Law is but a heathen word for power.

A. C. POWELL'S POSTULATE:

A man's respect for law and order exists in precise relationship to the size of his paycheck.

OAK'S PRINCIPLES OF LAWMAKING:

1. Law expands in proportion to the resources available for its enforcement.
2. Bad law is more likely to be supplemented than repealed.
3. Social legislation cannot repeal physical laws.

MARSHALL'S FIRST LAW OF THE LEGISLATURE:

Never let the facts get in the way of a carefully thought out bad decision.

MIRAGLIA'S RULE OF LAW:

Never make a major policy change based on a close vote.

HELLMAN'S HOMILY:

We do not have to agree with people to defend them from injustice.

FULLER'S RULE OF LAW:

The more laws, the more offenders.

LAW OF LEGISLATIVE ACTION:

The length of time it takes a bill to pass through the legislature is in inverse proportion to the number of lobbying groups favoring it.

UNDERLYING PRINCIPLE OF LAW:

Anything not expressly forbidden is permitted.

ANDREW YOUNG'S RULE:

Nothing is illegal if a hundred businessmen decide to do it.

ANONYMOUS AXIOM:

In a thousand pounds of law there's not an ounce of love.

BERGEN'S LAW:

There's nothing worse than a stupid law.

SPRECHT'S RULE OF LAW:

Under any conditions, anywhere, whatever you are doing, there is some ordinance under which you can be booked.

MCCANDLISH'S LAW OF UNJUST BUREAUCRACY:

Any system of justice in which ignorance of the law is no excuse, but in which there are too many laws for any one person to know and remember, is by definition unjust.

MURPHY'S LAW OF GOVERNMENT:

If anything can go wrong,
it will do so in triplicate.

BISMARCK'S SAUSAGE PRINCIPLE:

People who love sausage and respect
the law should never watch either
one being made.

JACQUIN'S POSTULATE ON DEMOCRATIC GOVERNMENT:

No person's life, liberty, or property is
safe while the legislature is in session.

**MARTIN LUTHER KING JR.'S
OBSERVATION:**
Injustice anywhere is a threat
to justice everywhere.

JUAREZ'S THIRD LAW:
A plea for justice is often
a claim for injustice in
one's own favor.

THE FIFTH RULE OF POLITICS:
When a politician gets an idea,
he usually gets it wrong.

WILLKIE'S LAW:

A good slogan can stop
analysis for fifty years.

GOETHE'S OBSERVATION:

Laws are inherited
like diseases.

TODD'S POLITICAL PRINCIPLES:

1. No matter what they're
   telling you, they're not
   telling you the whole truth.
2. No matter what they're
   talking about, they're talking
   about money.

THE WATERGATE PRINCIPLE:

Government corruption is always
reported in the past tense.

FRANCE'S
RULE OF FOLLY:

If a million people believe a foolish thing,
it is still a foolish thing.

SANTAYANA'S
OBSERVATION:

Fanaticism consists of redoubling your
efforts when you have forgotten your aim.

DUCK'S
POLITICAL PRINCIPLE:

Any campaign reform only lasts until
the powers regroup.

GROVE'S GUIDING PRINCIPLE:

Legislation is never intended to guide the man with vision. But it should protect that vast majority which is without it.

SPANDER'S LEMMA:

The great thing about democracy is that it gives every voter a chance to do something stupid.

HORACE'S POLITICAL PRINCIPLE:

If voting could change anything, there would be a law against it.

GOOD'S RULE FOR DEALING WITH BUREAUCRACIES:

When the government bureau's remedies do not match your problem, you modify the problem, not the remedy.

KATZ'S LAW:

Men and nations will act rationally when all other possibilities have been exhausted.

THE GOLDEN RULE OF ARTS AND SCIENCES:

Whoever has the gold makes the rules.

THE THREE LEAST CREDIBLE SENTENCES IN THE ENGLISH LANGUAGE:

1. "The check is in the mail."
2. "Of course I'll respect you in the morning."
3. "I'm from the government and I'm here to help you."

MAIN'S LAW:

For every action there is an equal and opposite government program.

CAMERON'S LAW:

An honest politician is one who, when bought, will stay bought.

BROWN'S RULES OF LEADERSHIP:

1. To succeed in politics, it is often necessary to rise above your principles.
2. The best way to succeed in politics is to find a crowd that's going somewhere and get in front of them.

MILES' LAW:

Where you stand depends on where you sit.

FIBLEY'S EXTENSION TO MILES' LAW:

Where you sit depends on who you know.

WALTON'S LAW OF POLITICS:

A fool and his money
are soon elected.

**PARKER'S LAW OF
POLITICAL STATEMENTS:**

The truth of any
proposition has nothing to do
with its credibility and vice versa.

AMERINGER'S AXIOM:

Politics is the gentle art of getting votes from the poor and campaign funds from the rich by promising to protect each from the other.

ADLER'S RULE:

It is easier to fight for one's principles than to live up to them.

BOOKER T. WASHINGTON'S RULE:

You can't hold a man down without staying down with him.

ARMEY'S AXIOM:

You can't get ahead while getting even.

LOVKA'S FIRST
POLITICAL PRINCIPLE:

There is no sincerity like a
politician telling a lie.

PEROT'S OBSERVATION:

The only thing most politicians stand for is reelection.

NOWLAN'S LAW:

Following the path of least resistance is what makes politicians and rivers crooked.

SHAFFER'S LAW:

The effectiveness of a politician varies in inverse proportion to his commitment to principle.

HUNTER'S LAW:

No matter how dishonorable, every politician considers himself honorable.

WILSON'S LAW OF POLITICS:

If you want to make enemies, try to change something.

TUPPER'S POLITICAL POSTULATE:

Those who sit astride the fence have few directions from which to choose.

ABOUREZK'S LAWS OF POLITICS:

1. Don't worry about your enemies. It's your allies who will do you in.
2. The bigger the appropriations bill, the shorter the debate.
3. If you want to curry favor with a politician, give him credit for something that someone else did.

POLITICAL POLLSTER'S RULES:

1. When the polls are in your favor, flaunt them.
2. When the polls are overwhelmingly unfavorable (a) ridicule and dismiss them; or (b) stress the volatility of public opinion.
3. When the polls are slightly unfavorable, play for sympathy as a struggling underdog.
4. When too close to call, be surprised at your own strength.

POULOS' POLITICAL COROLLARY:
A good slogan beats
a good solution.

GALBRAITH'S LAW OF POLITICS:
Anyone who says he isn't
going to resign, four times,
definitely will.

NEWMAN'S RULE:
Crime does not pay…
as well as politics.

KILPATRICK'S COMMENT:

We have surrendered the silly notion that politicians should be above politics.

LBJ'S LAW:

If two men agree on everything, you may be sure that only one of them is doing the thinking.

HEINE'S LAW:

One should forgive one's enemies,
but not before they are hanged.

HOWE'S LAW:

There is some advice that is too good—
the advice to love your enemies,
for example.

LAWRENCE'S LAW:

A diplomat is someone who can tell you
to go to hell in such a way that you will
look forward to the trip.

FROST ON DIPLOMACY:

A diplomat is a man who always
remembers a woman's birthday
but never her age.

POTTER'S LAW:

A rumor doesn't gain credence
until it's officially denied.

CALVIN COOLIDGE'S COMMENT:

You don't have to explain
something you never said.

EVAN'S LAW:

Once you give up integrity,
the rest is easy.

NAPOLEON'S OBSERVATION:

Rascality has limits;
stupidity has not.

THOMAS JEFFERSON'S RULE:
Delay is preferable to error.

SYRUS' LEADERSHIP PRINCIPLE:
Anyone can hold the helm
when the sea is calm.

PODNOS' LAW:
One is tolerant only of that
which does not concern him.

LEGAL
RESEARCHMANSHIP
AND
LAW SCHOOL LAWS

FORDHAM'S RULE OF RESEARCH:

The larger your law library,
the longer it takes to discover
that you don't have what
you need.

GORDON'S LAW:

If a research project is not
worth doing at all, it is not
worth doing well.

MURPHY'S LAW OF RESEARCH:

Enough research will tend to support your client's position.

FELSON'S LAW:

To steal ideas from one person is plagiarism; to steal from many is research.

WILLIAMS AND HOLLAND'S LAW:

If enough data is collected, anything may be proven by statistical methods.

DARROW'S COMMENT ON HISTORY:

History repeats itself. That's one of the things wrong with history.

THOMPSON'S PROPOSAL:

Any proposal can be made to fit any fact by incorporating additional assumptions.

FIRST LAW OF LEGAL PROGRESS:

The advance of jurisprudence can be measured by the rate at which exceptions to previously held laws accumulate.

Corollaries:

1. Exceptions always outnumber rules.
2. There are always exceptions to established exceptions.
3. By the time one masters the exceptions, no one recalls the rules to which they apply.

SOUDER'S LAW OF SCIENCE:
Repetition does not establish validity.

The Legal Exception:
Precedence implies validity.

HORWOOD'S SIXTH LAW:
If you have the right data,
you have the wrong problem.

MAIER'S LAW:
If the facts do not conform to your
position, they must be disposed of.

PRIMARY RULE OF HISTORY:

> History doesn't repeat itself—
> historians merely repeat
> each other.

PAVLU'S RULES
FOR ECONOMY IN RESEARCH:

1. Deny the last established
   truth on the list.
2. Add yours.
3. Pass the list.

COLEMAN'S
COMMENTARY
ON SANTAYANA:

Those who fail to learn from the past are
condemned to repeat history class.

BATES' LAW OF LEGAL RESEARCH:

Research is the process of going up
alleys to see if they're blind.

PERSIG'S POSTULATE:

The number of rational hypotheses
that can explain any given phenomenon
is infinite.

MR. COOPER'S LAW:

If you do not understand a particular word
in a piece of legal writing, ignore it. The
piece will make perfect sense without it.

Bogovich's Corollary:

If the piece makes no sense without the
word, it will make no sense with the word.

HARPER'S MAGAZINE LAW:

You never find an article until you replace it.

DUGGAN'S LAW OF LEGAL RESEARCH:

The most valuable quotation will be the one for which you cannot determine the source.

Corollary:

Your opponent will know the correct attribution of the quotation—and the context which makes it inapplicable to your case.

DOLIN'S LAW OF RESEARCH:

The library will have every back issue of a journal except for the issue you need for your research.

WEINER'S LAW OF LIBRARIES:

There are no answers, only cross-references.

HANSEN'S LIBRARY AXIOM:

The closest library doesn't have the material you need.

MURPHY'S RULE OF THE TERM PAPER:

The book or periodical most vital to the completion of your term paper will be missing from the library.

Corollary:
If it is available, the most important page will be torn out.

SEIT'S LAW OF HIGHER EDUCATION:

The one course you must take to graduate will not be offered during your last semester.

LAWS OF CLASS SCHEDULING:

1. If the course you wanted most has room for "n" students, you will be the "n+1" to apply.

2. Class schedules are designed so that every student will waste maximum time between classes.

   Corollary:
   When you are occasionally able to schedule two classes in a row, they will be held in classrooms at opposite ends of the campus.

3. A prerequisite for a desired course will be offered only during the semester following the desired course.

ROMINGER'S RULES FOR STUDENTS:

1. The more general the title of a course, the less you will learn from it.
2. The more specific a title is, the less you will be able to apply it later.

NATALIE'S LAW:

You never catch on until after the test.

THE STUDENT'S TAUTOLOGY:

The teacher is never absent on the day of the exam.

PRESCHER'S LAW OF EXAMS:

If you don't know the answer, someone will ask the question

LAWS OF
APPLIED TERROR:

1. When reviewing your notes before an exam, the most important ones will be illegible.

2. The more studying you did for the exam, the less sure you are as to which answer they want.

3. Eighty percent of the final exam will be based on the one lecture you missed about the book you didn't read.

4. The night before the contracts midterm, your Ethics instructor will assign two hundred pages on corporate conduct.

   Corollary:
   Every instructor assumes that you have nothing else to do, except study for their course.

5. If you are given an open-book exam, you will forget your book.

   Corollary:
   If you are given a take-home exam, you will forget where you live.

6. At the end of the semester, you will recall having enrolled in a course at the beginning of the semester—and never attending.

MEREDITH'S LAW FOR LAW SCHOOL SURVIVAL:

Never let your professor know
that you exist.

KISSINGER'S AXIOM:

University politics are vicious precisely
because the stakes are so small.

BAXTER'S LAW:

An error in the premise will appear
in the conclusion.

GROYA'S LAW:

What we learn after we know
it all is what counts.

BARRY'S RULE:

If you stop to think, remember
to start again.

STEINER'S PRECEPTS:

1. Knowledge based on external evidence is unreliable.
2. Logic can never decide what is possible or impossible.

FEINBERG'S PRINCIPLE:

Memory serves its own master.

YOUNG'S LAW:

It is when you trip over your own shoes that you start picking up shoes.

PLUTARCH'S RULE:

It is impossible for anyone to learn that which one thinks one already knows.

LEGAL
EXPERTSMANSHIP

HIRAM'S LAW:

If you consult enough experts, you can confirm any opinion and support any position.

WEINBERG'S COROLLARY:

An expert is a person who avoids the small errors while sweeping on to the grand fallacy.

MARS' RULE:

An expert is anyone from out of town.

REYNOLDS' LAW OF EXPERTISE:

The further the expert witness has traveled to testify, the more he will be believed.

AKERS' LAW:

Your expert witness will demonstrate his expertise by equivocating during the trial.

BOHR'S LAW:

An expert is someone who has made all of the possible mistakes in a very narrow field of study.

GIOIA'S THEORY:

The person with the least expertise has the most opinions.

RUDNICKI'S RULE OF THE LEGAL EXPERT:

Only someone who understands something absolutely can explain it so no one else can understand it.

WEBER'S DEFINITION:
An expert is one who knows more and more about less and less until he knows absolutely everything about nothing.

RYAN'S LAW:
Make three correct guesses consecutively and you will establish yourself as an expert.

GRIFFIN'S LAW:

Statistics are a logical and precise
method for saying a half-truth
inaccurately.

UTVICH'S LAW:

One accurate
measurement is
worth a thousand expert opinions.

VAN ROY'S
FIRST LAW:

If you can distinguish between good advice
and bad advice, then you don't need advice.

DE NEVERS' LAW:

Never speculate on that which
can be known for certain.

MANLY'S MAXIM:
Logic is a systematic method of
coming to the wrong conclusion
with confidence.

LA GUARDIA'S LAW:

Statistics are like expert
witnesses—they will testify
for either side.

FIRST RULE OF
APPLIED MATHEMATICS:

Ninety-eight percent
of all statistics
are made up.

HENDERSON'S LAW:

The less you say, the less
you have to retract.

BILLING'S LAW:

Silence is one of the hardest
things to refute.

FAHNSTOCK'S LAW OF DEBATE:

Any issue worth debating
is worth avoiding altogether.

HARTZ'S LAW OF RHETORIC:

Any argument carried far enough
will end up in semantics.

THE MUNROE DOCTRINE:

A little inaccuracy sometimes saves tons of explanation.

HUTCHINS' LAW:

You can't outtalk a man who knows what he's talking about.

TATMAN'S RULE:

Always assume that your assumption is invalid.

MULLINS' OBSERVATION:

Indecision is the
key to flexibility.

WHITEHEAD'S RULE:

Seek simplicity,
and distrust it.

COUVIER'S LAW:

There is nothing more frightening
than ignorance in action.

ULMANN'S RAZOR:

When stupidity is a sufficient
explanation, there is no need to
have recourse to any other.

MILLER'S LAW:

You can't tell how deep a puddle is
until you step in it.

Segal's law:

A man with one watch knows
what time it is.

A man with two watches is never sure.

Clarke's law
of revolutionary
ideas:

Every revolutionary area—in science,
politics, art, or whatever—evokes three
stages of reaction. They may be summed up
by the three phrases:

1. "It is impossible—don't waste my time."
2. "It is possible, but it is not worth doing."
3. "I said it was a good idea all along."

CLARKE'S FIRST LAW (ADAPTED):

When a distinguished but elderly lawyer states that something is possible, he is almost certainly right. When he states that something is impossible, he is very probably wrong.

JONES' LAW OF ACCOMPLISHMENT:

Anyone who makes a significant contribution to any field of endeavor, and stays in that field long enough, becomes an obstruction to its progress—in direct proportion to the importance of his original contribution.

VON NEUMANN'S AXIOM:
There's no sense in being precise when you don't know what you're talking about.

LUNSFORD'S RULE OF LEGAL CONSULTATION:
The simple explanation always follows the complex solution.

TUCKER'S COMMENT:
It makes sense, when you don't think about it.

PHILLIPS' RULE:
The best defense against logic is ignorance.

LEGAL
ACCOUNTSMANSHIP

EMERY'S LAW:

Regulation is the substitution
of error for chance.

CLARK'S LAW:

When a lot of people are doing
something stupid, the reason for it
will be found in the tax laws.

HARNER'S TAX PRECEPT:

If tax law requires a choice
between two options, it will
become apparent that you made
the wrong choice only after it is
too late to change that choice.

BISHOP'S TAX LAW LAW:

Changes in tax law occur either too early or too late for you to take advantage of them.

BLACKWELL'S AUDIT PRINCIPLE:

The tax audit will occur for the year of your biggest error.

O'BRIEN'S PRINCIPLE (THE $357.73 THEORY):

Tax examiners always reject any item with a bottom line divisible by five or ten.

Buckwald's Law:

As the economy gets better, everything else gets worse.

Wiker's Law:

Government expands to absorb revenue and then some.

Westheimer's Rule:

To estimate the time it takes to do a task: Estimate the time you think it should take, multiply by two, and change the unit of measure to the next highest unit. Thus we allocate two days for a one-hour task.

THE GUPPY LAW:

When outrageous expenditures are divided finely enough, the public will not have enough of a stake in any one expenditure to squelch it.

Corollary:
Enough guppies can eat a treasury.

SPENCER'S LAWS OF ACCOUNTANCY:

1. Trial balances don't.
2. Working capital doesn't.
3. Liquidity tends to run dry.
4. Return on investments won't.

GRESHAM'S LAW:

Trivial matters are handled promptly; important matters are never solved.

LYNDON'S LAW:

Kickbacks must always exceed bribes.

BRIEN'S LAW:

At some time in the life cycle of virtually every organization, its ability to succeed in spite of itself runs out.

LAW OF INSTITUTIONS:

The opulence of the front-office decor varies inversely with the fundamental solvency of the firm.

EDWARDS'
TIME/EFFORT LAW:

Effort x Time = Constant

a) Given a large initial time to do something, the initial effort will be small.

b) As time goes to zero, effort goes to infinity.

Corollary:

If it weren't for the last minute, nothing would get done.

HERTZ'S RULE:
The richer the client, the greater
the display of distaste when
receiving the bill.

SPINOLA'S BUDGET PRINCIPLE:

A budget is just a method of worrying before you spend money, as well as after.

CADE'S LAW OF BUDGETING:

The larger the budget, the less effectively the funds are allocated.

THE 90/90 RULE OF PROJECT SCHEDULES:

The first 90 percent of the task takes 10 percent of the time, and the last 10 percent takes the other ninety.

WINGFIELD'S AXIOM:

Accuracy is the sum total of your compensating mistakes.

INSURANCE COMPANY DICTUM:

Millions for defense, but not one cent for damages.

PARKS' LAW OF INSURANCE RATES AND TAXES:

Whatever goes up, stays up.

JUHANI'S LAW:

The compromise will always be more expensive than either of the suggestions it is compromising.

FIRST LAW OF MONEY DYNAMICS:

A surprise monetary windfall will be accompanied by an unexpected expense of the same amount.

HORNGREN'S OBSERVATION:

Among economists, the real world is often a special case.

GLYNN'S LAW:

The amount of aggravation inherent in a business transaction is inversely proportional to the profit.

THE RULE OF ESTATE DIVISION:

Items most difficult to divide or liquidate will not have been accounted for in the will.

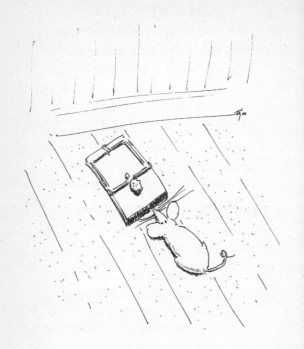

CRANE'S LAW:
There ain't no such thing
as a free lunch.

LEGAL
BUREAUCRACTICS
AND
HIERARCHIOLOGY

THE PITFALLS OF GENIUS:

No boss will keep an employee who is right all the time.

AIGNER'S AXIOM:

No matter how well you perform your job, a superior will seek to modify the results.

ROGERS' RULE:

Authorization for a project will be granted only when none of the authorizers can be blamed if the project fails but when all of the authorizers can claim credit if it succeeds.

JR. PARTNER'S LAW OF REWARD:

The one who does the least work
will get the most credit.

Corollary:
Your best ideas are immediately adopted
by the senior partners as their own.

GATES' LAW:

The only important information in
a hierarchy is who knows what.

WILSON'S LAW:

A person's rank is in inverse relation
to the speed of his speech.

GRIZZARD'S SLED-DOG PRINCIPLE:

Only the lead dog gets a change of scenery.

THE BUREAUCRACY PRINCIPLE:

Only a bureaucracy can fight a bureaucracy.

PARKINSON'S LAW OF BUREAUCRATIC DELAY:

Delay is the deadliest form of denial.

JOE'S LAW:

Your inside contact in the organization is the first person to be let go in the reorganization.

FOX ON BUREAUCRACY:

A bureaucracy can outwait anything.

Corollary:
Never get caught between two bureaucracies.

HOFFSTEDT'S EMPLOYMENT PRINCIPLE:

Confusion creates jobs.

SOPER'S LAW:

Any bureaucracy reorganized to enhance efficiency is immediately indistinguishable from its predecessor.

OWEN'S THEORY OF ORGANIZATIONAL DEVIANCE:

Every organization has an allotted number of positions to be filled by misfits.

Corollary:

Once a misfit leaves, another will be recruited.

MOLLISON'S BUREAUCRACY HYPOTHESIS:

If an idea can survive a bureaucratic review and be implemented, it wasn't worth doing.

JACOBSON'S LAW:

The less work an organization produces, the more frequently it reorganizes.

MCCARTHY'S MAXIM:

The only thing that saves us from
the bureaucracy is its inefficiency.

COURTOIS' RULE:

If people listened to themselves more often, they would talk less.

SWEENEY'S LAW:

The length of a progress report is inversely proportional to the amount of progress.

MORRIS' LAW OF LEGAL CONFERENCES:

The most interesting paper will be scheduled simultaneously with the second most interesting paper.

COLLINS' CONFERENCE
PRINCIPLE:

The speaker with the most
monotonous voice speaks
after the big meal.

TRAHEY'S LAW:

Never dump a good idea on a
conference table. It will belong
to the conference.

LACKLAND'S LAWS:

1. Never be first.
2. Never be last.
3. Never volunteer for anything.

LAW OF TRIVIALITY:

The time spent on any item of the
agenda will be in inverse proportion
to the sum involved.

ACHESON'S RULE OF THE BUREAUCRACY:

A memorandum is written not to inform
the reader but to protect the writer.

PLANER'S RULE:

An exception granted becomes a right
expected the next time it is requested.

ENGLE'S LAW:

When you stand up to be counted,
someone will take your seat.

GOURD'S AXIOM:

A meeting is an event at which
the minutes are kept and the
hours are lost.

OLD AND KAHN'S LAW:

The efficiency of a committee meeting
is inversely proportional to the
number of participants and the time
spent on deliberations.

SHANAHAN'S LAW:

The length of a meeting rises
with the square of the number
of people present.

MITCHELL'S LAWS
OF COMMITTOLOGY:

1. Any simple problem can be made insoluble if enough conferences are held to discuss it.

2. Once the way to screw up a project is presented for consideration, it will invariably be accepted as the soundest solution.

3. After the solution screws up the project, all those who initially endorsed it will say, "I wish I had voiced my reservations at the time."

MATILDA'S LAW OF SUBCOMMITTEE FORMATION:

If you leave the room, you're elected.

KENNEDY'S COMMENT ON COMMITTEES:

A committee is twelve people doing the work of one.

COBLITZ'S LAW:

A committee can make a decision that is dumber than any of its members.

THE ABILENE PARADOX:

People in groups tend to agree on courses of action which, as individuals, they know are stupid.

KIRBY'S COMMENT ON COMMITTEES:

A committee is the only life form with twelve stomachs and no brain.

LAW OF COMMITTO-DYNAMICS:

Those most opposed to serving on committees are made chairpersons.

CHAPMAN'S COMMITTEE RULES:

1. Never arrive on time, or you will be stamped a beginner.

2. Don't say anything until the meeting is half over; this stamps you as being wise.

3. Be as vague as possible; this prevents irritating others.

4. When in doubt, suggest that a sub-committee be appointed.

5. Be the first to move for adjournment; this will make you popular—it's what everyone is waiting for.

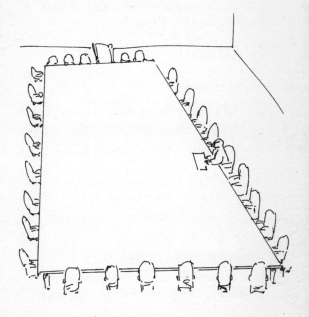

PHILLIP'S LAW OF COMMITTEE PROCEDURE:

The only changes that are easily adopted are changes for the worse.

PARKER'S RULE OF PARLIAMENTARY PROCEDURE:

A motion to adjourn is always in order.

MCKERNAN'S MAXIM:

Those who are unable to learn from past meetings are condemned to repeat them.

ADVANCED MURPHOLOGY

TYLCZAK'S PROBABILITY POSTULATE:

Random events tend to occur in groups.

ZYMURGY'S LAW OF EVOLVING SYSTEMS DYNAMICS:

Once you open a can of worms, the only way to recan them is to use a larger can.

COIT-MURPHY'S STATEMENT ON THE POWER OF NEGATIVE THINKING:

It is impossible for an optimist to be pleasantly surprised.

THE CARDINAL CONUNDRUM:

An optimist believes we live in the best of all possible worlds.
A pessimist fears this is true.

HIGDON'S LAW:

Good judgment comes from bad experience. Experience comes from bad judgment.

OGDEN NASH'S LAW:

Progress may have been all right once, but it went on too long.

SIMON'S LAW OF DESTINY:

Glory may be fleeting, but obscurity is forever.

SCHOPENHAUER'S LAW OF ENTROPY:

If you put a spoonful of wine in a barrel full of sewage, you get sewage.
If you put a spoonful of sewage in a barrel full of wine, you get sewage.

THE ROCKEFELLER PRINCIPLE:

Never do anything you wouldn't be caught dead doing.

LIEBERMAN'S LAW:

Everybody lies, but it doesn't matter since nobody listens.

Horowitz's rule:

Wisdom consists of knowing
when to avoid perfection.

Rule of the open mind:

People who are resistant to change
cannot resist change for the worst.

Denniston's law:

Virtue is its own punishment.

Corollary:
If you do something right once,
someone will ask you to do it again.

MASON'S LAW:

The one day you'd sell your soul
for something, there is a glut of souls.

PROFESSOR BLOCK'S MOTTO:

Forgive and remember.

EDELSTEIN'S ADVICE:

Don't worry over what other people
are thinking about you. They're too busy
worrying over what you are thinking
about them.

MR. COLE'S AXIOM:

The sum of the intelligence on the planet remains a constant; the population, however, continues to grow.

JONES' MOTTO:

Friends come and go, but enemies accumulate.

McCLAUGHRY'S CODICIL TO JONES' MOTTO:

To make an enemy, do someone a favor.

ZAPPA'S LAW:

There are two things on earth that are universal: hydrogen and stupidity.

THE IRE PRINCIPLE:

Never try to pacify anyone at the height of their rage.

LAW OF LIFE'S HIGHWAY:

If everything is coming your way, you're in the wrong lane.

DISRAELI'S DICTUM:

Error is often more earnest than truth.

HOLTEN'S HOMILY:

The only time to be positive is when you are positive you are wrong.

OLIVIER'S LAW:

Experience is something you don't
get until just after you need it.

GABIROL'S OBSERVATION:

The wise are pleased when they discover truth, fools when they discover falsehood.

FOSTER'S LAW:

The only people who find what they are looking for in life are the fault-finders.

FIRST RULE OF NEGATIVE ANTICIPATION:

Don't burn your bridges until you come to them.

VOLTAIRE'S LAW:

There is nothing more respectable than an ancient evil.

HOFFER'S LAW:

When people are free to do as they please, they usually imitate each other.

KIERKEGAARD'S OBSERVATION:

Life can only be understood backward, but it must be lived forward.

JAFFE'S PRECEPT:

There are some things that are impossible to know—but it is impossible to know these things.

MUIR'S LAW:

When we try to pick out anything by itself, we find it hitched to everything else in the universe.

THE AQUINAS AXIOM:

What the gods get away with, the cows don't.

LAW OF CONSERVATION OF TSURIS:

The amount of aggravation in the universe is a constant.

Corollary:
If things are going well in one area, they are going wrong in another.

THE LAW OF EPONYMY:

Any given law will not be
named for the person who
created it.

Corollary:
It's not who said it,
it's who named it.

KEYES' FIRST AXIOM:

Any quotation that can be
~~altered~~ changed will be.

LONG'S LAW:
Natural laws have no pity.

BOHR'S AXIOM:
The opposite of a profound truth may well
be another profound truth.

THE TWO RULES
FOR ULTIMATE
SUCCESS IN LIFE:
1. Never tell everything you know.

ELLIS' LAW:

Progress is the exchange of one nuisance for another.

GERHARD'S OBSERVATION:

We're making progress. Things are getting worse at a slower rate.

THE FIFTH (AND ONLY) RULE:

You have taken yourself too seriously.

Heard a good law lately? If you have, or if you've come up with one yourself and you'd like to see it immortalized in print, why not send it to us for inclusion in a future *Murphy's Law* book or calendar? If the law you send is from another source, please try to tell us exactly where it is from. Send your laws to:

Murphy's Law
c/o 2560 9th Street, Suite 123
Berkeley, CA 94710

or e-mail it to:

MurphysLaw2000@hotmail.com

Discover the Princely Pleasures of
KING & JOKER
and the Other Works of Peter Dickinson

* * *

"He is a true original, a superb writer who revitalizes the conventions of the mystery genre."
—P. D. James

*

"Peter Dickinson always has been an idea man, in addition to being an exceptionally deft writer.... [In] *King & Joker*, Dickinson once again comes up with a daring concept... a mystery story with an unusual detective, and with logical, well worked-out development. The result is typical Dickinson."
—*New York Times Book Review*

*

"A warm, raffish, exciting story which should charm you out of your everyday skin and improve your disposition for days."
—*Kirkus Reviews*

*

more . . .

"Dickinson again delivers."
—*Minneapolis Tribune*

*

"Each of his novels unfolds like an exotic night-bloomer, transforming an ordinary bit of daylight greenery into something magical, rich, and strange. . . . Wherever he turns his swirling imagination, Dickinson finds the mysterious in the familiar and writes mesmerizing whodunits."
—*Washington Post Book World*

*

"*King & Joker* is full of Mr. Dickinson's usual flourishes. . . . The author loves a plot convolution in much the same way that a lecher loves a voluptuous curve. . . . His characters are becoming more convincing with each book."
—**Anatole Broyard**, *New York Times*

*

"Peter Dickinson is always surprising, always inventive, always a terrific read. Whether he's giving us alternate royal families or the deepest secrets of ordinary mortals, he has an eye and a mind and a voice like no other."
—**Donald E. Westlake**

*

"The whodunits of British novelist Peter Dickinson are exceptional."
—*Newsweek*

*

"Peter Dickinson is the best thing that has happened to serious, sophisticated, witty crime fiction since Michael Innes."
—*The Sunday Times* (London)

*

"That man Dickinson is infuriating to his fellow writers—so versatile, so bloody brilliant at everything he tries."
—Peter Lovesey

*

"Peter Dickinson's gift to the crime story has been an imagination of unusual, even extraordinary, forcefulness.... Not only are [his] characters wonderfully vivid and his settings such that you remember them for years afterwards, but the actual prose is excellent."
—*Twentieth-Century Crime and Mystery Writers*

* * *

PETER DICKINSON, one of Britain's most celebrated mystery authors and two-time winner of the Crime Writers Association Gold Dagger Award, has written nineteen novels of detection and suspense, as well as over a dozen acclaimed books for children. Praised for having expanded the limits of the mystery genre with new twists, outrageous humor, extraordinary psychological perception, and unique settings, Dickinson has created imaginative works that "reviewers invariably pronounce...highly original, beautifully written, and rightly so" (*Washington Post Book World*).

Novels of Crime and Detection
by Peter Dickinson

The Glass-Sided Ants' Nest
The Old English Peep Show
The Sinful Stones
Sleep and His Brother
The Lizard in the Cup
The Green Gene
The Poison Oracle
The Lively Dead
King and Joker
Walking Dead
One Foot in the Grave
A Summer in the Twenties
The Last House-Party
Hindsight
Death of a Unicorn
Tefuga
Perfect Gallows
Skeleton-in-Waiting
Play Dead

PETER DICKINSON

KING &JOKER

THE MYSTERIOUS PRESS
New York • Tokyo • Sweden
Published by Warner Books

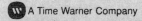

A Time Warner Company

MYSTERIOUS PRESS EDITION

This Mysterious Press Edition is published by arrangement with the author.

The Mysterious Press name and logo are trademarks of Warner Books, Inc.

Cover design by Jackie Merri Meyer
Cover illustration by Mark Burkhardt

Mysterious Press Books are published by
Warner Books, Inc.
1271 Avenue of the Americas
New York, NY 10020

A Time Warner Company

Printed in the United States of America

First Mysterious Press Printing: March, 1993
10 9 8 7 6 5 4 3 2 1

"So for a day and a night and yet another day Edward Duke of Clarence lingered at the portal of death. It is fruitless to speculate on how our nation might have developed had Eddy crossed the dark threshold. In due time, no doubt, his brother the Duke of York would have inherited the throne and reigned (presumably) as King George V, to be succeeded in turn by ... by whom? The glass of imaginary history reflects nothing but vague mists. Perhaps by now the world would have known a Republic of Great Britain. Perhaps George, bluff and sailorly, would have steered a course towards a more active, less amenable monarchy. Or perhaps all would have been very much as we know it today, with only the head on our stamps and coins different.

Fruitless indeed to speculate. For, to the relief of the Royal Family and the well-concealed amazement of the Royal doctors, the future King Victor I withdrew with painful slowness from that shadowed threshold and returned to the living world and to the arms of his betrothed, Princess Mary of Teck. She saw to it that he never knew another day's illness."

(from *King Victor I*, an unpublished fragment by Lytton Strachey)

FAMILY TREE

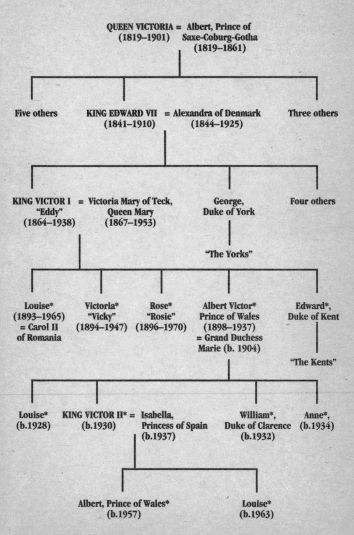

QUEEN VICTORIA = Albert, Prince of
(1819–1901)   Saxe-Coburg-Gotha
                (1819–1861)

Five others   KING EDWARD VII = Alexandra of Denmark   Three others
               (1841–1910)   (1844–1925)

KING VICTOR I = Victoria Mary of Teck,   George,   Four others
"Eddy"   Queen Mary   Duke of York
(1864–1938)   (1867–1953)

                                        "The Yorks"

Louise*   Victoria*   Rose*   Albert Victor*   Edward*,
(1893–1965)   "Vicky"   "Rosie"   Prince of Wales   Duke of Kent
= Carol II   (1894–1947)   (1896–1970) (1898–1937)
of Romania   = Grand Duchess
                                           Marie (b. 1904)

                                                              "The Kents"

Louise*   KING VICTOR II* = Isabella,   William*,   Anne*,
(b.1928)   (b.1930)   Princess of Spain Duke of Clarence   (b.1934)
                                 (b.1937)   (b.1932)

               Albert, Prince of Wales*   Louise*
               (b.1957)   (b.1963)

*Miss Durdon's babies

◆ 1 ◆

THE FIRST "JOKE" that Princess Louise actually witnessed took place in the Breakfast Room at Buckingham Palace on the last morning of the school summer holidays.

Father gave one of his warning snorts and looked down at the typed list beside his place.

"Two hundred and five," he said. "Cease automatic supply of sealing-wax in guest bedrooms."

Mother put her spoon carefully back into her dish of Fortnum and Mason's Soya Porage (by appointment).

"Most certainly not," said Mother. "Hue cannot expect visitors to ask for sealing-huax huenever they huish to bestow a decoration on somebody."

"I'd have thought people who bestowed decorations carried the kit around with them," said Nonny.

Albert, not looking up from slicing his second raw carrot into accurate rounds, said, "Sheikh Umu certainly did. When he gave me the Order of the White Oryx he sealed it by folding a strip of silver over the corner of the skin it was written on and biting it firm with his teeth."

"Was it oryx skin?" asked Louise.

"Of course not," said Albert. "Umu's an ecology nut. That's why he hit it off so well. Last bloke he caught shooting oryx he had publicly castrated."

1

"I take it," said Father, "that there's no suggestion that we should provide strips of silver in the guest bedrooms."

"Couldn't one of the footmen make it his business to see that there's sealing-wax in the room when that sort of bloke comes visiting?" said Albert. He then did his usual trick of looking up for a moment from his carrot, staring like a highly intelligent blue-eyed orang at the person he was talking to, popping a slice of carrot into the hole in the middle of his wild ginger beard, and instantly starting on sixty silent mastications, still staring. Strangers found table-talk with the Prince of Wales tricky, but Father was used to it. He snorted more loudly.

"How often have I got to drum it into your heads," he asked, "that running a Palace is a labor-intensive operation? Here we are, having to make drastic cuts in expenditure, and that means drastic cuts in labor. The more activities we embark on, even to make apparent savings in material costs, the more labor we need. Remembering to put sealing-wax in the right rooms at the right times sounds a trivial chore, but it involves labor—not just by the footman concerned but also on the part of the Protocol Secretariat who have to communicate with him about which visits are relevant. A few more jobs like that and you find you're increasing your labor force by one, not cutting it."

"Then it huill be cheaper to keep sealing-huax in all the rooms," said Mother. She sifted sugar into her bowl and put it on the carpet for Balfour to lick. This was her technique for seeing that Balfour ate his ration of Soya Porage, though he wasn't supposed to eat sugar at all. Father banged his pencil on the table but didn't snort, a bad sign.

"We've reached item two hundred and five," he said, "and so far we've accepted a total of nineteen suggestions. What's the point of hiring an O and M firm if we turn down almost every damn idea they put up?"

"Nevertheless," said Mother, "there will be sealing-wax in all the bedrooms."

Only Father, halfway gone into one of his rages, failed to notice the perfect English accent. Louise tensed inwardly.

"Now look here . . ." shouted Father.

Nonny coughed.

"Oh, all right," said Father, making another little cross in the margin of the list.

Mother nodded, smiled and reached for her banana-shredder.

All at once, in that cough, in that yielding, in that nod and smile, Louise realized that Nonny was Father's mistress. Louise had just poured herself another cup of chocolate and had a piled spoon of sugar halfway to it; she didn't spill a grain, despite the bounce of inner shock, but carried it smoothly across and stirred the chocolate to a froth. When she was satisfied she glanced across the table at Nonny. Miss Anona Fellowes was leaning back in her chair looking, as usual, both amused and bemused. She had a glistening blob of honey near the corner of her wide mouth, and like everything else that happened to her it seemed to suit her. Louise remembered a time when at a shoot at Sandringham a Land Rover had started with a jerk and Nonny had tumbled out at the back, landing asprawl in tire-churned mud. About five men had helped her to her feet and as she stood up, shaky but laughing, Prince Bernard of the Netherlands had whispered to Louise, "So, now mud becomes the smart thing to wear."

Louise's first jolt of astonishment changed quickly to a more general surprise that she hadn't realized before. Thirteen years . . . no, that wasn't fair—babies are so self-absorbed that you can't expect them to notice things till they're six, at least—say seven years of knowing that Nonny was completely one of the family, despite only being Mother's private secretary. . . perhaps that was actually what made it harder to see that she was also one of the Family.

Louise sucked the froth off her chocolate and as she did so looked around the table. She knew no one would guess that she'd suddenly found out—it was a family joke how little she showed her feelings. Sometimes that was a nuisance, when everybody assumed that you were as happy as a sand-boy when really you were perfectly miserable, but other times it could be useful. She stirred again to try and whip up another layer of froth. Did Mother know? Of course she did, because Father and Nonny could never have kept it such a secret without her help, and not even *France Dimanche* had suggested it. Did she mind? She always seemed so fond of Nonny, not only in public but also "among ourselves." Perhaps it suited her. Everybody knows that short bald men like a lot of sex, and poor Father was certainly not tall and his head had been shiny right across the top ever since Louise could remember. You could be passionate about Mother—she was marvelous—but it mightn't always be easy to be passionate *with* her...

The second layer of froth refused to come. Louise shrugged and coldly decided not to think about it anymore until she'd had a chance to talk to Durdy.

The pinger pinged its warning that they had only ten minutes more to themselves. Father gave a last snort, turned the O and M list face down, rose and crossed to the sideboard. Breakfast was always the same on weekdays. Soya Porage, half a banana and low-calorie chocolate for Mother. Croissants, honey and China tea for Nonny. Orange juice, muesli and raw carrots for Albert. Weetabix, fried eggs and grilled streaky bacon and high-calorie chocolate for Louise. And for Father first a small cup of very hot black coffee, then a vast cup of milky tepid coffee, then two eggs laid yesterday by the Palace Wyandottes, boiled for two minutes and left wrapped in a hot napkin for another five, and finally, when the pinger pinged, two slices of York ham carved by himself from the ham under the silver dishcover on the sideboard.

"Really, this is too bad," said Father in a voice so curiously between laughter and anger than everybody looked around. He was standing back from the sideboard with the dishcover in one hand, like a distorted shield. On the dish where the ham should have been was what appeared to Louise to be a large cow-pat, palpitating with strange life.

"Hey! That's my toad!" said Albert.

Nonny gave a small scream with a giggle threaded through it. Mother rang the bell for Pilfer. Father pulled the corner of his moustache and put the cover back on the toad.

"It's got to have air," said Albert.

"Quiet," said Father.

Pilfer slid into the room, bespectacled, stooping, all in black.

"Your Majesty rang?" he said in his slightly nasal whine.

He spoke to Mother because he knew that Father, if he'd wanted something, would have shouted and Nonny would have gone and asked.

"My ham is not what it should be, Pilfer," said Father.

Pilfer's eyebrows rose above the rims of his lenses. He sniffed the air but seemed to detect no odor other than the usual mixture of coffee, chocolate, Soya Porage and Balfour. Then he slid to the sideboard and lifted the dishcover with a black-gloved hand. For three seconds he stared at the toad. Louise saw the toad blink back. With complete silence and decorum Pilfer fainted.

At once Father was crouched by the body, loosening the collar and straightening the limbs. Nobody said anything while he took Pilfer's pulse.

"Bert," he said. "Get on the house phone and tell them to send up a stretcher."

"Is it a heart attack?" asked Nonny. Louise could detect behind the sympathy and concern a note of pleasure at the drama of it.

"No, no," said Father. "Just a faint. Heart quite steady. Bloody silly of me."

"In that case," said Mother, "he must stay huere he is until he huakes up."

"Are you sure he's a union member?" said Nonny.

"There'd still be no harm in having a stretcher," said Albert. "There's nothing in the union agreement against that. Only against Father providing medical attention to union members without a second opinion."

"Except in an emergency," added Nonny quickly, but Father was already into his tirade about the idiocy of paying for a doctor for the palace staff when he, the King, was a qualified practitioner who had worked his way up every step of the medical ladder without cutting one damned corner.

"I suppose if I'd settled for being a vet," he shouted, "I wouldn't even have been allowed to operate on the bloody dogs!"

At this moment Louise saw Pilfer's eyelids flicker and the color begin to seep back into his cheeks. Father was too angry to notice.

"Stretcher's on the way up," said Albert unnecessarily

clearly. Louise guessed that he also had seen Pilfer coming to, and wanted to spare the poor man's feelings by letting his faint seem to continue until he was out of the Royal presence. But the sound of his voice drew Father's temper as a golf-club draws lightning.

"And get that frog out of here!" he bellowed.

"It's a Blomberg toad," said Albert.

"It's terribly handsome," said Nonny.

"What's its name?" asked Louise.

"Amin, of course," said Albert. "I saw the likeness at once."

"No," said Mother. "You will not call it that. President Amin may well be misguided, but he is a head of state."

"You call your dogs after Prime Ministers," said Albert.

"That's different," said Mother, lapsing quickly back to her Spanish accent. "It began with Huinston. Do you remember darling Huinston, Lulu? And then there huas Baldouin, who huas rather a dull dog, but very affectionate . . ."

"And then," snarled Father, "we have to get a bloody stupid sentimental red setter and call it Attlee because some crass oaf on the Labour back benches asked a question in the House about our naming dogs after exclusively Tory Prime Ministers—just the sort of idiot interference with my private life which first stopped me going into the Navy and forced me to have a so-called socially useful training and then prevents me touching my own butler when he faints in the middle of my breakfast and anyway where's my damned ham?"

"But you like being a doctor," said Louise.

"That's got nothing to do with it, Lulu," said Father, suddenly mild and sensible at the sound of her voice. "I'd probably have liked being an admiral."

"You are an admiral," said Albert.

"A proper bloody admiral," snapped Father.

"But there will be no question of calling the toad Amin," said Mother.

"Certainly not," said Father. "You can call it Fatty if you like, Bert, but you're not going to tell anyone why. You hear? And now get it out of my breakfast room."

"Please can't we keep him for a bit?" said Louise. "I've

got to do a full biology project next term, and I want to do it about Blomberg toads. What does he eat, Bert, and how do you spell Blomberg? May I have a bit off your pad, Nonny?''

Nonny tore off a couple of sheets and swung them around to her on the Lazy Susan, then rose, drifted out into the lobby and came back a few moments later carrying an ordinary china dish with the ham on it.

"It was in the dining-room," she said. "Lulu dear, could you make a bit of space for me on the sideboard?"

Once more the great toad blinked at the light as Louise removed its dishcover and carried the salver back to her place. She was hardly settled before the First Aid men came in, and behind them Father's Private Secretary, Sir Savile Tendence. His bluff face pinkened and blue eyes popped and the rigid little bristles of his moustache seemed to twitch when he saw Pilfer supine on the carpet and the King not yet started on his two slices of ham.

"Sorry we're a bit late this morning, Sam," said Father, carving carefully away while the stretchermen fussed behind him with the body. "We've had a bit of a brouhaha. Pilfer saw a toad, fainted. Come and sit down. Give the poor man some tea, Nonny. What have we got on today, Sam?"

He always asked the same question and it was always unnecessary. All four members of the Family had in front of their places a typed form, one column for each member, showing all engagements for the week. Louise's entry for yesterday read, for instance, "11:00 A.M. HRH shopping. Clothes for new term. Jean Machine. Laura Ashley. 2:30 P.M. HRH open Sports Centre, Romford, Lady Caroline Tonge in attendance." Today was blank, at Louise's insistence. Tomorrow disgustingly said "08:50 A.M. HRH starts new term at Holland Park Comprehensive. Photographers." After that it was plain "School, School, School," and back to living a bit more like real people.

"This luncheon for Prince Albert at the London School of Economics Canteen," Sir Savile was saying. "We've made strong representations that nothing special should be laid on by way of food. They normally include a vegetarian menu. I understand, though, that a demo is expected."

"That's all right," said Albert. "I'm hairier than your hairiest Trotskyite, and a good deal further to the left, if the truth were known."

"It's a demo by the British Meat Traders Association, I'm afraid, Sir."

"Well, I'll demo right back at them."

"Now, Bertie, huill you please be careful?" said Mother. "Poor Mr. Peart huas telling me only on Monday about how huorrying the EEC beef mountain is."

"Who would be heir to the throne of a nation of beefeaters?" said Albert. "At least it's better than . . ."

"All right, all right," snapped Father, just in time to stop him teasing Mother about bull-fighting. "We've got to get on. This is a new one here, Sam. What the hell's a semi-informal walk-about? I don't know how to walk semi-informally. I wasn't taught."

Louise decided that her first experiment was a failure. Blomberg toads didn't eat bacon-rind. She was turning the Lazy Susan to get at Mother's Soya Porage packet when the light rumble of wood seemed to break the toad's nerve. It lurched forward off the salver at a fast, ungainly waddle, scattering cups and cutlery over the mahogany. Nonny threw her napkin over it but it barged on, a spectral blob moving with the gait of nightmare. With his usual gawky deftness Albert nipped to the sideboard, picked up the dishcover, whisked the napkin away and brought the cover down on his pet like a candlesnuffer. Still it drove on, a silver tank, to the edge of the table where Albert had the dish ready. Gripping the handle of the dishcover, he coaxed the toad onto the dish, then lashed the cover neatly down with Nonny's napkin.

"Good God," said Sir Savile. "When you said Pilfer saw a toad I didn't think . . ."

"You're not the only one who didn't think," said Father. "Damn silly of me to spring the brute on Pilfer like that. I suppose it was OK Bert having me on, but what I did was distinctly over the line."

(There were three important but vague concepts that had ruled Louise's life ever since she first understood words— "Among ourselves," "Over the line," and "Putting on a show.'' Nonny was clearly ''among ourselves.'' So, in his quiet way, was Pilfer. But Sir Savile was not and nor was Mrs. Mercury, the housekeeper. McGivan, mysteriously, was, in a way which the other security people—Theale and Sanderson and Janet Fletcher, for instance—were not. ''Among ourselves'' you could say and do what you liked—things which if you'd done them elsewhere would have been ''over the line.'' When you weren't ''among yourselves'' you were always to a greater or lesser extent ''putting on a show,'' wearing your public face, behaving as though it were the most natural thing in the world that forty photographers should turn up to take pictures of a teenage girl going to school. If Sir Savile hadn't been in the room it would have been possible to hold quite an interesting discussion about whether playing a practical joke on Pilfer was, in fact, ''over the line,'' because although Pilfer was a servant he was also ''among ourselves,'' and had been ever since, as an underfootman, he had shown Father how to build his first radio set and speak along the crackling ether to other radio nuts in places like Brazil and Oregon. You could discuss and disagree about ''over the line,'' but ''among ourselves'' was a set of relationships which you simply knew, without thought, in much the same way that baby chimps know from the grunts and grimaces of their elders the hierarchy of the group they live in, without even knowing that they know.)

Father's last remark had caught Albert at about his forti-eth chew at a carrot-slice, so he had to wait another twenty before he could protest.

''Me!'' he said at last. ''It wasn't me! Damned silly thing to do! Somebody might have put that dish down on a hot plate! And anyway I've more respect for toads than to play practical jokes with them.''

''Then who was it?'' said Mother, accentless and angry.

Everybody made not-me shrugs and grunts.

''What's this?'' said Louise, picking up a torn scrap of paper off the table. ''I think it must have been under the toad. I think I saw it fall off the dish when Bert picked it up.''

''Yes, that's right,'' said Albert.

The paper was blank. Louise turned it over. On the other

side was a single scarlet cross, scrawled with a thick felt pen.

"Oh, Lord," said Sir Savile. "It's another one."

"What do you mean?" said Albert.

"We've had a couple of other practical jokes, while you and the Princess were still in Scotland, Sir. The joker left a red cross like that both times."

"What were the jokes?" asked Louise. "Were they funny?"

"We won't go into that now," said Father with a sudden snap of temper. "D'you think this really matters, Sam? I mean, it's a nuisance, but we're used to this sort of thing. Only this joker has a bit more sense of humor than most."

"That's what's bothering me," said Sir Savile. "OK, there's always going to be the odd frustrated little tick who gets his own back with a silly practical joke. We've seen 'em, time and again. but I can remember old Toby, before I took over, warning me about the other sort. I can see him, clear as if it was today, sitting in the armchair in my office and puffing that horrible black pipe of his and saying 'What you've got to watch out for, me boy, is a *real* joker. They're the type that don't let up.' And he told me a long story about the trouble they had with a run of practical jokes right back in your great-grandfather's time, before the First World War. Never caught the blighter. Turned out to be a junior equerry. Died in the trenches, and his lawyers sent old Toby a sealed envelope confessing everything. Point about his jokes was that they could be funny, in a rather vicious sort of way. For instance, Trooping the Color once, he managed to scatter getting on for a thousand stink-bombs all over Horseguards Parade. He knew the drill, you see, and didn't put 'em where anyone was going to walk till you got several companies of guardsmen tramping about. Never knew when they weren't going to step on another one, you see. Ghastly stink, ladies fainting in the stands, guardsmen going bright green, horses shying like a circus—wish I'd seen it, though I expect if I had I'd have been too angry to laugh. Another time, visit of the French President, 1909, he managed to get itching powder on the harness for the Glass Coach. Horses bolted halfway down the Mall with King Edward, Queen

Alexandra, President and his missus all aboard. Half the stable staff got the sack, but our joker didn't care. He'd seen the Glass Coach bucketing down the Mall at a hand-gallop, with the King and Queen sitting there stiff as pokers, looking as though that was the way they always received State Visitors. And another thing about that joker—he left his signature too. So if old Toby didn't like it then, I don't like it now.''

For Louise there were several ghosts in the Palace—not the sort of hauntings that get into books, but memories so strong that the person remembered seemed almost solid enough to come stalking along one of those stretching corridors. For instance, Queen Mary, after whom the liner had been named, had died nine years before Louise was born, but there were still people in the palace who could imitate her icy accent and super-regal stance with such accuracy that Louise seemed to know and fear her more than she knew some living people. Sir Toby Smythe was another such ghost, having come to the Palace to work for the Master of the Household in the reign of Edward VII, and in 1922 becoming Private Secretary to Louise's great-grandfather, Victor I, and only retiring on Father's twenty-first birthday at the age of seventy-six. Louise knew all about Sir Toby; and his pipe; and his annual hiking holiday in German *lederhosen* which had got him thrown into Norwich jail as a spy in 1917; and his gallant but vain swim for help from the yacht in which Louise's grandfather, the Prince of Wales, had drowned in 1937; and the ins and outs of his campaign against the other great ghosts (including Queen Mary) to see that Father, when he became King a year later at the age of ten, knew something about the actual lives of his subjects; and the firewatching on the Palace roof during the Luftwaffe raids; and all that. Louise didn't much care for Sir Savile, mostly because he'd been on what she thought was the wrong side in the fight over whether she ought to go to a state school or to a dismally snob fee-paying establishment, but she knew that if he called up old Toby's ghost to witness that something mattered, then it did. This was no time to bait Father, so she crossed out the word ''Todes'' she'd put at the top of her notes and wrote

"Toads," then listened carefully to everything that was said. Immediately after breakfast she planned to go up to the Nurseries and ask Durdy about Nonny and Father, and whether it was all right, but it would be useful to have something else interesting to talk about in case Durdy clammed up. The joker would be ideal for that.

In fact not a great deal more was said about him, because the fuss with the toad had already taken up half Sir Savile's twenty minutes. Nobody needed to look at a watch—Louise herself never wore one—because Mother had a clock in her head and at exactly the same instant each day she would fold her napkin into its ring and say "Huell, Nonny . . ." It was a signal for Father to rise. When the King stands, all stand. The formal day—the day not lived "among ourselves" —had begun.

"I'm afraid we're a bit behind schedule, Sir," said Sir Savile. "I'm supposed to brief you about the Mali Ambassador—the FO are a bit jumpy there. I've made a tape of their briefing."

"Toshack's a damned fusser," said Father. "I wish the FO would move him to another desk. I read the despatches last night, but I suppose I'll have to listen to the bloody tape on my bog. Thanks."

Father marched away. Sir Savile held the door for Mother and Nonny, saw that Louise and Albert weren't ready to leave, gave that curious heavy nod of his which was the vestigial remains of a court bow, and went. Albert yawned with relief.

"That makes you look like a sea anemone," said Louise. "All tendrils sticky red."

He snarled at her like an ogre and picked up Father's list of suggestions from the O and M firm.

"He oughtn't to leave this about," he said. "We don't want a lot of rumors floating around about who's getting the push. Where'd we got to?"

"Two oh five. Sealing-wax."

He flipped through the sheets.

"That's the last of that section," he said, "Ah, now we're really getting down to brass tacks. 'Section Four.

Domestic Arrangements for Royal Family. Two oh six. Princess Louise to advertise her services as a baby-sitter.' ''

"Come off it. They wouldn't put that first."

"Careful, Lulu. You mustn't get a reputation for being brainy. The GBP doesn't go for brains."

(This abbreviation for Great British Public was clearly "over the line" but just as clearly ineradicable. Even Mother sometimes slipped into using it.)

"Shut up," said Louise. "I'm going to go and tell Durdy about the toad. Bert, can I do next term's project on it?"

"Course you can. I'll give you a hand," said Albert, still running his eye down the list of royal comforts the O and M men wanted to chop.

"I suppose I couldn't take him to school tomorrow. I'd love to see some of those photographers faint."

"Princess Louise and friend. Is this her first romance? Better not, Lulu . . . Hey! Look at this!"

Startled by the tone of genuine shock Louise craned to read the line he was pointing at. "Three twelve. The transfer of Miss Durdon to a suitable nursing-home would represent a saving of £1620 p.a. in medical and other expenses."

"Durdy!" whispered Louise.

"They must be mad!" said Albert.

◆ 2 ◆

SEVERAL YEARS AGO, in her horse-mad period, Louise had placed an imaginary double oxer and a water-jump across the Upper West Corridor which led to the Nurseries. The horse-madness was long cured, but still, if there was nobody about, she used to jump the obstacles. If anyone was watching she merely sailed over them in her mind's eye with the stop-watch ticking away the seconds needed to beat Harvey Smith's clear round. This morning she walked through them without even noticing.

Training had enabled her to suppress her reaction to the discovery about Father and Nonny. Royalty have to learn to behave like that. If a Queen is busy smiling and shaking hands with the wives of Australian officers and somebody whispers in her ear that her small son has fallen out of a tree and broken his collar-bone, she carries on smiling and shaking and slots motherly worries into the back of her mind until she can bring them out and cope with them. (This had actually happened to Mother.) In the same way Louise had slotted the Nonny business away until she could go and ask Durdy about it. Now, as she approached that moment, she realized that although she didn't think she was shocked, it was still a shock in a different way, a quite new kind of thing. So she couldn't assume that Durdy would be able to make it all come all right, as she always had so far when Louise had been troubled. This was something that belonged right outside the Nurseries.

In the old Night Nursery Kinunu was doing Durdy's ironing. This was quite unnecessary, except that for a hundred years a nursery maid had always done the ironing after breakfast and it comforted Durdy to smell that faint prickle of scorching still.

"Good morning, Kinunu," said Louise.

"Morning, mithmith," said Kinunu, turning and giving a little curtsey which, like everything she did, seemed unconsciously to mock the same action as performed by other people. It was difficult not to think of Kinunu as Siamese, because her big-eyed, flat-featured face ended in a little pointy chin just like a cat's. In fact she came from a small Malayan hill-tribe, and had been chosen by Durdy from a set of photographs after the last nurse had left in tears. She'd turned out to be able to speak almost no English, and Father said her nursing qualifications were pretty rum, but she was the only nurse Durdy had never quarrelled with and then bullied into resigning. She was very small, barely taller than Louise, and she was cat-like in another way too—you instinctively wanted to pick her up and put her on your lap and stroke her to make her purr.

They still called the room the Night Nursery though nobody slept in it, and it was completely changed from the old days. It smelt of hospitals. A washing machine stood in one corner, and a small laboratory bench under the window, but the most intrusive newcomer was the monitor screen and set of dials on the table against the inner wall. With these, whoever was in the room could hear every sound in the Day Nursery, see every inch of the bed that now stood there, and check temperature, breathing, pulse and a dozen other details about the patient who lay in the bed. There was a similar screen and set of dials in the little side-room, once Durdy's own, where Kinunu now slept.

Because Kinunu's English was so poor there was no real need to switch off the screen and speaker, but the Family had got into the habit with other nurses before Kinunu came, so Louise did it now. Then she gently opened the door into the old Day Nursery.

Miss Ivy Durdon, MVO, lay as always motionless in her
iron-framed hospital bed with its head against the wall
opposite the fireplace. She lay as still as the dolls on their
shelf, as still as the pudgy pastel children lifting up their
hands to greet the squirrels and blue-tits in the framed
Margaret Tarrant print of "All Creatures Great and Small."
Apart from the bed and the console of instruments beside it
everything was exactly as it always had been since Louise
could first remember it. Though no child was now likely to
fall from the windows, the bottom halves of each sash were
still barred with white-painted iron outside the glass. The
gas fire burped and whimpered behind the brass-railed mesh
fireguard. The cuckoo clock tocked its wooden note. Its
enemy, the Mickey Mouse alarm clock, stood on the mantelpiece with its arms at five past eleven, in a gesture of
permanent surrender, never changing unless the Nursery needed
to be woken early for something like a Coronation or a
Balmoral journey—never used now at all, in fact. The card-
board parrot nodded in the light draught between the windows.

Louise tiptoed across and kissed the blue-veined alabaster
forehead. Brown eyes opened and lilac lips smiled.

"Good morning, Your Highness," said the squeaky old
voice. "Someone's up early. Has someone done her business this morning like a good girl should?"

"Do you still ask Father that, Durdy?"

The lips tightened to keep a secret. Louise climbed onto
the rocking-horse and nudged it into motion. It was a proper
rocking-horse with long curved rockers, and as you swayed
it to and fro it gradually worked itself across the ancient,
mottled green carpet. The Union had once tried to have it
screwed to the floor after a stupid maid had rocked it to
sweep under one end and then let it rock back onto her
fingers; they'd said it was a potentially dangerous piece of
industrial equipment. Durdy had stopped any of that nonsense, of course.

Louise wasn't sure where to begin—now she was here
she saw that she couldn't talk about item 312 on the O and
M list—it'd only worry Durdy and Father would never let it
happen. There was the toad joke, but if she started on that
Durdy might get tired before they ever got around to Nonny.

"How old am I, Durdy?" she said.

"Thirteen and a quarter, darling."

"Am I old enough to be told things?"

"What the eye doesn't see the heart doesn't grieve over."

"That's nonsense, Durdy. You can grieve a lot more over not seeing things."

"Some people are so sharp they'll cut themselves."

"Not me. Bert's the clever one. Is there always a stupid one and a clever one?"

You got side-tracked into questions like that with Durdy. Now she lay with closed eyes, remembering. Louise noticed a hank of gold wool on the rim of the darning-basket and deduced that Mother had started a new stool-cover yesterday evening.

"Your great-grandfather," squeaked Durdy suddenly. "When he was just Prince Eddy they all said he was a fool, but when he became King Victor he was good enough to beat His Imperial Majesty of Germany, and everybody used to say *he* was a very clever young man. They're the sort that trip over their own feet."

Durdy viewed the history of her own times as a series of clashes between crowned heads. She herself had changed the nappies on the very bottoms that later sat on most of the thrones. For her the chief horror of the Second World War had been that the enemy hadn't got a proper ruler, and so it had seemed to her a vague and shapeless evil, something (Louise thought) like Sauron in *The Lord of the Rings*. Father said that the war had only really come alive for Durdy with the entry of the Japanese Royal Family on the other side.

Louise saw a way back to the Nonny problem.

"Queen Mary must have helped a lot," she said. "She cured Great-grandfather of his bad habits, didn't she?"

"Little pitchers have big ears."

"It must be very difficult for Kings. Poor Father. Does that sort of thing run in families?"

Durdy could move some of the muscles in her face but not others. Her smile was still all right, but when she was displeased the down-turn at the corners of her mouth gave her the look of an ivory devil-mask.

"Please, Durdy."

"Who's been telling tales?"

"Nobody. I just guessed."

"There's nine wrong guesses go to make a right one."

"I guessed at breakfast this morning. It wasn't really a guess. Mother was getting angry and Father hadn't noticed and Nonny coughed and I *knew*."

The devil-mask vanished.

"High time too," squeaked Durdy. "I was begging His Majesty to tell you only last week—no, I'm a liar, this very Monday it must have been—but there's none so deaf as won't listen."

"Father's not very good at listening. Poor old man, he has to listen so much to people in his job, I expect it's a relief to him not to listen to the Family. It's not really a bad habit, is it? Oh dear—I don't mean I think Nonny's a bad habit either."

Durdy said nothing. Eighty years of rearing children had made her an expert in waiting to see which way the cat would jump.

"It all depends what Mother thinks, doesn't it?" said Louise.

Still no answer. You learn not to discuss the feelings of your employers in front of their children.

"When did it begin, Durdy? Nonny I mean? Was there anyone before her? All the Kings in the history books chop and change like anything, don't they?"

Durdy's sniff was not loud, no longer the potent warning it had once been. Just as baby pheasants know that they must cower at their mother's brief chuckle when a hawk-shape floats above, so generations of small princes had learnt to bite short what they were saying at the sound of Durdy's sniff.

"I'm sorry, Durdy. I didn't mean..."

"Tittle-tattle."

"No! I mean it *is* interesting and I *am* inquisitive, but that doesn't matter. You see, now I know it changes the way I feel. I'm very fond of Nonny...in fact I suppose I love her...I'd never thought about it...that's what matters, isn't it? I've got to know how to feel."

"There, there, darling. I didn't mean it. I knew you weren't that kind. I'll tell you that His Majesty and Miss

Fellowes were very great friends when Her Majesty was still in that convent of hers.''

"But did Mother know when she married Father? All right, you needn't tell me, Durdy—I bet she did. *And* she had to become a Protestant!''

Durdy, a bigoted anti-papist, smiled with great satisfaction.

"And all she got in exchange was being allowed to open a lot of jam factories and bridges! I think it's a scandal! I'm not going to stand for any of that! I'm going to start a Princesses' Lib movement—I'll write to all the cousins and order them to join. *We're* going to marry for love, yum yum. You can be patron, Durdy.''

Sometimes Durdy's head twitched on the enormous pillow. This meant, Father said, that her will to move had been so strong that the paralyzed muscles had actually responded a little to the signal from the brain. For a moment Louise thought that she'd been trying to laugh at the joke—she used to have a lovely squeaky cackle—but then the tiny indrawing of the withered lips showed that the joke had gone too far.

"Fair's fair, Your Highness. May I trouble you to change the subject?''

Louise gave an irritable extra impetus to the rocking-horse which made its rockers growl on the floor for the next few swings. When Durdy said "Fair's fair" it meant that the argument was now settled and that none of the squabbling children should dare complain. And when she used the ancient protocol whereby only those of royal blood, however young, could change the subject, then the subject got changed. Louise had heard her do it to Father.

"Oh, well,'' she said. "I'll tell you about the toad. Somebody snitched Father's ham this morning, and when he went to carve his slices there was this gigantic toad under the dishcover.''

"Disgusting!''

"Oh, Father didn't mind at first. He thought Bert had put it there. In fact he put the cover back and called Pilfer in and complained about the ham being off and Pilfer lifted the cover and fainted, but not too badly, Father said. Then Sir Sam turned up and found out that none of us had done it and started to take things very seriously, and told us about a joker who'd caused a lot of trouble in old Toby's time . . ."

"I remember that. Yes indeed. There was a nigger ambassador coming to present his credentials—we didn't have so many of them in those days—and somebody hired a lot of other niggers to dress up and come along and pretend to be the one. The real nigger got turned away. I believe it caused an Incident."

"Wow! This one's stuck inside the Family so far. He leaves a red cross. The toad was the third joke but Father wouldn't tell us what the other two were—I bet *you* know, Durdy—won't you tell me? Please."

Sniff. Ah well.

"It's funny that they should take it so seriously," said Louise. "I mean, Bert's always playing practical jokes—in fact it runs in the family, doesn't it? Poor grandfather was a great practical joker, and so was King Edward, wasn't he? Did he ever play a practical joke on you, Durdy?"

"Not on me, darling. But I remember one Christmas at Abergeldie—I don't know what we were doing there at Christmas, it was usually Sandringham—when he was still only Prince of Wales. He came to visit his grandchildren in the Nursery one evening; it was bathtime and we had a very pretty little Scots under-nursemaid we'd just taken on. I was nursemaid and Bignall was Nurse. His Royal Highness had some ice in his drink and he slipped a piece down the back of this girl's uniform. The poor child giggled and squealed and blushed like a beetroot. Bignall did *not* take it in good part."

"It sounds a pretty feeble sort of joke to me. What became of the girl? Did she get sacked for giggling?"

"Those that ask no questions will be told no lies."

"Oho. So something had happened, and not that sort of something. Great-great grandfather—Edward VII—was in the history books, and on TV even, with all his sex life public property. The royal past was covered by a fog like the exhaust from a juggernaut lorry, a trail of mystery swirling along behind, only gradually settling. Great-great-grandfather's ruttish habits were now mostly plain to see. Great-grandfather was still half covered by the discreet cloud. As Prince Eddy he'd been dissipated—you were allowed to know that, but still not exactly what his dissipations had consisted of. But then he'd almost died, and then he'd married Great-granny, and one shock or the other had sobered him up and in the end they'd become King Victor I and Queen Mary, loved and respected through the fog. Poor Grandfather...

"Why do we always talk about my *poor* Grandfather, Durdy? Was it just because he got drowned before he could become King, or was it because he had Queen Mary for a mother and Granny for a wife?"

"Her Royal Highness is in a very nosey-parker mood this morning."

"Oh, Durdy, you're impossible. I bet he was dissipated too." Sniff.

"I'm serious," said Louise. "I mean I'm not serious about Grandfather being dissipated, supposing he was. I don't see how it matters now. But I am serious about Father and Mother and Nonny. I think they've done very well by Bert and me. We're very lucky with them, managing so tidily, and keeping us all happy. I mean really happy. What I hate is *mess*."

For a moment Louise thought that Durdy was going to do another of her sniffs, but instead she opened her eyes and said, "There's someone in the Night Nursery."

Louise couldn't hear anything, but Durdy had always had hearing of extraordinary sharpness. Every rebel mutter she had picked up. If she'd been Pope at the time (Albert once said) she'd have heard Galileo's exact words. I beg your pardon, Mr. G, but exactly what still moves? Come on, spit it out. I'll have no secrets from *my* Curia, *if* you please. And if anything the paralysis of her body had made her senses sharper still.

Now Louise caught the light pinging buzz from beyond the door, which meant that Durdy had pressed the two outer fingers of her left hand, the only two parts of her once busy body that she could still control, down on the buzzer that lay beneath the bedclothes. After a few seconds the door opened and Kinunu came prancing in, smiling as if she'd been enjoying the most marvelous illicit joke. She did her mocking curtsey to Louise and came on around the bed, where she contrived both to smile and frown at the dials of the apparatus that stood where the bedside-table should have been. Louise never looked at this, never even noticed it, managed to cut it out of her consciousness because, like the monitor camera, it was an intruder on the ancient order of the Nursery. It was there to keep Durdy alive, to monitor her breathing and pulse, to adjust the temperature of the bed, and twenty other things which Louise didn't understand. Father had pinned up a chart above it, showing where all the needles ought to be. Kinunu peered to and fro between the chart and the machines. At last she turned to the bed.

"All OK mithmith," she said.

"I daresay," said Durdy sharply. "And who's your friend, Miss?"

"Pleathe?"

"I heard a man's voice in the Night Nursery, Miss."

Kinunu hesitated but didn't seem at all to mind the bullying bite of Durdy's tone. If anything it only increased her look of wicked innocence.

"Come in here, whoever you are," called Durdy.

A shoe squeaked. The door moved as though the wood itself were shy. McGivan came creeping in.

McGivan. Albert's account of how he had been found went like this: Father had been opening a new police station at Inverness, and that had involved the inspection of a guard of honor of police constables. Father (Albert said) had been in the uniform of a Colonel of the Black Watch, kilt and all. There he had been, His Britannic Majesty, Fid Def etcetera, pacing blue-kneed through Inverness-shire drizzle, pausing at every fifth dummy to utter a gracious remark. One (asthma, poor sod) two (whiskey) three (can that moon face be the start of Addison's Disease? Remember to tell his Chief to have him checked) four (mild astigmatism) five—"Well, officer, and how long have you been in the Force?" "Twelve year, fower months, Sirr." "You look very well on it." "Thank you, Sirr." One (pity his mother didn't have those jug-ears operated on) two (nothing much visibly wrong there) three (whiskey) four (coronary in a few years) five—"Well, officer . . . hello, haven't we met before?" "They made me shave the moustache, Sirr." "Shouldn't happen to a dog! But where have I seen you?" "In your wee looking-glass the morrn, verra like." "Good God! Chief Superintendent, were you aware that this officer bears a strong likeness to me?" "Yes, Your Majesty. We felt it was a choice between his removing his moustache or not taking part in the parade. It was his decision which." "Ahem! Uh! Ahem!" (That was Albert's version of how Father swallowed his fury at this interference with the personal liberty of one of his subjects.) "Yes, of course, Chief Superintendent. Difficult situation for you. Still ... What's your name, officer?" "McGivan, Sirr." "Well, McGivan, I would be very pleased if you would grow your moustache just as it was. Otherwise I'd have to shave mine off and that'd be an expensive business because they'd have to change all the stamps, you know."

This was one of Albert's party pieces. Despite his own jungly hair he managed to do both Father and McGivan so well that it made even Mother laugh. Louise could see, instant to her mind's eye, how McGivan's brow wrinkled like a spaniel's at the notion of it being his fault that the stamps of the United Kingdom had all to be changed. She could also sense how the Chief Superintendent (Albert made him lanky but pompous) fretted at the knowledge of Father's anger and his own lack of grasp of its cause, and his eager promise to check out the suspect coronary and Addison's disease. And then Father pulling at his own moustache to hide his smile at the thought of the fun he could have with a double.

"What on earth do you want him for?" Nonny had asked.

"Oh, all sorts of things," Father had said. "He'll be both useful and amusing. Anything where he doesn't have to say much. He could swear in Privy Councillors like nobody's business, for instance, or . . ."

"Vick. No," Mother had said.

"But don't you see how much spare time it would give me? I could . . ."

"No."

"All right—perhaps not Privy Councillors, but there's all sorts of other idiot appearances I have to make . . ."

So in a way it was a good thing that Father's scheme hadn't worked. McGivan was amusing, but not useful. It was astonishing that two men so alike—with the same high color, the pale pop eyes, the shiny dome amid the sparse relics of gingery hair, the little drooping moustache, the arms too short even for the pudgy body—it was astonishing that despite all that they should look so different. Albert said it was like chimpanzees—you laugh at their parody of human behavior because they're so inhuman. If they looked more like us, they'd seem less funny. So McGivan was a joke because, despite being the spit image of the King of England, every movement he made—every blink, every frown of worry, every anxious smile, every shuffle of his tiny feet—was totally unroyal. That had been obvious the moment Father had first led him in, dressed in identical suits (Father's clothes never fitted, but with him the shabbiness was somehow arrogant; with McGivan it was mingy), and stood with him in Tweedledum and Tweedledee pose in the drawing-room. He'd been desperately shy, very snuffly and Scottish, poor man. After a couple of drinks he'd made a surprisingly passable shot at doing Father's voice. But when he'd at last been eased out of the room Mother had shaken her head.

"Nobody huould mistake him for you, but nobody," she'd said. "He is not a King, Vick. You are, in spite of everything. Even Mr. Huillie Hamilton huould know the difference."

"Nonsense, darling. What do you think, Nonny?"

Nonny had put on the innocent-little-child look she used when she was about to make one of her rather creepy jokes.

"He might do for your lying-in-state, I suppose."

So here was McGivan, amusing but not useful, creeping around the Nursery door, smiling and frowning and trying not to rub his hands together like a comic grocer. These days he wore his moustache waxed into neat points and spoke with an accent broader than he'd ever used in Scotland. It was as though, feeling he'd been a failure in looking like the King, he'd now determined to look and sound as different as possible.

"Come in, Mr. McGivan," squeaked Durdy. "And how are the ankles?"

"Verra much improvit," said McGivan. "It's the liniment His Majesty prescribit, ye ken."

"Still there's nothing like Pommade Divine, I always say," said Durdy. "And what can we do for you, Mr. McGivan?"

McGivan hesitated.

"Och," he said, "aweel. I was after askin' Her Royal Highness a few questions aboot yon eencident wi' the toad at breakfast. I am instructit to investigate, ye ken."

Nice for McGivan to have something to do, thought Louise. Officially he was one of the security police at the Palace, but there wasn't much in that line anybody felt like trusting him with. In one early episode he'd been sent on some outing as Albert's bodyguard, had got lost and then had made such frantic efforts to rejoin his Royal charge that the local police had arrested him. Albert had had to bail him out.

"Fire ahead," said Louise. "I don't think I noticed anything special until Father lifted the lid."

"The whole Family was no verra obsairvant the morn," said McGivan. "Noo, Your Highness, when ye cam into the breakfast-room, who was there, besides yourself?"

"Oh, I was first down. I usually am. Mr. Pilfer had only just rung the gong. I suppose that makes me chief suspect, because I'm pretty sure nobody went fiddling around with the ham-dish after I came in."

"Och, you and Prince Albert are already eleeminated. Baith o'ye were in Scotland when Her Majesty had the misunderstanding with the advertising agency, and also when the eencident occurred in His Majesty's toilet."

"In Father's loo! Honestly? What incident, for God's sake?"

(Albert said it was really Durdy's fault that Father's time on the loo each morning had become part of the Palace ritual almost as sacrosanct as, say, the Changing of the Guard. No wonder everybody had been so stuffy about the nature of the earlier jokes.)

McGivan coughed and looked away. Durdy sniffed.

"Oh, all right!" said Louise. "What else can I tell you?"

Painstakingly McGivan took her through all the details of the toad-finding and Pilfer's faint, seeming most interested in things that couldn't possibly be any help. Her impatience must have showed.

"Ye ken I must ask questions of the serrvants," he said. "And I canna do that unless I can tell them I have questioned the Family equally severely."

"Yes, but surely you want to start with who knew about the toad? I think Prince Albert said it only arrived yesterday."

"Correct," said McGivan. "I checkit the box mysel'. It could have been a bomb, ye ken?"

"But who else knew? That's the point."

"Aweel, Sergeant Theale crackit a wee bit joke aboot it. Was Constable Sanderson there? I dinna mind. And there'd be the messenger who took it to the Prince. Aweel. Aye, yon's a guid suggestion, Your Highness. Verra guid for a lassie. I'll investigate on those lines. Aye."

With another monstrous snuffle he crept away. Kinunu giggled as he left, but Durdy sighed.

"Are you tired, darling?" asked Louise. "Shall I go?"

"Not tired, only old," whispered Durdy.

"How old? Don't tell me. As old as your tongue and a little older than your teeth. Right?"

Durdy smiled peacefully and closed her eyes. Louise bent to kiss her forehead, nodded to Kinunu and tiptoed away. Walking back down the corridor, she took the oxer and the water-jump each with an absentminded bound. Visiting Durdy always made things seem all right—Nonny and Father, for instance: in half an hour that had stopped being a strange new portent and became something that Louise had known and accepted all her life, without knowing that she did so. In fact as she went down the stairs she was thinking neither about that nor about the clearly impossible suggestion that Durdy should be moved to a nursing-home, but about the joker. An incident in Father's loo! Wow! It was funny but it was also a bit uncanny. In some ways Father was a very secretive person, so not many people in the Palace would be aware of how much his morning ritual mattered to him. That meant that either the joker had been dead lucky in his choice of target or he was one of those who knew—somebody "among ourselves."

• 3 •

"How old? Don't tell me. As old as your tongue and a little older than your teeth. Right?"

Miss Durdon felt her face smile, felt the brush of lips on her forehead, listened to the loved footsteps tiptoeing away, heard Kinunu's giggle and shut it out of her mind. My last baby, she thought. My very last. The thought drifted her away, back and back . . .

A sunlit terrace. Great lumpish hills, brown and mauve with heather. A dark pine plantation. Heavy grey stone walls below fanciful turrets. Over all this the sunlight, northern and pale. On the lawn between the castle and the pines at least twenty lolling dogs, and on the terrace a tea-time ritual, with wicker chairs, cake-stands, four tall ladies all in black, two kilted servants holding silver trays, a funny little Indian in a turban pouring out tea. The ritual centers on a stout little grey-faced lady whose solid outline is made vague by billows of black lace. She has an Aberdeen terrier on her lap. Her face, sulky in repose, smiles with sudden eager sweetness as into the picture walk three small girls in white, wearing wide white hats. Durdon sees them from behind. The smallest girl, Princess Rosie, gives a couple of skips of happiness but Princess Louise hisses her back to propriety. They curtsey to the old lady whose pudgy little hands make a patting motion against her legs, causing the girls to settle like white doves around her knees. The

Indian gentleman hands her a plate and the old lady takes a
knife and cuts a rock bun into equal sections which she
gives to the girls as though she were feeding three of her
dogs. Durdon watches all this with anxiety—that Munshi,
she thinks, how can you tell if his hands are clean? The old
lady smiles along the terrace and speaks to one of the other
ladies, who beckons. Durdon checks that the baby in her
arms has not started an unprincely dribble and walks forward, less nervous than she'd expected. The old lady scuffs
the terrier off her lap and holds out her arms for the baby.
As Durdon rises from her curtsey and passes the royal
bundle across their hands touch. The Queen looks straight
into her eyes.

"I have not seen you before, have I? What is your
name?"

"Durdon, Ma'am. Nurse Bignall has the influenza, Ma'am."

"You are not very large, are you?"

"No, Ma'am."

"Never mind. I believe children like small people, and
you certainly look healthy. Where were you born?"

"Thaxted in Essex, Ma'am."

"I know the place. Excellent people. Wait. I think I shall
hand you back the Prince directly. They are not so amusing
until they can talk, are they?"

"I love them when they're tiny, Ma'am."

"But you love us too, Durdy?"

(Princess Rosie, three and a half, wide-eyed with sudden
alarm under the starched hat-brim.)

Durdon smiles quickly down at her, anxious to take the
baby back and not be thought pert or intrusive.

"Tell the child outright, Durdon. It is wrong to let them
fret."

"Yes, Your Highness, of course I love you too."

"And my highness loves you."

The Queen, whose speaking voice is rather light and
high-pitched, gives an extraordinary deep-throated chuckle.
Princess Vicky, aged six, loses her frown of fright at Rosie
speaking out of turn before Great-grandmama. The Queen
seems not to have looked away from Durdon's face during
all this time but she has somehow noticed Vicky's anxiety.

"No," she says. "Princess Victoria shall hold the Prince for me. You may retire, Durdon. I see that you will be with us for a long time, and will have other opportunities for nursing the little ones."

She nods decisively, as though settling a dispute between provinces of her Empire. Durdon backs away, terrified of tripping over one of the dogs and sprawling down in a vulgar flurry of petticoats, but at the same time content to see Vicky's back bent to coddle her living doll. . . .

The time-drift quivers and for a hideous few instants Miss Durdon is standing in a vaguely seen corridor and hearing a voice screaming "Durdy! Durdy! Where's Durdy!" That is Vicky dying of cancer at the age of fifty-two, a convert to Christian Science, refusing drugs but shouting in the delirium of pain for an older comfort. It happened in America and Miss Durdon hadn't been there, but they'd told her about it. Now she uses her strong will to push the imagined scene from her mind and coax the drift back to that earlier time, the time of her first babies. . . .

Abergeldie, the Prince of Wales's Scottish home, a few miles down the road from Balmoral. (However often the drift takes her back to this scene, Miss Durdon can never remember why the Prince should have been up there at Christmas, when he'd normally have been at Sandringham, nor why his grandchildren should have been visiting him without their parents. All that is vague, but the details of the actual event are as sharp-edged as a photograph.)

Bathtime in the Nursery suite. Two brown hip-baths on the floor. Small bright-pink bodies nestled into vast white towels. Steam, and the smell of talcum and Wright's Coal Tar Soap, and the drift and hiss of a Highland storm against the shutters, and the new electric light very yellow. Nurse Bignall rigid by the fire with the hairbrush in her lap. Princess Rosie, nearly four now, turning away from the fire already wise enough to hide her grin of relief as the torture ends; her new-brushed hair floats with no weight above her shoulders, glinting in glistening waves. Durdon gives Vicky a last reassuring surreptitious hug, then makes her slip from her lap and go to let Bignall tug at the tangles of her coarse, intractable hair. Sober, Bignall does this with energetic pleasure, like a minister rooting out sin; tonight she has made herself a pot of "tea" before bath-time, a brown liquid which she drinks cold, without milk. Catriona is drying Princess Louise. Durdon can't stop glancing at the new under-nursemaid; she is extraordinarily striking with her pointy-chinned small face pinkened by steam and nervousness, her red-gold hair piled under her cap, her full bust and tiny waist accentuated by the starched white apron of her uniform. Vicky's first suppressed whimper is followed by the slap of the back of the brush on flesh.

"Stand still!" growls Bignall. Durdon feels herself stiffen. Three times more, she says to herself, and I'll take the brush out of that witch's hands and face the consequences. Oh, if only. . .

As the door opens the whole room seems struck into stillness, as though they were all posing for a photographer.

"Curtseys, girls," says Bignall in her soldiery voice. Rosie does a beauty in her nightdress—grace will out, Vicky a gawky one, Louise a mere token in her towel. But Bignall, trying to lead the dance, stumbles and only saves herself by grabbing the fender. The tubby, bald, slab-faced, bearded gentleman in the doorway appears not to notice.

"Don't let me interrupt you," he says. "I felt like a change of company, my dears. You're lucky. I wish I had pretty ladies to bathe me."

Rosie laughs. She loves Grandpapa—but then she loves everybody. The Prince of Wales closes the door and strolls to the fire, where he rests his cigar on the mantelpiece. The wild, foreign reek of it joins the plainer nursery smells. The ice tinkles faintly in the top of his tall glass of hock and seltzer. Bath-time proceeds, but only to the next whimper. No slap, but the brush was poised until Bignall remembered that there was a stronger power than hers in the room now.

"Here, you!" barks the Prince. "You're doing that too roughly. It is not the child's fault that her hair has knots in it. You—you're doing nothing. You brush the Princess's hair."

Vicky tiptoes across to Durdon, too intelligent not to

dread the consequences, despite the immediate relief. Durdon doesn't even dare to look at Bignall. This'll make it happen, she thinks as she begins to brush. What'll she do? What'll I do? She'll wait till we're back in England. Then she'll . . . yes, she'll go to Duchess May with a bottle of "tea" and say she found it in my drawer. She'll say she found it up here, so she'll go the moment we get back. I won't have time to prove anything. It'll be her word against mine. Vicky would bear me out, but I can't . . .

A sudden giggling scream and a man's deep chuckle. Durdon, though she is tense as a terrier, manages not to jerk at Vicky's hair as she looks around. Catriona appears to be having a fit, throwing her arms about and wriggling her whole body like a snake. Her cheeks are as red as a ripe apple and her giggles are made worse by her efforts to control them. Only her feet somehow remain respectful of the royal presence, as if they were glued to the floor. Rosie is crowing with laughter, Vicky smiling, Louise looking disgusted.

"What happened?" whispers Durdon.

"Grandpapa put some ice down the back of her dress," breathes Vicky.

Bignall stalks forward, a black pillar, a storm.

"Sir, I must request you to leave my nursery," she says. "The children are over-excited."

The Prince swings round, amazed. His cod-like eye stares at her and wavers. In the instant given her Durdon raises her right hand to her lips and tilts her wrist with her fingers cupped round an invisible glass. At once she turns back to the thicket of dark ringlets.

"Stand closer to me," snaps the Prince's voice.

"Sir?"

"Do what you're told, woman. Now breathe in. Out. Again. You've been drinking. I thought so. Get out of the room."

"Sir!"

"Get. Out. Of. The. Room."

Footsteps. A gasping sob. The door. His voice again.

"You there. What's your name? Durdon. Come here."

Fully calm she puts the brush down and walks across to

him, stopping when there is barely a foot between them. He is not a tall man, but her eyes are level with the first diamond stud of his gleaming shirt-front and she has to raise her head to his. She takes slow, deep breaths and lets them out, as if showing the Princesses how to do their regulation breathing exercises at the window each morning. The Prince's breath smells of his cigar, and something else, musky and fierce.

"Right. You take charge for the moment," he says. "I will write to the Duchess tonight. Now, you, girl. What's your name?"

"Catriona McPhee, Sir," whispers the child.

"Come here. I shan't hurt you. Stand there."

He puts his dumpy little hands on her shoulders.

"Now breathe in," he says. "Out. Again. Hm. I like a sweet breath."

They stand there for some seconds, the Prince staring at the girl and the girl looking back at him with her head half turned away, her bosom rising and falling under the snowy stiff linen. Suddenly he grunts, a slow and meditative sound, then wheels away to the door. At once Vicky, usually so hesitant, darts across the floor and catches at this sleeve, pulling him down so that she can whisper in his ear. When he straightens, his cold opaque-seeming eyes stare at Durdon. He nods and goes.

As the door closes Rosie, inexplicably, bursts into tears.

Time-drift again, but not far, not far. The current that floats Miss Durdon into the first two of those sharp-lit bays now always nudges her into their once-forbidden neighbor.

A sob in the shadowed dark, and another. Nurse Durdon is awake at the first and sliding her sheets back at the second. For a moment the shadows seem to lie in the wrong direction, and then she remembers that Bignall is gone, and the smell of her and the fear of her, and now she is Nurse Durdon and has the tiny room between the Blue Nursery in which the baby Prince has his cot and the Pink Nursery where the Princesses and Catriona sleep. Their nightlights cast shadows through the two open doors, making angular patches of dim yellow on the ceiling of the middle room. It is icy cold. The glitter of moonlight off snow-swathed slopes is sharp as a spear through a crack in the shutters. The sobs half-stifle, then still completely as Nurse Durdon creeps bare-footed into the girls' room.

Vicky is deep in dreams and no mistaking, though she sleeps frowning as always. Rosie has actually missed Bignall for a couple of days but in her sleep she has forgotten the loss and lies like a child made by God to express His pleasure in children, a sinless joy. Nurse Durdon has never heard Louise cry, or even sigh, and she sleeps with that look on her face as though she were already Queen of a flat kingdom full of honest, dull subjects. Catriona . . .

Her eyes are shut, but her pretty little features are taut and even in the dimness a tear glistens on her long lashes. Nurse Durdon crouches by the bed.

"Hush, hush," she whispers. "You'll wake the children. It's only a nightmare."

"Och, but I'm frightened."

"It's only a nightmare. Go back to sleep, you silly girl."

"I canna sleep. I havena slept a' nicht. I'm frichtened."

"The idea! Here of all places!"

"Aye, here of a' places."

"I'm getting cold. Listen. If it will help for this one night I'll treat you like one of the little girls and take you into my bed. That's what I do when they have nightmares. But I won't do it again, I promise you that."

Nurse Durdon tries to imitate Bignall's gait as she stalks back to the middle room. Of all things! As if nursing four children weren't enough, to have to nurse the nursemaids too! But Catriona's body is so beautifully warm, as warm as fresh bread and as easy to hold as little Rosie's, that the stiffness and irritation quickly ebb away.

"If only there was never any men in the world," sighs Catriona.

"God made them for a purpose," whispers Nurse Durdon. "We must not question His ways. Are you worried about some young man in your town?"

"Och, no!"

"What's the matter, then?"

"I canna tell ye."

"It's not anything to do with the children?"

"No."

"And you haven't stolen anything?"

"No, no!"

"Or done anything else like that?"

"No."

"Then there's no harm in telling me. I'll help you, whatever it is."

"Ye canna."

"Of course I can. I know—one of the men here has been pestering you."

Silence, but the sudden stiffness of the soft body gives the answer. Poor child. Abergeldie is full of male servants, stifling in the musty rituals of their duties and then idle for hours. How their eyes must follow a child like Catriona. How, given the chance, they will tease her—and worse.

"Never mind, child. I can look after you. I can see that your duties are changed so that you aren't left alone."

"Ye canna. Ye canna."

"Of course I can. The duties of the nursery staff are my responsibility now."

A sob.

"You're being silly, Catriona. You will be all right, now you've told me."

"Och, didna ye speir what he did to Nurse Bignall?"

"The Prince!"

"Aye. Him."

"Oh, you poor child! Yes, I see. No doubt that's why he came up to the nursery in the first place. But he cannot touch you here at Abergeldie, my darling, not with the Princess here. And when we go back to England we will not be in the same house with him, and he has his own lady friends there, and . . ."

"Och, but he'll hae me in the end. He's the snake and I'm the wee bird in the heather. He'll hae me in the end."

They lie in silence for a while until Nurse Durdon realizes that Catriona has begun to weep again, without sobs, a helpless welling of slow tears. She lifts her head and kisses the salt lashes and runs a comforting palm along the soft back, as she would with a hurt child. With a wriggle like that of a fresh-caught salmon in a ghillie's rough hand Catriona throws her arms round Nurse Durdon's shoulders and drags her down to kiss her fiercely on the mouth. She is strong, and half again Nurse Durdon's weight. She fights the first shying buck of surprise and revulsion, forcing heads and bodies together.''

"Let me go! Let me go!"

"Na. Na. Be kind wi' me. Ye're sae bonny and wee. I love ye."

Catriona pleads on and on in whispers until, frightened and slow, Nurse Durdon relaxes into softness where touch tingles, breath smells of sweet fruit, nerves and muscles float in happy warmth. She finds that the muttered love-words her lips are saying twang with old Essex vowels. It is as though she had laid proper-spoken, careful Nurse Durdon neatly aside, like the dress and apron folded on her chair, and was Ivy, simple Ivy, in the caressing dark.

Mostly Miss Durdon found it unpleasant to have no feeling at all in her paralyzed body, not even to know except by smell when she had wetted or soiled herself; if the electric circuits in the apparatus by the bed were to fail, then she would not feel the fall in temperature except as a slowing in the activity of her mind and a drowning into sleep. But in one way the lack of a palpable body was a gain. For sixty years, while she had work to do and a chosen life to live, she had shut Catriona McPhee out of her mind, but now that the work was over almost every day she allowed the time-drift to take her back and eddy her round and round that one Christmas at Abergeldie. Unhindered by any sensations from the used-up scrawn that lay on the bed, smooth-skinned limbs would form invisible round her central will; they would feel again the stiffness of tight-buttoned boots and tight-laced whalebone, the crackling glossy crispness of fresh-starched caps and aprons—so like the crackling surface of the snow that had been touched by each day's clear but feeble sun and then restarched by each night's ruthless frost. It needed a little more will-power to shut out the endless, surf-like drumming of London traffic from

across the Palace garden, where the buses and taxis growled
up Grosvenor Place to Hyde Park Corner, but it was no
effort for Miss Durdon to close her eyes and see the spaniels
gamboling along a glittering slope, and the Princesses se-
date in their furs like little squirrels but with brilliant eyes
and glowing cheeks, and Catriona—Cat—Kitten—with her
wild animal look, wearing her uniform like armor against
the sword-sharp glances of the men who paced along the
swept paths.

Twelve days, eleven nights. Nurse Durdon during the
diamond days, cased in that armor, careful and loving,
watching the girls—Vicky especially—relax and lose the
edge of wariness, discover that they were now free to live in
the rejoicing instant, with nothing to pay into Bignall's iron
till at the end of it. Ivy during the caressing, trembling,
whispering nights.

That eleventh night.

"Och, and I love ye."

"Now you dan't, Kitten. You just love to be stroaked.
Shh. You lie still—I mun tark wi' you."

"I winna listen."

"Shh, shh. Lie still, Kitten, still. I'm goin' to tell the
Duchess as she mun find you a good pleace in another
family. I can meake her do that. Shh. Listen. This cawn't
last—it mun all end in tears. When we go South, deay after
tomorrer, we'll be in a real big nursery, wi' two more
meaids beside. But it's not only that, Kitten. I mun choose.
I mun choose now. Oh, Kitten, Kitten, you've bin tearing
me in two—two people you've meade me. Oh, Kitten, I
love you, more'n you'll ivver love me or anyone, but I
cawn't live like that. I cawn't be two people. Not all my
deays I cawn't. I mun choose . . ."

She has to go on saying it to be sure it's true. She has to
name the choice before she can make it. Catriona (it will be
fifty years before Miss Durdon, exploring these long-lost
shores again with the knowledge and equipment of a life-
time's navigation, can draw a true map of the girl's nature—
feeble and stupid about everything except herself, but there
gifted with the strength of will and intuitive intelligence

which intensely selfish people often possess) Catriona pretends not to understand.

"Ye needna Ivy, ye needna. We're daeing naething sinfu'. When it comes tae marrying, what mon wi' ken the difference?"

"Oah, it's not that, Kitten, not that. I love you, but I mun steay wi' my girls, and I cawn't teake you wi' me. Spose nobody nivver found out, still it's be like that Bignall and her tea. I mun be their Durdy, alweays there, all deay, all night, as long as they've need o' me. The Duchess cawn't do that, and she'll be Queen one deay, and further from them than ivver. They might as well have no mother at all. Doan't cry, Kitten. The Duchess'll find you a nice family, doan't cry..."

But they are both crying now, sobbing in each other's arms, Ivy for her own death, for hands that will never again gentle a lover's limbs, that will never kiss lips or whisper love-words. And Catriona...

Nurse Durdon believes that the child is working her way back into her nightmare and tries to reassure her by nursery means, in the "well-spoken" accent she has so carefully acquired.

"There, there. It's nothing to be afraid of. I'll explain to the Duchess and she'll find you a place where the Prince will never come."

"Och, but he'll hunt me doon. I've speired it in his ee. He'll hae me i' the end! He'll hae me i' the end!"

◆ 4 ◆

O N HER THIRTEENTH birthday Louise had been
interviewed by a rather sugary lady from *Woman's
Hour* about the whole business of princessing. Louise
had been so anxious to point out that some of the apparent
advantages aren't really that hot that the interview had come
out rather whiny. It had been a bore when Mother had made
her do the whole interview again, but listening to the tape
Louise knew she'd been right, even though second time
round she'd sounded rather more sugary than the inter-
viewer. The GBP had loved that.

One example she'd chosen in the whiny interview had
been that she was allowed to do her homework in the Palace
Library. This ought to have made things like Geog and Hist
an absolute doddle, with all those reference books to draw
on, but it was pitted with hidden traps.

At one end of the scale were the books which had been
acquired to help Great-grandfather—Victor I—understand
something about the Empire he ruled. Everybody agreed
that Queen Mary had worked wonders with King Victor and
turned him into a model monarch, but even for her the
improvement of his IQ had been a struggle. He needed
constant stimulation to keep his attention for a few pages, so
he had been supplied with books (or where these were not
available with typed reports bound in marbled boards) written in very simple English and full of startling stories, with

little nuggets of information scattered here and there. Louise found these enjoyable but distracting reading, and also dangerous to copy from. If a Princess has the bad luck to include in a Geog essay a sentence such as "The natives of South West Africa are very degenerate and will never be fit to govern themselves," then the Princess's mother, or somebody, will make her write the whole essay again. It's no use simply crossing the sentence out, because who's to know that her Geog teacher isn't a Maoist who will send a photostat of it to the underground press?

At the other end of the scale were Father's books. Father didn't like anything simple, except detective stories. Louise sometimes thought that he really didn't enjoy reading things if he thought there was a danger that another member of the Family might understand them. For instance if he needed to mug up a few conversational tidbits before meeting the Ambassador for Upper Volta, he'd send for tables of the incidence of river-blindness and a pamphlet on the latest attempt to breed mildew-resistant varieties of cassava. Of course there were in-between books, but Father had insisted that Mrs. Suttery, the Librarian, was not to help her find them.

On the other hand the Library was a good place to work. All those stacked shelves, and the green-lamped reading-desks, and the busts of Plato and Aristotle and Shakespeare and Dante with his cracked nose—work was what they seemed to expect of you. On the third night of term Louise had a history essay, a real peach for which she'd only needed to look up a few dates, because it was on a subject in which she'd had a deep and almost personal interest ever since she'd first been read the story at the age of five. She became so carried away that she had trouble keeping her handwriting tidy enough for Mother's exacting standards, and her last sentence carried her onto fifth side of paper.

". . . so Elizabeth was bang right to execute Mary, and she knew exactly what she was doing, and anybody who says different is talking sentimental rubbish."

Still full of pent-up vehemence which she'd been unable to release in the confines of the essay, Louise signed her own name in the blank area of paper and underlined it with a baroque curlicue of the sort her heroine used to draw. She shut the book from which she'd got the dates with a snap as final as the fall of an axe. Mrs. Suttery looked up from gathering her belongings into her bag. She was a tall, hollow-cheeked woman with intensely white hair and sad brown eyes.

"Finished already, Your Highness?" she said in her twittering voice.

"I'm early, you're late, Mrs. Suttery," said Louise.

"Yes, I'm afraid so."

"I expect you've been busy."

"Not really. No more than usual. You know, when you're worried everything seems to take longer."

"I'm sorry you're worried. Is it anything . . ."

"I'm afraid not, my dear. We're all worried, you know. It can't be helped. We all know that there've got to be cuts. In a way I'd almost rather I was one of them, because it would be so awful staying on and thinking about the people who've had to go. Oh dear—I shouldn't be talking to you about it, really."

"I hate it," said Louise. "I bet they choose all my favorite people. It's horrible."

"Well, I must get back to Alexander," said Mrs. Suttery, bravely changing the subject (which technically she wasn't supposed to do). "He's moulting again. Never fall in love with a Blue Persian, my dear. Good-bye."

"Good-bye, Mrs. Suttery."

Outside the cones of light from the desk-lamps the Library was full of autumn dusk. The clock—just like an old Post Office clock in its plain brown case—said twenty to seven. Mother wouldn't be ready to read the essay until seven. Louise's defence of the Virgin Queen had left her full of impetus, like that of a horse which has cleared its round so easily that it insists on looking for fresh fences to jump. She strolled over to see what Mrs. Suttery had been doing— pasting in the week's press-cuttings, it turned out. The big cutting-book lay open so that the glue could dry. Louise grinned again at the picture of Albert offering an enormous carrot to a round-faced farmer dressed as John Bull and carrying a placard saying "Beef put the G into GB."

Mother had been quite angry about that. Below it were five photographs of Louise herself walking through the school gates. She looked at them with a slightly irritated interest. A quite pretty, rather cool-looking round-faced blonde child with a satchel under her arm. Jeans and check shirt. It was the look of coolness that irritated her, because she remembered that moment as one of sudden near-panic. A year before she had walked through those gates for the first time into a very bad six weeks of friendlessness, curiosity and suspicion, which she'd only got through because she'd been able to talk to Durdy about it. It had been her own choice, after a long and obstinate battle, to go to a State School, and she'd known all along that she'd have to make it work, but she'd nearly failed. Then things had settled down and she'd enjoyed herself, so it was strange that the new year should begin with a sudden return of those old miseries, and stranger still that they shouldn't show at all. She ought to have been used to it: the *Daily Mail* had once tried to saddle her with the nickname of "The Ice Princess," but mercifully it hadn't stuck. It wasn't true—it only looked true. Julie, her best friend at school, was always gesturing and grimacing, but Louise had slowly discovered that inside this dramatic shell was a rather cautious and calculating person, a little too grown-up to be quite happy. Louise herself was the other way round and sometimes it worried her. Still, it came in useful for putting on a show.

Her eye slid to a nasty little paragraph in the *Daily Mirror*, pointing out that for the Princess to walk to school wasn't quite as democratic as it looked, because she'd been taken as far as Kensington Palace in a Rolls, and only walked from there. Nothing about it usually being only one of the Triumphs, and the Rolls being used that day because Mother was visiting Granny...

"Tittle-tattle..." she said aloud, doing rather a good imitation of Durdy's sniff.

The word, lingering among the silent books, reminded her of something she wanted to know. She crouched her way along the shelves behind Mrs. Suttery's desk until she reached the volumes of press-cuttings for 1954. One of them had a more used look than the others—that'd be the

Wedding, first marriage of a reigning British Sovereign since 1840. How long had they been engaged? Say a year. Lugging out one of the early 1953 volumes Louise laid its spine on the floor, shut her eyes and let it fall open at random, at the same time making behind her eyelids a picture of what she wanted to see—Nonny, laughing, creamy-skinned, in that strange half-swaying stance of hers which even the wide-hipped skirt of the New Look wouldn't be able to hide. She opened her eyes.

BLACK BLOOD?
Does Princess Isabella Carry a Fatal Disease?

Violently Louise shut the yelling headlines away, raising a cloud of dust which made her cough. No she doesn't, she thought, so you're stupid, arncher, and I hope your paper was one of the ones that went bust! She leafed around in the volume before that one, but found nothing except a back that might have been Nonny's in a picture of Father welcoming Mother at Victoria Station, but even by then she'd lost interest in her original search and begun to think more about Mother.

("Durdy, who's your top Queen? Mine's Elizabeth, and the rest nowhere."

"Ah, I've no book-learning, darling. It never did anyone much good, I always say."

"Oh, come on, Durdy—you've known a lot of Queens. You met Queen Victoria, didn't you?"

"Only just the once, darling. She was a real Queen. Queen Mary was a real Queen. Some of those continental Royals were a mousy lot, of course. But Her present Majesty—she's a real Queen too, and don't you forget it.")

Mother had given up so much to marry Father. She'd had changed her religion at the risk (she still seriously believed) of eternal damnation. She had come to live in a damp climate among people who hadn't any of her own feelings about the meaning of monarchy but treated it half the time as a glorious peep-show and half as an expensive way of causing traffic jams. And now it turned out that she had done this knowing that Father really loved somebody else. And still she had made it work.

With its chuckling whirr the Library clock chimed seven. Louise heaved the cutting-book home, scrabbled her homework together and left. Halfway along the corridor she remembered that they were saving money now, so she scampered back to turn off the Library lights.

Mother was at her little gilt writing-desk under the left-hand window of her private drawing-room. Annette evidently hadn't yet come round to draw the curtains, but the reflection from the desk-lamp made the space beyond the glass look as black as deep night. Mother managed to lean over her work without in any way bending her spine; this, and her shiny dark hair pulled tight back to her nape, and the even pallor of her arms and face, made her look like a doll from Queen Mary's collection, one of the expensive Parisian family whose flesh was the finest wax. Louise paused in the doorway, still tinged through all her consciousness by her thoughts in the Library. I'll always see her like that, she thought. She walked quietly forward and slipped her essay onto the desk.

Mother finished her sentence and picked it up without a word. That was OK, Louise thought—just another part of Mother's endless duties. She was perfectly fair. If something was "over the line" so that the whole thing had to be done again, she'd always explain why. If work was messy she'd say so but never permit any changes because that was teacher's business. Her spelling, luckily, was worse than Louise's. This evening as she turned the first page she began to smile, which was strange enough to be worrying, and when she'd finished she put the paper down and sat there tapping the arrogant signature with a long fingernail.

"I couldn't help it," said Louise. "I got carried away. I don't think they'll mind."

"Of course not, darling. It is very amusing, and strong. And of course Elizabeth huas right, though in my own history books I huas taught that she huas a great devil. But have you ever huondered how she felt? Huat huas it like to huait so long, and then to let herself pretend to be tricked into signing the order? Nobody could love her, you know—not the huay they all loved silly Mary. Is it enough to be right?"

Mother had turned to Louise as she spoke and now she let her long pale arms fall in a gesture of appeal. Automatically, like a bird obeying its innate response to stimulus, Louise slid onto her lap, though there wasn't really room because of the desk and the hard gilt chair creaked with the extra weight.

"I love you anyway," she said as the cool arms closed round her.

"I huas not aware that hue huere talking of personal matters," said Mother. "Last time you sat on my lap I could kiss the top of your head. Soon I shall only be able to kiss your chin."

"Am I too heavy for you? People don't hug people enough."

"Don't you believe it. Huen I huas much smaller than you are now some of those terrible old German cousins came to stay. Huenever they saw me they huould pick me up and hug me and insist on a kiss. They huere huomen, but they had moustaches, and even in Madrid they huore huool next to the skin, huich made them smell like dirty old sheep, except that their breaths smelt of aniseed."

"Oh, both sides have got to want to. It's got to mean something. Do you want to?"

"Just now, yes, in spite of your filthy hands. Huat on earth have you been doing, Lulu?"

"Oh, I finished my homework early and started looking at something in the old press cuttings."

"Which year?"

It didn't need the perfectly pronounced W to tell Louise that she'd trodden on a mine, hidden in the grass of the soft meadow through which she'd just been strolling. Deliberately she pulled herself closer into Mother's stiffened embrace.

"Before you were married," she said. "That's why I'm a bit sloppy this evening. I was thinking how marvelous you are, and how foul people can be, and what a lot you've given up. And I do love you—it's just that I don't get many chances to show it."

It wasn't any good. She'd made it worse.

"Well, I love you, Lulu," said Mother, "and I know I am not very good at showing it. I'm sorry. You'd better go and wash, darling, because I don't want to have to change this dress before dinner."

There was no shake in her voice, no glimmer of wetness in her eye. Her kiss was as precise as the full stop at the end of a sentence.

"Sorry," said Louise as she disentangled herself. "Don't move. I'll tell you if I've left any marks . . . I think your dress is OK but there's a little blotch on your neck. Do you mind lick? Oh, Mother, don't be silly. Sit still. There. I'm glad you haven't got a moustache and you don't smell of aniseed and old sheep, but I'd love you even if you did. I think that's all right now. Bye."

Only when she was out of the room did she realize that she'd left her essay on the desk, and that it wouldn't be fair to go back and collect it now. Mother would bring it along to supper. Somehow her face managed a smile at Annette when she met her bustling along the corridor, but really she felt as upset as Mother had been. The only thing she could think of was that Mother hadn't really accepted Nonny as easily as she'd pretended to, and that there was something about it in the cutting-books which still hurt. And yet Durdy had said it was all right . . .

Mother did bring the essay to supper. All the Family were at home, for once, and Father insisted on charades afterwards. They had a laughing evening, and Louise managed to push her sense of danger and hurt deep down and close the lid on it. But next afternoon when she went to the Library to start her homework she had to wait in the doorway to let out a couple of the Palace porters who were pushing a rubber-wheeled trolley piled with slabby green volumes. Inside she found Mrs. Suttery looking harassed.

"Hello, Mrs. Suttery, have you had the removals men in?"

"Yes, thank heavens. I've got rid of all the press-cuttings before 1960, except the wedding volume. Lovely empty shelves—just what a librarian dreams about."

"Where've they gone? Are you going to burn them?"

"Good heavens, no! They've just gone into store. I've been wanting to move them out for simply ages."

Louise smiled. One of the likeable things about Mrs. Suttery was that she was a less practiced liar than most of the Palace staff.

• 5 •

"BLIGHTER HAD A GO at me last night," said Sir Sam.

"But you foiled him," drawled Albert.

They were standing with Louise on the slope of lawn below the West Terrace. Further down, on the level, Mother and Father were talking to Mr. Farren, the Head Gardener. A little to the right Mr. Jones was arranging his tripod, watched by Commander Tank, the Press Secretary. Louise hated photograph sessions. The less formal they were the more trouble they seemed to be, with endless fiddling to achieve the apparently snapshot effect. Usually Mr. Jones was quick and clever, but even so there was a lot of waiting about.

"Foiled him?" said Sir Sam sharply. "Far from it. It was dashed annoying. I had to attend the reception in these trousers—thank God His Majesty's not like King Edward. Old Toby told me he once heard Edward blow his top about the width of braid on a guest's lapel. Pin-striped trousers with a boiled shirt! Whew!"

"What happened?" asked Louise.

"Oh, it was just silly and tiresome. My office has a bathroom, you know, and I keep a few clothes in the wardrobe there. Can't always be dashing home every time I've got to change. Hadn't left myself much time last night—never do—it's pretty well automatic—I reckon to get out of these duds and into tails in four minutes flat. Fact, it's so automatic that I was into my trousers before I realized that the blighter had scissored both legs off at knee-level!''

"You must have looked like a boy scout in mourning," said Albert.

"That's right," said Sir Sam. Even on almost-private occasions such as this he used his royal-joke smile—neat, eager, appreciative, but at the same time vaguely nervous, as though feeling that things could quickly get out of hand if much more of that went on.

"But you've got a spare pair of pants, haven't you?" said Albert. "I remember last week, when Mrs. Kissinger spilt her borscht in your lap, you snapped your fingers and somebody twinkled off, and a couple of minutes later you disappeared behind the service screen and popped out all immaculate, like a quick-change turn."

"Yes, of course I've got spares. Fact, I'd three suits of tails and two dinner-jackets up there, each with two pairs of bags. They'd all had the treatment."

"What a waste," said Louise.

"English tailors are no good at trousers anyway," said Sir Sam. "If I were a rich man I'd have my jackets cut in London and my bags in New York. Anyway, there they were, all hung up on their hangers. The blighter had even had the insolence to take off only one leg of those pairs and hang them up so that it didn't show. He'd had plenty of time. My secretaries push off at five-thirty and then I have a session with HM until six. And, you know, that pair Mrs. Kissinger chucked the soup over, I suddenly remembered they'd only just come back from the cleaners. They were still in their box in the outer office. Done him, by God! I thought. But by heavens he'd found it, done his deed, folded the trousers neatly back and pinned his diamond red cross to them! Hello, you're wanted."

This year Commander Tank, after taking his mysterious soundings of public feeling, had come up with a number of subliminal targets to be aimed for in the annual Royal Wedding Anniversary photo. It had to demonstrate a strong sense of family unity, of course. It should hint that the Royals were helping to fight inflation by doing things for themselves, but not overtly suggest that they were on their uppers. Whatever they were doing should be rather English and middle-class, because the last official photographs had shown them at a champagne picnic on President Giscard d'Estaing's country estate, and so on. These effects were to be achieved by showing His Majesty and the Prince of Wales planting a Queen Isabella rhododendron to mark the anniversary, Queen Isabella herself standing by and looking pleased. So far so good, except that Mother had always thought the color of the flower that bore her name brash and unsubtle, and Mr. Farren loathed having holes dug in his turf. Louise now presented an added problem, because in the interview with the sugary lady she had said that she hated anything to do with gardening, and this had struck the GBP, that nation of gardeners, as a charming eccentricity. In the end Commander Tank decided that she could lie in the foreground doing her homework, clearly of the Family but not—when it came to planting rhododendrons—with it.

As photographic sessions went it wasn't bad. The rain held off. Albert shovelled earth out of the barrow with a will. Father, majestic even on his knees, tendered the roots into place. Mother held the shrub upright with a smile that implied some ancient enemy was being buried alive beneath it. Louise's homework was French, a language in which she'd been bilingual since she was four (though with a slight Spanish accent), so she got some of it done in spite of the distractions. Mr. Jones clicked for the last time and said "Thank you." Albert produced a bunch of plastic tulips he'd kept hidden in the barrow and popped them in round the shrub. Father bellowed, snatched them out and started pelting him with them and with clods of earth. Mother laughed. Albert scampered away across the lawn, an ape-man in jeans. By the time Louise had gathered her books he'd caught up with Sir Sam and was talking earnestly to him.

"... might have been anything," Sir Sam was saying as she came in earshot. "A plain flat box. Cleaner's name on top, but somebody'd put a couple of files on it, so that was covered up."

"Then I don't believe he found it, just like that," said Albert. "It's too much. Prowling round your bathroom looking for extra pairs, yes. But I know what your office is like . . . what happened when the messenger brought the box up?"

"I wasn't there. When I got back Mrs. Anker said 'Something's come—I think it must be your borschty trousers.' "

"You see," said Albert, suddenly sounding remarkably like Father, which happened when he was seriously interested in anything, "that means the joker's made a mistake this time. He's narrowed the field. If you get going on it at once you ought to be able to find everybody who knew that your pants had come back from the cleaners—there can't be many."

"I'll make a small bet there won't be any."

"Well, you'd lose," said Louise. "McGivan told me he'd checked your toad, Bert, in case it was a bomb, and Sergeant Theale had made a joke about it. I bet that happens with all the boxes that come."

"Yes of course it does," said Sir Sam. "It's standard procedure. I wasn't thinking about the security staff."

"Well, I think we ought to," said Albert. "It's going to be a bit tricky because they're the ones you'd naturally get to investigate anything. But you see, not many people knew about my toad either. They did."

"They could have told somebody," said Louise.

Albert reverted to his usual slightly quacking gabble.

"Oh, sure," he said. "We've all seen the staff passing on tidbits out of the corners of their mouths. 'Sir Sam's trousers what Mrs. Kissinger threw the soup over have come back from the cleaners.' Not very high on the rumor scale, Lulu."

"I meant your toad, you fool," said Louise.

"Sergeant Theale's got a curious manner," said Sir Sam. "I hope it's not him. He's a very good man, otherwise. Well, if you're right ten pairs of trousers will be a small price to catch the blighter."

His frown vanished with an audible click as he turned, suave and smiling, to thank Mr. Jones for coming and make sure that Commander Tank fed him into the machinery for easing such people out of the Palace. As he moved away

Louise saw that Mother was still holding the shrub and Father was still shoveling the earth round its roots.

"Hell," said Albert. "I'd better go and help. I wish he felt he could leave it to Farren."

"I don't," said Louise. "The papers are going to say he planted it himself, so he's got to."

"Lucky he doesn't feel the same about foundation stones, or he'd finish up building the whole hospital."

"That's different. Bert?"

"Uh?"

Louise looked at her parents. Though Mr. Jones had gone they still seemed posed and artificial against the sweep of the lower branches of the big cedar, with the edge of a storm bruise-blue behind its apex and the slant light of evening slotting between the heavy horizontal branches.

"Do you know about Nonny?" she said.

"Yes, of course. Mother told me when I was about ten. I've always felt it was funny they should make such a song and dance about telling you."

"Mother told you?"

"Yes, of course. Why?"

"Something happened yesterday which made me think she minds more than she pretends to."

"I think you're wrong. What sort of thing?"

"Well . . ."

With a little stumble of hesitation Louise explained about the essay, and her talk with Mother, and the sudden sense of rejection as soon as she mentioned the press-cuttings.

". . . and when I went to the Library next day," she finished, "I found they were moving out everything before 1960."

"What! All the good wishes about my birth, and poor old Masefield's extraordinary poem in *The Times*?"

"Oh, Bert!"

"Sorry. I know what you mean, but I think it's something else. I don't know what—you do hit reefs with Mother, though. Something happened when I was born, for instance— I've never found out what. Are you worried?"

"A bit. I'm glad I asked you, though. I don't like the idea of living with a sort of lie. I mean . . . Look at them now."

They watched the King of England straighten, put his hand to the small of his back and do a mock hobble round to Mother. She said something. He put his arm round her waist and together they watched Mr. Farren brush the last of the loam from his lovely turf.

"It's funny how things become symbols," said Albert in his Archbishop Coggan voice. "Father's not interested in plants, and Mother doesn't like this one, but now they've made it mean something to both of them. I make these observations from the standpoint of one who is destined by birth to become a symbol himself, in his own humble way."

"I'm glad it's you and not me," said Louise.

Slowly, with linked arms, Mother and Father began to stroll along the lawn, not towards the Palace but sideways, parallel with the lake.

"That's nice, isn't it?" said Nonny's voice from behind them. "It seems a pity to interrupt them."

She was walking down from the terrace, looking very secretarial with her specs pushed up on her forehead and a pad in her hand. She smiled vaguely at Louise as she swept past with her long-legged bouncy stride.

"No, watch," muttered Albert, somehow guessing that Louise felt it was not just prying but actually risky to do so. Their Majesties seemed to hear Nonny coming, for they swung and stood there, still arm in arm but in a faintly formal stance, as though they were now posing for a much more old-fashioned picture of married harmony. Nonny seemed to sense this too, for she turned her last stride into a curtsey so low that she unbalanced and almost fell sprawling. It was Mother who helped her to her feet and then, as if greeting her after a long separation, kissed her warmly on both cheeks. The three of them moved off together, Mother in the middle with her arms round the waists on either side of her. Behind them Nonny's pad lay where she had dropped it with its upper sheets gesturing feebly in the light breeze.

"They're putting on a show for us," said Louise.

"Yes. But it's a show of something real. I don't think they laid it on, Lulu. It happened."

"I don't understand it, really."

"Nor do I, but it's a functioning system. If you muck around with it it'll break down."

"What do you mean?"

"Don't ask too many questions."

"I wasn't going to. I'm not like that. It's just . . . Anyway that's interesting about Sir Sam's trousers. I'm having tea with Durdy tomorrow. It'll make her laugh."

Durdy did laugh. Anything that discomforted Sir Sam was balm to her heart, provided it didn't in any way upset the members of the Family. Louise fetched the crumpets out of the corner cupboard (Kinunu put a fresh packet there every day, whether or not the old one had been eaten—the O and M men would soon stop *that* if they found out) and was sitting on the brown rug by the gas fire toasting one on the old telescopic brass toasting-fork whose prongs were the horns and tail of a grinning devil and whose handle had once been a pudgy angel but was now worn with use into an abstract blob.

"Mother was telling me about some horrible German cousins," she said. "They smelt of sheep and aniseed and kept picking her up and kissing her. Did you ever meet them, Durdy?"

"Yes, darling. They came to your grandfather's funeral."

"Kissing *and* crying?"

"I soon put a stop to the kissing."

"How on earth? They sound like a real kissing mafia."

"I borrowed Lady Elizabeth Motion's little girl who was just coming out with the measles."

"But didn't that mean that Father and the Aunts got the measles too?"

"They'd had it, darling. I always saw that *my* children got the infectious diseases as soon as they were old enough. If I heard of a suitable child with mumps I'd borrow him at once. Why, I even borrowed one of the Ribbentrop boys to give your Aunt Anne the chicken-pox. But their German Highnesses weren't to know my little ways, were they? And your grandmother was always too far up in the clouds to remember who'd had what."

"Durdy, you're marvelous. I wish Mother had had you to protect her from the kissing mafia."

"Nanny Cramp was an excellent Nanny, darling. She did the best she could in very trying circumstances."

At the first faint whiff of burning Louise withdrew the fork until its prongs were stopped by the criss-cross mesh of the fireguard. Reaching over the brass rail at the top, she reversed the crumpet and thrust it back to within half an inch of the red-gold elements.

"North Sea Gas isn't really so bad for this," she said. "I think Father just made a fuss because it was different. I suppose when you've been toasting crumpets the same way for forty years . . . what trying circumstances, Durdy?"

"Oh, it was enough to try the patience of a saint, Nanny Cramp said. Everything so formal all the time! When Queen Ena went bathing there'd be these two great big soldiers in their best uniforms with their guns, and they'd march into the sea beside her until it was deep enough for her to swim in. Nanny Cramp once saw them standing there, staring out to sea, with only their heads sticking out of the waves. Ridiculous! And if you were a Royal, everywhere you went in the Palace there'd be footmen all along the corridors to shout ahead that you were coming. Just fancy! The notions it might give a child!"

"And all that going on with poor Uncle Carlos dying too."

"No, that was later, after they'd abdicated. They had to be very careful with him all the time, of course. Still, it's no use crying over spilt milk."

Louise withdrew the fork again and with flinching fingers snatched the crumpet off and on to her plate, where she smothered it with butter. Her mouth began to salivate as the melting juice drooled into the doughy craters.

"Would you like a corner of my crumpet, Durdy?"

"Just to keep you company, darling."

When Louise popped a tiny triangle of crumpet between the thin violet lips a stream of spittle began to flow uncontrollably from the corner of the mouth. This always happened, so she had a tissue ready and mopped with it until Durdy stopped her slow chewing and the stream died.

"Thank you, darling," said Durdy. "You mustn't let yours get cold."

"I've put it in the grate. It'll be quite hot."

It wasn't of course, but it was worth having a tepid and congealing crumpet in order to perpetuate the rite of giving Durdy a corner of your food "just to keep you company." And the next one would come piping from the fire.

"I've got to go and have tea with Granny tomorrow," said Louise. "Shall I give her your love?"

"My respects, Your Highness."

"Oh dear. You know, I rather like her. I even like her being so awful. Sometimes I think I'm the only one who isn't afraid of her. Whatever she does, she can't touch me. I'm just out of her range. It's funny."

Durdy said nothing. Privileged though she was, perhaps she felt it wasn't her place to take part in the criticism of might-have-been Queens.

"It's difficult to think of Grandfather really loving her," said Louise. "Actually it's difficult to think of him doing anything, except drowning. I'm pretty sure what Victoria was like—almost as if I'd met her—and King Edward, and Great-grandfather and Queen Mary, but all the picture I have of Grandfather is a man with big eyes, wearing white flannels and looking worried."

"He was a lovely baby. How I remember the fireworks! He came after three girls, you see."

"Don't give me that! Remember I'm the President of Princess's Lib, Durdy. Anyway it's against the law now. When Bert has children there'll be a little man watching to see that the girls get exactly the same number of fireworks as the boys. Just think—if it hadn't been for Grandfather we'd have had a Queen Louise—only I shouldn't have been here to see it, of course, and anyway they'd probably have made her call herself Elizabeth or something. Did Grandfather come and toast crumpets when he was grown up, like Father does?"

"I had to take a firm line about that. People used to say that he never wanted to leave the nursery, so Thursday visits were all I would permit. Sometimes you have to do things which fair break your heart."

"Do you think he'd have made a good King, Durdy?"

"It's not for me to say, Your Highness."

"Oh, come off it. I suppose if King Victor turned out all right there's no reason why Grandfather shouldn't have— only I can't believe Granny would have been as much help as Queen Mary. A bad start doesn't really seem to matter much. I suppose Father really had an unfairly good start, being a boy King and refusing to run away during the war—I bet you had something to do with that, Durdy."

"We settled it between us, Queen Mary and Mr. Churchill and I. Your Grandmother is not to be blamed, darling. She never really understood what the English are like, you see."

"I suppose when all your own Family have been shot for not clearing out soon enough you're a bit inclined to want to scoot as soon as danger threatens. I'm glad Father stayed. It's like him, isn't it? And then everyone was eating out of his hand by the time the war was over."

Despite her promise to Albert, Louise found herself continually edging the conversation nearer the mystery. It was like a scab which isn't quite ready to come off—you know it'll bleed if you pick it, but the itch is too strong to resist. Durdy seemed unconscious of the path they were taking.

"He got on very well with those Labour people," she said. "He used to say that if he'd had a vote he'd have voted for Mr. Attlee, but I daresay he was only teasing."

"I suppose all that helped a lot when he wanted to marry Mother. He got his own way over that, didn't he?"

"His Majesty gets his own way about most things. He was a terror in the nursery. Once he climbed out of that window, over the bars, and hung on and said he'd drop unless I took him to the zoo."

"Who won?"

"It isn't about winning or losing, darling. I persuaded him to come in without making any promises, and a little while later he went to the zoo with the Prince. That was the last time he saw his father."

In conversation with Durdy one King led to another and you just let it happen. Normally Louise would have gone on with the interesting subject of Father being a terror, but the itch was too strong.

"What had they all got against Mother?" she said. "When I was looking at the newspaper cuttings I saw a stupid headline about hemophilia, but that was all right, wasn't it? I mean in spite of Uncle Carlos?"

In the silence, broken only by the wooden tock of the cuckoo-clock, Louise heard Durdy begin on one of her sniffs and then turn it into a sigh.

"If you want to know about all that, darling, you will have to ask His Majesty. I never understood it. Now may I trouble you to change the subject, Your Highness?"

"No, Durdy, that won't do. We did genes in biology last term, and sex-linking, and I told Father how funny it was seeing all the cousins in a table in a science book, and he just said it wasn't funny at all. I thought he was going to shout at me, but then he went gentle and told me that Mother wasn't a carrier and he wouldn't have been allowed to marry her if she had been, and so I wasn't either. And he asked me not to talk about it anymore."

"So that's that," said Durdy.

But the scab was bleeding now.

"No it isn't," said Louise. "Something's wrong, something to do with Mother. I upset her badly the other day and now I'm frightened I might do it again. And I'm beginning to think it must be something to do with me. I mean, it's funny their telling Bert about Nonny when he was ten, and then not telling me at all. Darling Durdy, couldn't you explain to Father . . . look, at first I was just inquisitive and I suppose that was wrong, but now the way you're all going on is making me feel . . . oh, I don't know . . . as though there was something wrong with me which everybody was afraid to let on about."

"There's nothing wrong with you. Word of honor, darling. Nothing whatever."

"Oh, I know there isn't really, in my mind. But with another part of me . . . it's like those nightmares you have which you can't remember when you wake up, only you know they're there. If you could remember them they'd be all right. That's why I can't stop myself asking questions.

OK, I'll change the subject. Miss Durdon, be so good as to
entertain me with the story of Lord Curzon and the elephant
and the bad banana.''

Although the Princess had gone, time refused to drift.
Perhaps the tiny taste of melted butter and crumpet was still
too strong. The drum of traffic too seemed curiously nag-
ging. Miss Durdon was worried, and too tired with it to cut
these last moorings and float free. She ran over the talk in
her mind until she got to the Princess who might have been
Queen . . . three Princess Louises there'd been, she thought,
and weren't they different! As different as chalk from
cheese. The first one hadn't really been Miss Durdon's
child, she had been Bignall's—a plain girl, seldom smiling,
always a foreigner in Miss Durdon's own Kingdom (though
when she was a Queen in her own right she'd refused to
employ any nurse for her children unless the woman had
first been interviewed by Nurse Durdon—an insistence that
caused some diplomatic frettings during the Kaiser's War).
It was strange that Vicky, though there were only thirteen
months between them, should always have been a native of
that Kingdom, even in the ghastly days of her dying . . . Miss
Durdon shut the image away by conjuring up the second
Louise—a subject of that Kingdom, of course, a perfect baby,
took her feed on the instant, slept all night, sat on her pot like
a soldier . . . it wasn't fair the way you couldn't help loving
some less than others, and do what you could they knew it. On
the scrap screen in the corner was a picture of HRH Princess
Louise in a pleated skirt and an eyeshade like the beak of a
bird playing in the quarterfinals of the Women's Doubles in the
first post-war Wimbledon; and she still wrote once a month
from Rome, long loose scrawls which only His Majesty could
read, telling Durdy gossip about film-directors and cardinals
mixed in with worming the Pekinese . . . still trying to grasp
that little extra parcel of love which the tree could never
bend down to let into her reach. And the third Louise.
    "My last baby. My very last."
    As though her old lips had whispered a spell the moorings
unloosed themselves of their own accord.
                        * * *

The little window-seat is hard and awkward. Misty-bright light of the northern dawn streams through the panes onto the blotchy, wrinkled, writhing creature on Miss Durdon's lap as she unwraps the warmed towel and, heedless of the tiny threshing limbs and the rasping shriek from the lungs, dresses the new-born girl for the first time. The baby is so light that every time she lifts her it feels as though she's going to toss her in the air by mistake, but Miss Durdon is used to this sensation. It's always like that. By the time of each new birth your arms have become used to lifting the baby before, without noticing how it's put on weight, so when they once more lift a really tiny one they feel as if they were trying to float up like gas-balloons at a fairground. . . . As the warmed flannel begins to shield it the baby's yelling slackens, but it is still making that stuck-pig noise when the last little wrestle of getting the arms into the jersey-sleeves is over and Miss Durdon can lay the small downy head into the hollow below her collar-bone and begin to soothe the back as it retches for fresh air to yell with. In thirty seconds, almost as sudden as if she'd turned the wireless off, a yell becomes a sob and the next sob is no more than a suck.

"Thank God for that," murmurs the King, still in his shirt-sleeves, staring out over Loch Muick at the interfolded slopes of heather beyond. "Why do babies always have to get born in the middle of the night?"

"Because it's the quietest time, of course," says Miss Durdon. "I expect if you look in your books you'll find that the sort of animals that rummage around at night have their babies in the day. It stands to reason."

"Durdy, you're a marvel. I bet you're right. I'll look it up as soon as we get back to civilization. I wonder if anyone's thought of it before."

"Course they have. You don't have to think of it—you just know it."

"Ah, but you're not a scientist. There might be a paper in it. Shouldn't be too difficult to collect the statistics. I'll ask old Zuckerman. Now, you know what happens next."

"What happens next is that *you* get some sleep, young man. So off to bed with you now."

He looks exhausted and no wonder. His face is white in the color-draining light and sweat has dried his moustache into rats-tails. But he shakes his head.

"Got to think things out. What's the time? Four twenty. OK, I rang Tim at Allt-na-giubhsaich when? Just about eight last night. He'll have got on to the Home Sec by nine, say. It'll have leaked to Fleet Street somewhere soon after midnight—Tim'll probably be staving off the local newshound by now. I wonder where the nearest Privy Councillors are. Let's say they'll be coming down the glen by noon. Do they still have to bring an Archbishop? Dashed if I know. I'm going to get a good deal of stick for letting it happen like this, Durdy."

"If you don't face trouble, trouble will come to your door. That's what I always say."

"I know you do, except when you say 'Never trouble trouble till trouble troubles you.' But you're right. We'll make a song and dance about it. Sir Derek will back me up there was not the slightest hint she'd be three weeks premature."

"Don't you worry. When they see my lovely new baby they won't think about anything else."

The King laughs, still frowning. A faint voice comes from the bed."

"You like her, Durdy? She's up to standard?"

"Oh, she's beautiful, beautiful. I thought I was never going to have another one."

"I should think not, at your age," says the King. "How old are you, Durdy?"

"As old as my tongue and a little older than my teeth."

"You're eighty-two. I shall have you made a dame for services to obstetrics."

"Don't be silly. I wouldn't say no to an MVO, though. That's more my place."

"Hell. Perhaps you're right. Anyway, this is the line we'll take. OK, I was a bit pig-headed coming up to Glas-allt Shiel only three weeks before the kid was due, but medical opinion was that the Queen needed absolute peace

and quiet—and dammit, I am pig-headed. Everybody knows
that. And after all it is one for the history books—when was
the last time a reigning monarch delivered his own daughter? We'll put on a show—you too, Durdy. Don't you go
biting off journalists' heads the way you usually do, or it's
no MVO for you."

Sniff.

The King laughs again and returns to the bedside where he
talks low-voiced and tenderly. Miss Durdon stares out of the
window at the gleaming loch, and the slabs of pine plantation and the treeless slopes of heather sweeping down to the
left of it. Somewhere over there, only ten miles away
beyond Conachraig, lie Balmoral and Abergeldie. But where
does Catriona McPhee lie? Where is that granite headstone?
It is sixty years since Ivy last saw her and almost that since
she last thought of her, but now she suddenly remembers the
wild face dim in the glow from the nightlights, eyes closed,
tears on the long lashes. She is startled. The baby snorts on
her shoulder. Ah well, she thinks, it's only natural.

◆ 6 ◆

HOLLAND PARK COMPREHENSIVE SCHOOL disgorges its pupils in tides. At one moment all the channels from it seem choked with strollers and scurriers; satchels swing, jaws champ gum, bikes wobble between the groups, last messages are shrieked. A minute later only one gloomy straggler mooches past. Then the next tide floods out.

Louise deliberately timed her leavings to coincide with one of the tides. At first she'd done it in order to baffle the odd unimaginative photographer who might be hanging around for an informal snap, but now it was more for the sake of her bodyguard. He, poor man, came in for a good deal more chiyiking than she did, but if she went out in a crowd and didn't even glance at him he could usually tag along without being noticed.

The day after her crumpet tea she walked, as usual, with Julie and Jerry as far as Church Street, where the other two caught their respective buses home, then on alone past the antique shops as far as York House Place, where she could cut through to Kensington Palace Gardens. She was just coming out of the narrow, brickwalled path to the wide avenue where the Foreign Embassies drowse beneath the plane trees when the man appeared.

He was about twenty, very tall, red-haired, with a thin, clean-shaven worried face. He wore an expensive brown jersey, dark trousers, suede boots. He took a quick but gangling pace from behind a tree, almost as though he were about to say "boo!" Without thought Louise put on her public face, the small non-committal smile and the glance of intelligent interest.

"Shall I show you something, little girl?" he whispered.

His hand was at his trouser-zip when the bodyguard reached him. There was a rapid, dance-like flurry and then the two men were standing with their backs to Louise, the stranger held in an efficient arm-lock. He didn't struggle but threw back his head and began to crow swear-words, making them sound like a chant at a tribal dance. Louise turned away and crossed the avenue where she waited while the uniformed policeman guarding the gate of the nearest Embassy came striding down, talking as he did so into his shoulder radio. Only when he recognized her and saluted did she remember to take off her public face. Another policeman arrived from lower down. There were no questions. The stranger was still chanting his litany of dirt when the bodyguard handed him over and turned to follow Louise. It was Sergeant Theale. She waited for him.

"Thank you very much," she said. "Poor man. What'll they do with him?"

"That's out of my hands, Ma'am."

Sergeant Theale looked small for a policeman, but this was really because he was very neatly made and within the limits of bodyguarding was a snappy dresser. He managed to achieve the same light tan all the year round. His face looked faintly Irish, flattish and small-nosed, and his hair was light brown and close curled. He held a Commonwealth Games Bronze Medal for the four-hundred-meter hurdles. In contrast to McGivan he always managed to look happy. He wasn't Louise's usual bodyguard.

"Where's Mr. Sanderson?" she said.

"Dentist, Ma'am. Came on sudden with toothache, so I stood in for him. I only got to the school with a couple of minutes to spare."

"I'm glad you did," said Louise. "Not that he'd have done me any harm, really, but it's a bit shaking ... I know it's out of your hands, but could you put in a word for the poor man? I'm sure he needs help."

"He needs a good belting if you ask me, Ma'am."

Suddenly Louise saw what Sir Sam meant when he talked about Theale's curious manner. There was a twist of tone towards the end of his sentences which made them sound as if he thought they were funny. It was very distinctive, though he probably didn't know he was doing it. Louise put on her public face and took it off again.

"Please see what you can do," she said, turning towards Kensington Gardens. "No, please don't drop back. I know I don't look as though I minded, but... anyway, I'd rather not face my grandmother for a bit—besides, she won't have finished practicing. Let's go and look at the ducks."

It was one of those September days which you sometimes get after a poor summer, as if July were trying to remind you what it could have done if it hadn't been too busy raining. Half a dozen kites were up and four big model yachts were racing on the Round Pond. Loose Labradors and Dalmatians lolloped about. The green of some of the trees was mottling towards yellow, and a gang was working with chain-saws at two elms, dead of the disease. It was warm enough, in spite of the breeze, for Louise to take off her jersey and fold it into her satchel. While she was doing this a slim black boy in a yellow shirt came up to her. He must have been about ten.

"Can I have your autograph, please Miss, um, Your Highness?"

"Now, move along there please," said Theale.

"No, wait a sec," said Louise. "I'd better explain. I'm not allowed to sign autographs—it's one of the rules. Oh, you've actually got your book. Hell! I know what, I'll draw a duck for you and put my initial in. Will that do?"

"They'll all say I did it myself, Miss."

"No they won't, because Sergeant Theale will witness it. And anyway you're not to show them, because then they'll all be here tomorrow and I'll never be able to come and look at the ducks again. That's why it's a rule... there. It's a pochard, I think. Thank you, Sergeant. OK?"

"OK," said the boy. "So long. Thanks."

Louise watched him go. A moment before he'd been an

individual. Now he plopped back and became part of the murky waters of the GBP.

"Sorry, Mr. Theale," she said. "I can't help bending the rules some of the time, but I needn't have dragged you in."

"That's all right, Ma'am."

They strolled on. Louise felt edgy. She hadn't realized that Theale was such a stickler, and wished now she'd gone and sat quietly at Kensington Palace waiting for Granny to finish. Still she was stuck with her decision, and it was up to her to start the conversation.

"Have you got any grandmothers alive, Mr. Theale?"

"No family at all, Ma'am. My parents died in a coach crash three years back, and they were the last."

"Oh, I'm sorry."

(The correct form of words added "That must have been a great loss to you," but something told Louise they weren't needed.)

"I'd not seen them for three years before that. He travels the fastest who travels alone."

"I shan't get very far in that case. Sometimes it feels as though everybody in the whole world was some sort of cousin."

"There's some pretend they are. Some I know."

"Oh, yes. My father keeps an album of Rightful Kings of England. It's one of his hobbies. He's got about thirty at the moment, including two Black men and one Chinese. He says he's going to give a special Garden Party where they can all meet each other, but of course he won't do it. It wouldn't be kind."

Theale grunted. While she was speaking Louise had been watching a grossly fat small boy trying to catch a pigeon; his mother/nurse/au pair was busy with an endless kiss with a young man on a bench. Theale's unexpectedly informal reply made her think that she had touched some sort of a sore point with him, but then she decided that she must have offended him by her attitude to the whole princessing scene.

"You have to joke about it some of the time," she said, "or you'd go mad."

"There's jokes and jokes, Ma'am," he said. "The Prince is a great joker, and none of us mind that. It makes for a bit of brightness in our lives sometimes. But now, you take this

customer who's been playing tricks in the Palace—I don't
go for that at all. It's not just that they're a nuisance, and
bad for morale, and that. To me whoever's doing them is no
better than that feller back there who tried to commit a gross
indecency in front of you. That's what this joker in the
Palace is doing—committing a series of gross indecencies. I
hope it's going to be me as catches him, that's all.''

Louise decided he was genuinely angry, though she could
never have told it from his tone. As always his speech ended
on a slight lilt that was almost a chuckle.

''Do you like working in the Palace, Mr. Theale? I mean,
it's a bit of a backwater, isn't it?''

''It's an honor, Ma'am.''

''That doesn't stop it being a backwater. I expect a lot of
honors are, really. Suppose you could choose your next
posting, when it happened and where, how much longer
would you like to stay?''

''Just under two years,'' he said promptly. ''That's one
good thing about the job, the hours are pretty regular, which
you can't say of a lot of other police work. Makes it a whole
sight easier to study for my next go of exams.''

''Are you looking forward to them?''

''You bet . . . Ma'am.''

''So'm I. I'll be doing my O-levels almost the same time.
We must remember to wish each other luck. What's the
time—I don't carry a watch.''

''Getting on half past four.''

''My grandmother ought to have finished practicing now.
Thank you for the walk.''

''Thank you, Ma'am.''

As Louise changed out of her jeans into the deliberately
''sweet'' frock which she'd dumped at Granny's on the way
to school, she thought about Theale. Until he'd mentioned
the joker she'd clean forgotten Albert's suggestion that it
might be somebody from the security office, Theale himself,
even. No, she decided, not him. It wasn't just his being a
stickler—the joker might well be like that—you'd need to
have a bit of an obsession with Palace ritual to want to muck
it around. But it was hard to think of anyone so keen on his

own career running the risks with it that the joker ran; and there was his voice, with that curious chuckle in it—Louise instinctively felt that somebody who talked like that without noticing it must have no sense of humor at all, and the joker's jokes had been pretty funny, in their way. Besides, Theale's reaction to the joker had been so like his reaction to the poor man outside the Embassies that she almost felt that if Theale was the joker he'd have had to have hired the man to go there and jump out at her. No, not Theale. It would be impossible to explain to Sir Sam, and difficult even to Albert . . .

Louise brushed her hair, slipped into her special Granny-visiting low-heeled shoes and went out into the hall. Upstairs Granny's harp was still sending its acid tinklings into the musty, mourning air, so there was time for her to shut herself into the dotty old mahogany phone-box in the hall, ring home and ask for the Press Office.

"Hello, is that Katie? It's me. Yes. Have you had anybody ringing up asking for lurid stories? Oh, good—only a bloke jumped out at me on my way back from school—I don't think he thought I was anyone special, just a passing girl, poor man. No, Sergeant Theale arrested him and handed him over to a couple of bobbies from the Embassies. I just thought I'd better warn you. Yes, quite all right, just sad for him. Look, Katie, can you ask the Commander to see if he can fix it so the man doesn't get charged? That'd be marvelous. No, he was quite young—it was sad. Thanks—see you."

Somehow that exorcised the specter of the red-headed man and made Louise feel quite light-hearted as she trotted up the stairs towards the harp-music. She opened one leaf of the big double door and tip-toed into the music room. There bright day streamed through tall windows, twinkled off veneered wood and polished brass, but still seemed somehow to leave shreds of ancient gloom floating between the sun-shafts. It was the same with all those polished surfaces—no doubt every one of them was speckless, but still the room felt as though the dust had gathered in it undisturbed since the night the news came of Grandfather's drowning.

Granny had her back to the door and seemed not to have noticed its movement. She crouched at the harp with her

head pressed close against the frame as though she were
listening to whispered messages beneath the notes. Her
bare, scrawny arms made angular shapes as they reached for
the strings. She was wearing her music-clothes, shapeless
swathes of black and grey lawn which made her look
(Albert said) as though she'd got half way through the
Dance of the Seven Hundred Veils and then given up. Her
hair was a brighter orange than last time.

Louise simply waited, listening to the notes without
understanding them. It's a twangling instrument, she thought.
That's what. Hey! I bet Shakespeare had a tin ear, like me.
Everybody keeps saying how musical he must have been,
but then you get a word like "twangling" which gives it
away. And what about that corny old Duke—or was he a
Prince?—no, only a Duke—asking for a bit of music all
over again? And then being surprised when it didn't come
off? If you were musical you wouldn't muck around like
that, and you wouldn't be surprised when it didn't work. It's
only that old Shakes knew the sort of things he was
expected to say and said them better than anyone else . . .
something about a cat's guts—that shows he knew what it
was like *not* to be musical, so think again, everybody . . . but
it's funny how even if you've got a tin ear you can tell that
it's almost over . . . any minute now . . . she knows I'm here
of course . . .

Ping. Twangle. Plockity-plock. Punggg. Head flops. Arms
flop. Count five. Swing to audience. Smile.

Sure enough the Dowager Princess of Wales swung round
on her music stool like a harbor crane. The deep maquillage
of her cheeks was all runnelled with tears which were still
streaming from the corners of her jade-green eyes. She rose
groggily and stood blinking at the intruder. Then she pretended to realize who it was, shrugged her pointy shoulders
and produced a bitter little smile.

"And now I have ruined my face," she said.

"At least it means I can kiss you properly without
spoiling anything," said Louise as, with slight gritting of
the will—as if forcing herself to eat her unfavorite prawn
cocktail at a public meal, and smile while doing so—she
hugged Granny tight and kissed her on both cheeks. The

films of veiling made it feel as though she were clutching a cocoon of cobwebs. Granny chuckled through her tears and pushed her away. She looked pleased though.

"Was it because the music was so beautiful?" said Louise. "I wish I could understand about music."

"No, no, little owl, the music was nothing, a mere exercise, pooh, pretty little scales, chords, tinsel, you can play it without thinking, without feeling, which you see leaves you time to think stupid thoughts . . . no, no, I am not going to bore you with tales of your poor Grandfather (but what a King I should have made of him!) that is not why you come to this old harridan is it, little swan, of course not. No. I was thinking how soul-tragic it is for me that I shall never know—nobody will ever know—whether I am a great harpist (which I think I am, to be sure—but how can I be sure? *That* is the soul-tragedy). But you are my perfect audience, little sparrow, because you cannot hear it and have no need to lie to me!"

This was a much more typical snatch of Granny's talk than her opening remark had been.

"But everybody says you're terribly good," said Louise, quite truthfully.

"I am a horse!" cried Granny, throwing her arms wide and looking considerably more like an orange-crested vulture of some sort. "A horse with flashing eyes and a long white mane and diamonds all over my bridle—also I play the harp. So everybody says I play the harp very well—for a horse. Even myself, sometimes I think I am playing with hooves!"

She clenched her many-ringed fingers into fists and made pawing motions in the air.

"Ah, but for my destiny I should have known, the world should have known, that here is a great human soul that speaks through music! Neeeeeeeaaagh!"

The whinny echoed among the twinkling objects and seemed to stir the harp-strings into unheard murmurs.

"You're a great actress too," said Louise. "I'd love to see you on the telly."

"You must never mock at a soul-tragedy," said Granny, still clearly pleased. "Especially you, who will know the same soul-tragedy."

"Me!"

"You will never know whether you are beautiful, little gosling," said Granny sharply. "I will make a new face and then we shall have tea and I shall send stupid Beatrice away so that she will not interrupt our talk. Will you wait for me in the little sitting-room?"

"Fine," said Louise, bobbing into a small curtsey as she held the door for her. It was quite unnecessary, and probably not even protocol, but Granny had a rather Hollywood attitude to things like that.

Every three months the *Gazette* listed a change of lady-in-waiting to HRH the Dowager Princess, but no matter who got her name into print it was always Beatrice, Lady Surbiton, who did the job. Louise found Aunt Bea (she was no relation—it was just a courtesy title) in the clutter of the drawing room, looking as always hopelessly out of place among the rugs and icons. Aunt Bea was a dear old thing, large and white with tiny pudgy hands, always dressed in a rasping tweed skirt, dark green twin-set and double row of pearls. She was very short-sighted and tended to knock things over if they had been moved from their usual place— Granny sometimes rearranged the room for the pleasure of seeing this happen and then scolding her. Her voice was so soft that she made everything sound like a wicked secret. Louise was glad that she wasn't staying for tea because it was uncomfortable to listen to Granny using her as a pin-cushion (though according to Albert Aunt Bea had tried to commit suicide a couple of years back when Mother and Aunt Anne had conspired to relieve her of the role. Albert said she'd jumped out of a ground-floor window and twisted her ankle.)

"Hello, Aunt Bea. How's life?"

"Who is that? Oh, Your Highness, you did give me a start. I almost dropped this . . . er . . . this . . . only luckily I must have put it down somewhere before you came in. Life? Much as usual. Very quiet. Very, very quiet. Except, oh yes, the most extraordinary thing, a lot of grand pianos arrived this morning. Eight or nine. I was quite at a loss to tell the men where to put them until HRH woke up and sent them all away again. Apparently it was some sort of joke.

But I must say, my dear, that your Grandmother is perfectly capable of ordering nine pianos and forgetting to tell one about it, but of course she refused to see it that way, though she insisted on trying them all out and was quite tempted to keep two. You know, it made me feel quite uneasy. Jokes. Oh dear.''

Louise too felt a faint shiver of unease, like a creeping draught that seems to permeate an apparently cozy room. It was as though the jokes were a disease, and now it was spreading.

"Poor Aunt Bea," she said. "Let's talk about something else. How's Mike getting on in Canada?''

Aunt Bea launched into one of her long, sighing accounts of the great interest in her life, her delinquent grandson, heir to the Surbiton title, who seemed only to have to attend a pot-smoking party to make sure it was raided, only to have to borrow a friend's car without permission to run down a Lady Mayoress in it, only to have to go for a quiet Sunday walk in the country to disappear and emerge in the small hours of Wednesday morning blind drunk, stark naked, hammering on the door of some night-club performer's Mayfair flat. She hadn't really got round to describing the effect of Canada on him, and vice versa, when Granny's butler, Mr. Forster, came in with the first of the cake-stands and handed her a note written on bright green paper. She put on her pebble glasses and peered her way right through it.

"Oh, dear," she whispered. "It seems I'm not to have tea with you after all. Well, I've a lot of letters to write, I expect, so if Your Highness will excuse me . . .''

Poor Aunt Bea, thought Louise. What a bitch Granny can be. She'd have made a pretty grisly sort of Queen, too. I wonder if Sir Sam and the Palace machine could have kept her battened down. She'd have silvered his hair for him OK.

Granny had invented a tea-ceremony to suit her own personality. It involved a number of cake-stands and very tiny tea-cups, so that her guests spent most of their time levering themselves out of deep-cushioned chairs to fetch each other stamp-sized sandwiches and minicakes and fresh thimblefuls of tea. Albert used to bring his own whole-wheat sandwich and flask of applejuice so that Granny couldn't use him to treat Aunt Bea like a yo-yo. He wasn't often invited.

But today Granny came sweeping in in a black trouser-suit a-glitter with diamonds and glared at these arrangements. Instantly she rang the bell.

"I cannot think why Beatrice insists on using these ridiculous little cups," she snapped. "Ah, Forster, please take these cups away and bring us two of the big breakfast ones. Now, little owl, take one of these tiresome stands and fill it up with everything you need—tip the rest on the tray—then you can settle into your nest and chirp away. When my children were small I used to steal off to the Nursery to have a proper English tea—that is the only civilized invention of this nation, nursery tea. Durdon understood about tea. There were crumpets, always, toasted on the gas fire. What are you smiling at, little swan? You must be careful how you mock me. I have an uncertain temper. Everybody knows that."

"I had crumpets with Durdy yesterday."

"What! Is she still alive? Absurd!"

"She can't move and she can't feel but she's still more alive than anybody."

"Without that woman this country would have been a republic by now. How I longed to dismiss her—don't look so shocked, little wren, of course it was impossible, as if I were to suggest blowing up the Tower of London like Sir Guy Faux . . ."

"The Houses of Parliament, Granny."

"What does it matter? This country has no history. How many Kings have you assassinated? One! And you did that by committee. It simply shows that your Kings have no meaning for you, except as a peep-show. Seriously, little wren, suppose my father-in-law, that abominable King Victor, had died in youth, as he nearly did. Suppose my mother-in-law, Queen Mary, had married Georgie York, who was secretly very fond of her—only he could not show it, being so English. Why, then you would have had a quite different Royal Family from the one you have now. But do you suppose anything else would have been the smallest bit different? Pooh!"

"But that means even if you'd become Queen things would be just the same, Granny!"

"You must not be too clever with your Grandmother, little owl. For you are wrong. I would have been the meteor of change. Your poor Grandfather! By now—supposing Lord Halifax had not arranged for his so convenient drowning—by now I would be either in noble exile or gloriously reigning. I would have made him a true monarch. Think of it! With Oswald Mosley at our side—no Hitler war, no strikes, no communism, all Europe peaceful and disciplined, and at home respect for the social order and the arts! I had such plans for the arts in this nation of philistines!"

When Granny said shocking things it was important to look a bit shocked or she got huffy. Louise knew about Mosley from a Sunday paper article which Father had made her read, but had only the dimmest ideas about the other bloke. She let her eyes widen and waited for a pause.

"But that's thrilling!" she said. "How did you find out about Lord Halifax? Why doesn't everybody know?"

Delicately Granny picked up the icing off a little yellow cake, ate it and threw the cake itself into the fireplace.

"I have always known," she said. "It was a conspiracy of nonentities who did not dare let me become Queen. But until this day I have told nobody—I resigned myself to the dignity of defeat and my music. It is important to have secrets, and to keep them . . . and since you are so sweet to come and have tea with your tiresome old Granny I will tell you a little secret about yourself. Do you know how you were born?"

"Oh, yes. The doctors said Mother had to have peace and quiet so Father took her up the Glas-allt Shiel and I was born a fortnight premature and Father delivered me and Durdy helped and there was the most frightful fuss because you aren't supposed to be born without a lot of witnesses to prove that you haven't been smuggled in in a bed-pan. I'm afraid I know that already, Granny."

"Ah, but what you do not know is that you were *not* born prematurely. It was your wicked Father, wanting to do it all himself without the proper fuss and protocol . . . oh, he persuaded himself that it was for your poor Mother's sake . . . she is not a good bearer of children, dear Isabella—

not like me—she cannot feel what a godlike act it is to give
birth to a Prince—a little pain, pooh!—I smiled, I laughed
with triumph, I gave birth like a cat, purring, I wished to do
it before all the world, in Westminster Abbey, yes, and Ted
Elgar should write me a birth-anthem for those sweet little
choirboys to sing, with many many trumpets, so that the
child should know that he had truly been born a Prince. And
there would be public holidays and the bakers should bake
loaves of a special shape—oh! . . . but dear Isabella, who is
afraid of nothing else, wishes to creep away and give birth
in secret, because she is afraid of that. But of course it was
your wicked Father who put her up to it so that he could
play at being a doctor. Premature? Pooh! You were a
nine-month child if I ever saw one."

"But Mother's doctors must have known, Granny."

"Oh, my dear little gosling, when you are as old as I am
you will have learnt how these doctors stick together. The
crimes they hush up in their hospitals! And Vick is one of
them—and remember he can reward their little lies with
knighthoods and baronies and goodness knows what. So that
is *your* little secret."

"Thank you for telling me. I've always been a bit
worried about their going off for a lovely quiet holiday and
me barging in and spoiling it."

"There, there, little owl. You must be careful not to have
too sweet a nature. It is important that people should
understand that you have it in you to make them suffer."

Louise had her mouth full of chocolate Digestive biscuit,
so she made a grunting noise. Granny was not deceived.

"Pooh!" she cried, waving another of the cakes as
though it had been an elfin hand-grenade. "They will suffer
in any case. Let a people choose a saint to be their Prince, a
deaf, dumb, blind saint, he will cause them to suffer by his
saintliness. Your sweetness will hurt many people, people
you have never seen, because you are a Princess. It is better to
choose whom you make to suffer, as I do . . . but you do not
come to tea with me to hear sermons, but to talk gossip.
What is happening inside that hideous Buckingham Palace?
How is dear Sir Samuel?"

"Sir Savile, Granny. I know Father calls him Sam, but . . ."

"Nonsense! A Jew if ever I saw one—how is he?"

"Quite well, I think. Only before a big reception on Monday someone got into his dressing-room and cut the legs off all his evening trousers. He made it sound worse than if they'd cut off his own legs."

Granny nodded.

"And somebody ordered a great many bad English pianos to be delivered here this morning," she said. "Somebody in the Palace, who knew the ropes well enough to see that the gate-porters let them through. Oh, don't look at me like that, little owl—it was your brother Albert of course. He is angry with me because I no longer invite him to tea. You will tell him I am not amused."

"It wasn't Bert, Granny, honestly. We've had several of these jokes and two of them happened before Bert and I got back from Scotland, and the next one somebody used one of his toads for, which I'm sure he wouldn't have done."

"Good. I am capable of making life unpleasant for Albert but it would give me no pleasure, and I am now too old to waste time on matters that give me no pleasure . . . so! You have a joker in the Palace. It is of course all the fault of Harold Wilson."

"Oh, Granny! How can it be?"

"Why, of course, little owl, for not giving the King enough money to run his Palaces, and for allowing everybody to be paid absurd wages—what sort of a country is it that has no poor?—so that your father must tell his faithful servants, 'Go and find yourself a different job, because I can no longer afford to let you serve your King.' Then of course there would be a man—or a woman—no, it would be a man to cut off the trouser legs—who says to himself, 'So, I am to be thrown out after all these years of loyalty. I will have my revenge in advance, before I go, so that I can see it happening, and all they can do is sack me. They cannot any longer put me in dungeons or crop my ears or even send me to Australia.' That is how I would think, little wren, except that my revenges would be more cruel. Trousers! Pianos! Pooh!"

"I wonder whether you're right. I'll tell Albert, anyway. He was pretty upset about his toad."

"Toads! Pooh!"

Theale held the front door of the Triumph open and Louise climbed in without thinking. They were sliding under the plane trees when he spoke. That was surprising for a stickler, like not putting her in the back.

"Excuse me, Your Highness."

"Yes, Mr. Theale?"

"Four-ten this afternoon you were with me, up by the Pond?"

"That's right. Why?"

"Did you hear about the pianos?"

"Yes."

"So did I, and I thought while I was waiting for you I'd go down to the Gate-porter's, see how they let 'em through. Soon as they heard my voice they began to look at me pretty funny. Turned out that somebody'd rung them up, four-ten this afternoon, wanting to know whether the pianos had arrived all right. Said he was from the Red Cross."

"Oh!"

"That's right, Ma'am. And this chappie that rang up had the same voice as me."

"But . . ."

"Lucky I was with you, Ma'am. Normally this'd have been my afternoon off, except for Sanderson having the toothache."

"But who on earth . . ."

"There's one or two, Ma'am. There's Palace messengers don't hit it off too well with us in Security, for instance. I'd begun to think someone might be trying to lay for one of us."

"I think that's horrible—much worse than the jokes. But at least there's one good thing, Mr. Theale—it means everybody knows you're not the joker now, doesn't it?"

◆ 7 ◆

IT WAS A long time since Louise had been "sent for."

She was in Albert's zoo after school on Friday. It was going to be one of those dispersed weekends for the Family, which Louise so hated. Mother and Nonny were already on their way to Helsinki to open a British Week. Father was off in a couple of hours for a three-day tour of the north-east, Albert was driving down after supper to the Kents—he'd asked himself for the weekend in order to chat up Soppy Windsor. In the long-running Palace sweepstake on the eventual Princess of Wales the wise money was nowadays piling on to Lady Sophia Windsor. Mother had arranged for Louise to go down to the Yorks tomorrow morning, so Louise had arranged to keep her homework till then—it was a good deal more interesting that anything the Yorks were likely to lay on. She'd come to the zoo to tell Albert about Theale and the pianos—she hadn't had a chance earlier, because of his rush of official engagements before the start of his university term.

The zoo had once been King Victor I's gymnasium, built on Queen Mary's insistence and used with some reluctance by the monarch. It was a long, light room on the ground floor at the south-west corner of the Palace, with barred windows and unplastered stone walls. Albert had a laboratory bench against the left wall, but the rest of the space was taken up with tanks and cages. When Louise came in he

was coaching his mynah through a Jacobite epigram and
wouldn't let Louise speak, so she spent a minute or two
watching Fatty, the Blomberg toad, rearranging its bed of
leaves in its tank, and then moved on to play with the
lion-maned tamarin. This was a new arrival, a creature of
extraordinary beauty and appeal, a little gold ape with round
blue eyes—slightly pop, like Father's—and tiny, human-
seeming hands. It was very tame and would sit on your
shoulder and look for nits in your hair; but when you had to
put it back in its cage it would press its palms against the
glass and wail. Albert had been given it by some South
American President, and as soon as protocol allowed was
going to pass it on to a larger zoo where it could have the
space and company it needed. It was looking for a nut
Louise had hidden in her blouse pocket when the telephone
rang.

The mynah broke off its lesson to do a bit of ringing too.
Half the other animals, jealous of the attention it got,
gibbered or shrieked at it. Louise snatched up the phone and
put her finger over her free ear.

"Zoo," she said.

"Zoo to you too, Lulu," said Father's voice. "I've been
chasing you all round the shop. Could you come along to
my office?"

"Coming," she said, and put the receiver down with a
sense of being detached from the racket in the room. When
she'd settled the tamarin back into its prison she saw Albert
looking at her.

"I've been sent for," she said.

"Good God!" said Albert.

"Good God!" creaked the mynah.

"Just listen to that," said Albert. "You spend hours
trying to teach it something worthwhile and you get nowhere, and then it goes and picks up a chance swearword
it's only heard once. What on earth . . . Oh, sorry, Lulu,
none of my business. Good luck."

"Good God!" corrected the mynah.

Father's voice was diagonally across the courtyard, but of
course it was raining. This meant that Louise had to pass
through something like a quarter of a mile of corridors and

stairs. Though it was almost the weekend there were still plenty of people about, all of whom had to be smiled at as she passed. Don't be stupid, she thought. I haven't done anything wrong and anyway he's only my father with a small f. But still she was . . . not really frightened, no, but a bit more than nervous. Usually Louise felt not much different as a person from most of her friends—she was sure that all their families were pretty eccentric in some way or other and that princessing was something outside herself, outside the true, inner self—something only on the surface, like having a marvellous figure which made bricklayers whistle at you from scaffolding, or having a fearsome squint which made people on the bus stare for an instant and then look hard at the advertisements—but you could have either of those and still be pretty ordinary inside. Louise was sure that she was ordinary. That didn't change, just because she happened to be a Princess and live in a Palace. But now, marching along one of those stretches of corridor that felt and smelt more like an elderly, snobby hotel than a home in which real people lived real lives, she became aware of a process that was already beginning to happen to her: as she grew up, princessing would gradually infect the ordinariness, seeping into it, so that by the time she was as old as Mother she'd have stopped being an ordinary person and become an ordinary Princess. Right inside, perhaps, there'd still be a secret Louise, which nobody could reach, and she'd spend all her life defending its last few rights.

At the foot of the stairs up to Father's office she stopped, more for the sake of delaying the moment than in order to stare at the enormous painting of Kaiser Wilhelm greeting Edward VII on the station platform at Berlin. Father insisted on having this hideous thing hung where he could see it every day, because (he said) it was a perfect parable about putting on a show. Apparently Edward had taken into his head at the last moment to go and visit another part of the train—some pretty lady, Louise thought. He'd still been there when the train stopped, and had climbed out onto a bare platform. Meanwhile, fifty yards along, was the glittering scene of the Kaiser and all his court, red carpet, band for the National Anthems, the works, waiting to greet a King

who wasn't there. Edward had seen what was wrong and
had climbed back into the train to work his way down inside
and emerge at the proper place, but meanwhile somebody at
the other end had told the greeting party to look for the King
farther back . . . it had made an awkward start to the visit, to
say the least. But the official artist had painted the scene as
though everything had gone like clockwork, with the King
stepping down onto the carpet to be greeted by his smiling
nephew, with the courtiers standing like statues and the band
blasting away in the background.

It's part of Father's own defenses, Louise thought. It's a
way of telling himself every day that putting on a show isn't
the real thing. We have to live like that all the time,
reminding ourselves . . . Father's shouting at meals, Mother's accent, Bert's carrots and teasing—they're all ways of
giving the inside person a bit more room. Supposing we
weren't Royals and Father sent for me—I'd probably call
him Dad or something—I might be scared stiff but it
wouldn't be like this. One of the reasons why Granny is so
frightful is that she can't tell the difference between her
inside and her outside. She talks more about being Royal
than anyone, but she doesn't understand it, not really—and
that's why they're all so frightened of her. But I'm not. I'm
too ordinary, and I'm going to stay like that. So there.

Father was reading his way through a despatch box with
his usual incredible speed. His eye seemed to unzip each
page, but at the end he knew what was in it, initialed it and
laid it on the pile of ones he'd already read. Every now and
then he'd add a scribbled comment. Louise waited by the
door, looking round the ambiguous furniture and decor. It
was like one of those trick-perspective pictures: stare at it
and it looked like the room of a monarch who did a bit of
doctoring; blink and stare again and it became the surgery of
a doctor who happened to be King. The chaise-longue was a
handsome bit of furniture, but the retractable light-fitting
above it turned it into an examination couch; *Black's Medical Dictionary* leaned against *The Statesman's Year-book*; on
another shelf the wired hand and fore-arm of a skeleton
pointed menacingly at the ebony statuette of a naked kneel-

ing woman, souvenir of a Royal Tour in West Africa; and so on. It was all summed up in Father's favorite toy, which had been given him as a Silver Jubilee present by his colleagues at the hospital. This lay on a special display table and at first glance it looked like a large book open at two dashing James Gunn pictures of an imaginary King and Queen. But the pictures were painted on transparent film and so were those beneath them; as you peeled each layer back you found the monarchs first naked, then flayed, then exposing in succession their nervous systems, their innards, their veins and so on down to the bleached and grinning skeletons. Father loved it, but the rest of the Family thought it was disgusting. The room wasn't large or plush, but felt like a place where a lot of work got done.

Father stopped reading, stared at the paper for a moment, then wrote several lines of comment. When he'd added it to the pile he looked up.

"Sorry, Lulu," he said. "Some clever men can be bloody fools. Durdy says you want to talk to me. Hello, what's up? You don't have to wear that face in here."

"It's better than bursting into tears," said Louise. "Oh, hell! Sorry. Read some more despatches."

It must have been years since she'd last really cried. She let the sore little retching sobs come and go for a minute, then cut them short as sharply as an officer halting his platoon. As she mopped her cheeks she forced the djinn back into its bottle, corked it and threw it into her own deeps. She looked up to see Father watching her.

"I didn't realize things were as bad as that," he said.

"They aren't. It's just that on the way here I suddenly began to see how trapped we are, all four of us."

"I'm afraid I can't do much about that, Lulu," he said in a careful voice, as though he were afraid of seeming impatient. "And you've got to remember we get the hell of a lot out of it. It's stupid to pretend we don't. Whether it's actually worth it depends on who's doing the sums."

"Yes, I know. I don't know why I burst into tears. I suppose it was everything boiling up, and being sent for . . ."

"But you asked to be sent for."

"I know."

"Well, let's make a start on that. Why?"

"Is there anything wrong with me?"

He didn't seem surprised, but sat looking at her with his head on one side.

"What sort of wrong?" he said at last.

"I don't know. It's ... well ... did Mother tell you about when I brought her my essay about Elizabeth?"

"As a matter of fact, yes, but you tell me. It was a good essay, she said."

"I got A minus for it. But that's ... You see, we talked about Elizabeth a bit, and then Mother started talking about being loved, and I said I loved her and I sat on her lap and we began to have a bit of a cuddle—it can't have been very comfortable for her but I think she was liking it, and ... I'd been thinking about her before, and how marvellous she is, and then I was telling her we don't get enough chance to show each other we're ... I suppose a bit more than fond of each other ..."

Her voice dribbled away into doubt. He was still looking at her but there was an amused light in his eyes and he had begun to tease the corner of his moustache.

"You'll be all right," he said. "You're going to be damned attractive. You'll get all the cuddles you want."

"I'm not talking about that," she said furiously.

"Sorry, Lulu. I know you're not. It just crossed my mind. But it's more important than you think, whether you like it or not. Carry on."

"Oh ... well there we were, and suddenly Mother noticed how dirty my hands were and when I said I'd been looking at old press-cuttings she went all stiff and sent me away. And next time I went to the Library the cuttings were being moved out and Mrs. Suttery pretended that she wanted the space ... and one or two other things, and Durdy ..."

"You don't think we're all entitled to a little privacy, even from each other?"

"Yes, of course. That matters frightfully. But you see ... well, look, those press-cuttings had been there for ages and anybody could look at them. I know Bert read all about his own birth and Masefield's poem and so on. But as soon as *I* start looking ... it's as though there was something which I, specially, mustn't be told about. It's not because there's anything wrong with the thing, but because there's something wrong with *me*."

"You haven't got it into your head that you're a hemophilia carrier, Lulu? I give you my word of honor that you aren't."

"No," she said. "You said that before, and I know you'd tell me if I was. But look, of course you didn't have to tell me about you and Nonny, but it seems funny Mother telling Bert when he was ten, and then leaving me to guess. It's not as if I mind. In fact, provided Mother thinks it's OK I think it's a good idea, because it makes Nonny *really* one of the Family. Sorry. I shouldn't have said all that. That's none of my business."

"Yes, I see," he said. "Perhaps we've been a bit clumsy. Certainly Bella over-reacted about the press-cuttings. I thought so at the time, but she was so upset that I let her have them moved. I think one thing I need to know is why you were looking at them in the first place."

Louise never blushed, but there was an undertone of dry suspicion in his voice that made her feel as if she were going to.

"I wanted to find a picture of Nonny," she said. "I wanted to know if she was always so beautiful."

He laughed his big, raucous laugh, a curious sound coming from his neat and slightly podgy body. She could see him almost yawning with relief as he stretched to open a drawer of his desk. When he flicked the photograph towards her it twisted in the air so that she had to scrabble it off the floor.

It was an old one, originally black and white but now with yellowish tinges. Nonny was sitting on grass. A corner of chequered cloth and a chicken-bone on a paper plate showed that it must be a picnic—not a formal, Royal one, but a bit of non-posh scoff in the open air. She was wearing a very simple polka-dot dress and a hat that was no more than a dark wide halo of brim and looking up into the camera, which must have been held nearly vertically above her. Louise could almost hear her laughter, though even in reality it was only a soundless bubbling of pleasure in

herself and the world around her. (You had to know Nonny
very well before you found out that her pleasure might not
solely spring from the fact that she was talking to you at the
time.) She looked about eighteen, but you couldn't tell—she
still looked fifteen years younger than she really was.

Louise gazed at the picture, suddenly happy with Nonny's
own happiness and the way it had lasted across the years.
When she looked up she saw Father watching her with a
faintly teasing smile.

"Isn't she lovely?" she said.

"In her own way," said Father, almost as if he didn't
want to admit it to anyone else. "Would you like a copy?"

"Me? Oh . . . no, I only wanted to see. It's funny, she's
hardly changed, but in the photo she looks a bit like
somebody else."

"Who?"

(He didn't want to admit that either.)

"I don't know . . . just somebody."

"Some film star, probably. You've seen her in an old film
on the idiot box. Half of them were sweating their guts out
to look like that, and Nonny did it without trying. Sling it
back, Lulu—we haven't got all evening. I think I'd better
try and tell you why Bella was upset about the press-
cuttings. It'll mean going into a number of things we don't
normally talk about in the Family, but you'll just have to
stick it out. I may say that in my opinion you haven't fully
understood what's been happening to you. Though you may
believe you have accepted and even welcomed Nonny's
relationship with me and Bella, unconsciously you dislike
and resent it. Furthermore you are disturbed by your own
inability to show your feelings on the surface, and you feel a
need for a relationship, preferably with Bella, in which this
barrier disappears. And thirdly you are aware that Durdy,
with whom you have had a relationship of that sort, can't
last much longer, and you would like to arrive at a situation
where Bella provided a substitute. Am I being too tough?"

"No. That's all right. I don't mean that you're right—I'll
have to think about it—but it's better to say things than not
say them."

"Sometimes. In this case, certainly. You see, I think that

you said to yourself, unconsciously, 'Nonny and Father have rejected Mother and in doing so have rejected me. But Mother and I still can have each other.' So that afternoon with the essay you made the offer and for a while Bella appeared to accept it and then she appeared to reject you—and reject you for a reason concerned with our past history about which you had not been told. That's why you've been brooding so much about an incident which in other ways is rather trivial—the sort of thing which occurs in most families pretty often. Do you follow me?''

"Yes."

"Right. Well, I can't replace things as they were before that afternoon. All I can do is tell you as plainly and clearly as I can about how I came to marry Bella, and the relationship that we have built up between the three of us. Effectively I shall be trying to make you accept that we are a unit of three, and that nobody has rejected anybody, and that when we had children they were very much loved and wanted and still are. I think Durdy told you that Nonny and I were lovers before I met Bella?''

"Yes."

"OK, we'll start there. I was twenty-five, and that means that for the past seven years people had been parading possible wives in front of me as though I were some sort of judge at a dog-show. Most of them were nice enough and some remarkably pretty, but as soon as I met up with Nonny I was really rather spoilt for prettiness. OK, say it, but try not to interrupt too much.''

"Why couldn't you marry Nonny? I mean, even then it must have been possible for you to marry a commoner. It was after the war, wasn't it?''

"Of course it was, and of course that's what I wanted to do. There'd been a bit of a hoo-ha, but I could have ridden that out. The reason's pretty straightforward in one way, though in another way I still don't understand it—she wouldn't have me. She turned me down. I kept count. I asked her forty-three times and then I gave up. No, I'd forgotten I was telling you the plain truth—what happened was that she swore she'd stop going to bed with me if I asked her once more, and she meant it. She simply didn't want to be a Queen. As I say, I still haven't really figured out why.''

His voice had lost its lecturing tone and taken on such a note of grumbling outrage at that old rebuff that Louise almost laughed. She remembered her own feelings as she'd looked at the painting of the scene at Berlin Station.

"I know why," she said. "I can't tell you. Go on."

"Well, that's how things stayed for a couple of years and then I met Bella. I hadn't met her before for two reasons—first, she'd been in a convent most of the time, and second she didn't count as suitable. I'll come to that in a minute. I knew of her existence, of course. She's my third cousin.

"It was at a party at the Rothschilds' in Paris. I sat next to her. A dark girl, still a bit inclined to puppy-fat, not specially striking except for that marvellous pale skin, very serious. Now we're coming to an important bit, because I want you to try and understand that although I was, and still am, deeply in love with Nonny, with Bella it was—not exactly love at first sight—that's too banal a way of putting it. But by the end of the evening we both recognized that we needed each other. It wasn't just that I knew that I'd met an entirely suitable Queen of England—some of the others would have done for that. But we'd found a sort of complementarity, a recognition that we really did speak the same language—and you've got to accept, Lulu, that the language we're forced to speak is a pretty rare one these days. Of course I didn't know then that Bella felt the same about me, but I decided at once that she was the one I wanted. I also realized that I was going to have a fight on my hands—much more than if I'd announced I was going to marry Nonny, in fact.

"That's why I didn't tell anybody except Tim Belcher what I was up to until I'd found out what Bella felt. You at least will be able to guess what the hell of a job it was setting up private, apparently casual meetings between a bachelor King and a Princess of a Royal Family in exile. Once it took Tim and me a couple of months' spadework to set up ten minutes' chat at a perfectly appalling production of *Siegfried* in Bayreuth, and I had to sit through the whole damned *Ring* for it. Things got a bit easier when we roped Bella's sister, your Aunt Maria, in . . ."

"But she's a nun!"

"She's a very good woman with a real gift for intrigue. If they'd any sense they'd make her a cardinal. Where was I? Oh yes, after that things began to move a bit, and I proposed to her, in Durdy's Nursery, as a matter of fact, with butter running down our chins. She turned me down. There can't be many Kings who've been turned down by the first two women they've proposed to. I tried again several times. No go. It was damned puzzling, because I was pretty sure she liked me, and I knew from Maria that her family were keen enough on the idea to let her become a Protestant. It took me months to get it out of her, and even then she couldn't tell me direct—she had to put it in a letter—that she was secretly convinced that she was a hemophilia carrier. You did hemophilia in biology, I think."

"Yes. Last term."

"I was a fool not to think of it, or I'd have twisted their arms to change the curriculum."

"Why on earth? I'm all right."

"Oh, not for you, Lulu—for Bella. I think I'd better give you a quick run-down on the disease, because there are bits they won't have bothered to put in. Hemophilia, a thoroughly nasty, unromantic ailment. Genetic—that's to say one of nature's mistakes which can be passed down from parents to children. One of her commoner mistakes, and by no means confined to Royal Families. It's sex-linked, which means that boys get it from their mothers but girls have to get it from both mother and father for the symptoms to show up. Until the last twenty years it's been rare for a male hemophiliac to live long enough to breed, so for all practical purposes the popular idea has been right—that's to say that the males die of it and the women pass it on to the next lot of males. Not all of them, of course. On average, if a mother who is a carrier has two sons and two daughters, one son and one daughter will be OK, one son have the disease and one daughter will be a carrier. I imagine they taught you most of that."

"I didn't know women could get it at all."

"Well, they can, but it's irrelevant. Now, the crowned heads of Europe. Victoria carried the mutant gene for hemophilia without knowing it. Her father was fifty-two when she was born, so the odds are it began with an actual sperm mutation in him. She was horrified by the way it showed up among her grandchildren but she died, lucky old biddy, not realizing that it all began with her. The most famous sufferers were the Russian Royal Family, but it also showed up in the Spanish one. Your uncle Carlos died of it. Maria is a carrier..."

"But how can you know? She's never had any children. She's a nun, for God's sake."

"She's a nun partly for God's sake and partly because she's a hemophilia carrier. We'll come to that in a bit. First I want to point out that a great deal of romantic nonsense has been written about the disease, and put into films, making it seem rather beautiful in a decadent sort of way. I tell you it's ugly, painful and sordid. They make it seem like a slow welling of blood across alabaster skin while courtiers sigh and scheme in the background, but in reality it's joints swollen with black pus, and the child screaming with the endless pain. It's guts that won't stop bleeding—oh, we can do quite a bit for it nowadays, but when your Uncle Carlos was dying and your mother was a child watching it, it was hell."

"Poor Mother!"

"Exactly. Moreover they gave her a wicked idiot of a confessor who told her that her family were being punished by God with the disease. So in spite of everything that everybody told her she was convinced that she was a carrier too."

"But you must have known she wasn't, or..."

"*I* knew. You can do a test, and though it was pretty primitive in those days and though her family were a conservative lot, they'd had it done. That's why Bella came out of the convent and Maria stayed in. Blood is a complicated stuff and it takes a dozen different things to make it clot at the right time and not at the wrong time. Two of these things are called Factor Seven and Factor Eight. If you haven't got enough Factor Seven you've got Christmas

Disease, and if you haven't got enough Factor Eight you've got Classical Hemophilia. The symptoms are practically identical, but if you mix two batches of blood, one deficient in Factor Seven and one in Factor Eight, the mixture will clot. Now, although the symptoms don't show up in a woman carrier of either disease, in a way she can be said to have the disease, because although she's got enough of the relevant factor for her blood to clot OK, she still hasn't got as much as a healthy brother, and nowadays it's possible to test the blood for both factors. Bella's family was in fact the completely average family of the text-books, so there was a healthy brother, your Uncle Juan, and Bella's Factor Eight count was almost identical with his. I knew this because I persuaded her to have the tests done again. I thought that if *I* explained it all to her she'd be convinced. Of course what I found was that though I'd convinced her intellect I hadn't made the slightest dent on her emotional horrors.

"Then a funny thing happened. I'd got it into my head, not unreasonably, that the hemophilia business was really a transference from an even more deeply buried set of sexual fears. That's not the sort of thing one can conveniently discuss in a letter—not with Bella, at least—so I had to wait till we could set up another meeting. We spent a perfectly marvellous day riding along old mule-tracks in the Basse Savoie—it's incredible how much more private a mountain can be than a closed room—and thrashed the whole thing out. I felt that if I was going to force her into total frankness I couldn't do any less myself, so it all came out about me and Nonny. In fact Nonny and I had settled that if Bella accepted me we'd bite the bullet and split up . . . You tell me what Bella did, Lulu."

"Oh . . . of course . . . she'd have come and tackled Nonny. I don't think she'd write—she'd come and see for herself."

"You're a perceptive child behind that mask. Yes, she was fairly quiet for the rest of the ride, told me she'd think it over, got home, packed and came over incog—didn't tell me or anyone—found Nonny's flat—it was in Pavilion Road, just behind Sloane Square—and called on her without an appointment. Naturally they were a bit wary of each other to start with, but when I turned up a couple of

evenings later to tell Nonny how the campaign was going I
found Bella sitting there looking as smug as the cat that got
the canary. They'd really hit it off.''

"I'd love to have seen your face."

"I daresay. They almost made me feel a bit de trop. And
they'd come up with this idea of Nonny joining the establishment as Bella's secretary.''

"But surely somebody must have known . . ."

"Tim Belcher knew. Durdy guessed. I don't think anyone
else had an inkling. We had my mother to thank for that. I
know you get along with her OK, Lulu, but I think she's a
perfectly frightful woman, despite her bringing what brains
we are endowed with into the Family. If she'd heard the
slightest whisper about Nonny she'd have shoved her oar in
to cause maximum misery. So it was a possible arrangement. Though it was jolly for me, I didn't think it was fair
either on Bella or Nonny, but they insisted it was. Nonny
got what she wanted, which was to be to all intents and
purposes married to me without having to be Queen. Bella
was more complicated, but she'd been able to tell Nonny all
sorts of things she couldn't tell me, the most important being
her horror not of sex but of childbirth—not the pain, but the
idea of giving birth to babies who couldn't stop bleeding.
She thought she could face the prospect of producing an
heir, but you've got to remember that she was a convent-
reared Papist, and though she knew about contraceptives she
hadn't really come to terms with the possibility of her using
them. Furthermore she'd got it into her head, quite rightly,
that I was a pretty randy young man, and she'd felt that if I
wanted a lot of sex that'd inevitably result in a whole string
of babies—Royal Families tend to run largish, you know. So
from her point of view there was a rather sordid practical
advantage in Nonny being—well—available. So that you
don't get the wrong ideas I'd better tell you that Bella is in
fact capable of very considerable physical passion. It took
us a year or two to find it out, but it's there. It's very
important that you shouldn't get it into your head that
Nonny's function is to be a sex object and Bella's to be an
official wax-work Queen.

"In fact, though it's jumping ahead a bit, I'll tell you

another thing. In some ways Bella is a very simple-minded person, with an almost childish belief in the value of words. When we came to get married she absolutely insisted on our using a modern English ceremony. She had an out-and-out set-to with Churchill about it, because he wanted all the Thees and Thous but Bella insisted on my saying 'You' because that can mean two people as well as one. We had a private ceremony, just the three of us, with two rings, before the service in the Abbey. I wept like a baby. I think what moved me was Bella's absolute insistence all along that she would not accept the guilt of murdering the love between Nonny and me. She was barely nineteen.''

He sat in silence for a full minute, pulling gently at the corner of his moustache, which he normally only did when he was amused by something.

"You don't have to tell me any more if you don't want to,'' said Louise.

"Yes I do. We've left out the important bit, about the press-cuttings. You see, when a King only marries one wife, there's still a third party to the contract and that's the GBP. I don't mind saying that it was a damned unpopular romance, not what they'd been looking for at all. First of all, before anything was announced, there was my Government to win over. Churchill and Eden both hated it, but I fixed for Churchill to have a long session alone with Bella, and though in some ways he was a bit gaga by then he was still damned sharp about other things, and he spotted that I'd picked somebody who had the makings of a real Queen. So after that he grumbled but went along and did a bit to keep Eden in check. The FO still hated it, but I thought I could ignore them if I had the GBP on my side.

"In fact I made the biggest misjudgment of my life about the GBP. I thought there'd be the odd bit of sniping, but I'd had no idea of the shindy they'd manage to kick up. I'd reckoned on a general moan about Franco having been a pretty hostile neutral in the war, and of course they'd all have preferred a blonde—Bella didn't photograph very well in those days—and a scream or two from the idiot left. What I'd failed to take in was this—the GBP are a pretty irreligious lot, but they had—in fact they still have far more than most people realize—a sort of negative religion. They're hysterically anti-papist. I say 'hysterically' in a technical sense, because it doesn't come out like that. They suppress the impulse and let it erupt in other ways, and in Bella's case it was in a fantastic series of ludicrous assertions about hemophilia. It was like everybody's nightmares coming together in the image of one monstrous bleeding baby. It shook me badly, and Bella even worse. They refused to listen to reason. For instance, they cottoned on to the fact that my mother was a member of the Russian Royal Family and simply refused to listen when we told them that the hemophilia came to the Romanoffs via Alix, who married my mother's second cousin once removed and couldn't possibly have passed on the genes to my mother, so there was no question of our children inheriting the gene from both sides. They simply wouldn't let up. You've no idea of the bile and filth that got chucked at Bella. She's as brave as anyone I know, but there came a point when she wanted to call the whole thing off. I wasn't having that, so I forced old Churchill to let me do a broadcast about it all. I had several things going for me. For a start, though I can't claim any credit for it, I came out of the war with the GBP thinking well of me. Then I had got a genuine medical training—I've never ceased to thank old Attlee for that, whatever you may hear me say at breakfast—which meant I could put over that side of things. I told them that if I'd thought there was the slightest chance of our having hemophiliac children I'd never have begun on this. I told them what the disease was like—I let 'em see that I really cared. I didn't say straight out that I'd abdicate if I didn't get my way, but I managed to give that impression. I put over a pretty good performance—it was genuine, but it was a performance—and I brought it off. Within about a fortnight Churchill agreed that we could go ahead, and since then we've never looked back. I'd say that Bella was one of the most popular Queens in the history books by now, and has been for the past fifteen years.

"Of course I didn't convince everybody, but there was only one of those who mattered and that was Bella herself— she knew in her mind it was OK, but I'm afraid I didn't really grasp quite how frightened she was until Bert was on

the way. She had a very bad time. Carlos's death and the
filth the GBP had chucked at her and that appalling confessor she'd had all became mixed in her mind. For the last
couple of months she wasn't properly sane. She practically
lived in Nonny's arms ... if ever you begin to feel, Lulu,
that Nonny doesn't really care about anything very much,
remember that time ... well, in the end it was a perfectly
normal birth, for a first child. She hardly used the breathing
mask. Fine baby, just under eight pounds, with a decent
head of hair. First thing we did, while he was still squalling,
was to make a tiny nick in his calf and let her see the blood
congeal. Next three months she spent having her nervous
breakdown, letting herself go with all the horrors she and
Nonny had managed to keep at bay while she'd been doing
her duty and producing me an heir.

"So you see, Lulu darling, that anything that reminds her
of that time, or the period while we were having trouble
with the GBP, is bound to upset her. If she'd known the
press-cuttings were still in the Library she'd have had them
moved out long ago. But there's something else which
affects you in particular. I can assure you with absolute
certainty that there's no more chance of your being a
hemophilia carrier than there is of any other of my female
subjects being one. That is a medical fact. Your Factor
Seven is the same as Bert's and your Factor Eight is a bit
higher. Personally I think this is a good thing for you to
know about, but Bella can't get it out of her head that if you
start brooding on it you'll finish up by going through the
same horrors she did. There can't be many British Princesses
who've led less protected lives than you manage to, but
you've still got to put up with a bit of protection here and
there. Quite often it will be for the protector's sake, as
much as for yours. I think that's all. Any questions?"

"Was I an accident?"

His hand dropped from his moustache and his face took
on a tense look she'd only seen before when his constitutional role was forcing him to accept something he thought
morally wrong.

"What do you mean?" he said slowly.

"I'm sorry. Well, for instance, you know my friend Julie

at school. Her parents weren't meaning to have another
baby and did. She says it was her first victory against them
and she's gone on winning ever since. I just thought, after
what you've told me, that I couldn't imagine Mother going
through with having another baby on purpose. I wouldn't
mind being an accident. Honestly.''

He smiled and relaxed.

''Well, I suppose the answer's yes, in a way. There was a
good deal of pressure on us to have another child. But in the
end—it was the early days of the pill and your mother got
her sums wrong, and there you were, on the way.''

''Did she have as bad a time with me as she did with
Bert?''

''Bella? No. She worked out a way in which she could
face it.''

''Then Granny was right!''

''What the hell do you mean? You're not to believe a
single word my mother tells you, d'you hear? And you are
not to talk to her about any of this again, ever. She's . . . I'm
afraid those are orders, Lulu.''

''I'm sorry. We hardly talked about it at all, I promise.
She started it by telling me a quite different story about
Grandfather being drowned by the Secret Service on orders
from Lord . . . hell, I've forgotten his name.''

''Halifax. That's a perfect example. That story was invented
by Goebbels during the war as propaganda, trying to make
people think I was Churchill's prisoner and things would
have been different if there'd been a grown-up King in
charge. As a matter of fact my father never had any time for
Hitler. He said you couldn't trust a man who wore such
badly cut trousers. And there isn't a shred of evidence for
the Halifax story—even that man Hochhuth decided he
couldn't write a play about it. But here's your grandmother
still repeating it.''

''I thought it sounded a bit stupid, but you have to
pretend to be thrilled with Granny. Then she started talking
about secrets and said she'd tell me one about me, which
was that I wasn't born prematurely at all, but that you'd
arranged to go to Glas-allt Shiel so that Mother could escape
the flap. If you did, I think you were right. And I'll never

talk about it to anyone. You don't have to explain about Granny. I know about her."

"OK, OK, OK. Well, provided you promise not to take it as evidence that anything else she tells you could conceivably be true, I'll admit she wasn't far out that time. I wish you could have seen old Durdy sitting on the window-seat and purring at you. It was lovely."

"I hope Mother was pleased too. And you."

"Yes. Yes, of course, Lulu. But we were all absolutely whacked. It'd been a much tougher birth than Bert's—no horrors or anything, just much slower and more painful. It's odd how these things go. You'd have thought . . . Anyway, we were all pretty tired, but glad to see you."

"Who else knows?"

"Couple of doctors—I fixed them. I think Tim Belcher guessed—he was up at Allt-na-giubhasaich—and what's more he didn't approve. He didn't say anything, but a bit later he asked to leave the Palace. I miss him. That's the one thing I regret about the whole charade."

"It sounds a bit stuffy of him."

"Different people have different sticking-points."

"I suppose Nonny knew too?"

"Eh? Oh yes, of course."

He blinked and grinned at Louise.

"Glad you approve of her, Lulu. Has all this helped?"

"Oh yes . . . yes, a lot. Thank you, Father."

"There's one other thing—I hardly need say it to you, because you're such an old poker-face anyway, but perhaps I'd better. One of the problems about sharing a secret is that you have to learn to behave as though you are the only person who knows. Even when you're alone with other people who know you've got to keep up a habit of acting and talking as though they didn't, and so must they. Otherwise one day somebody's going to make a mistake. You can talk things over with Durdy if you want to—I do myself—but nobody else unless you are expressly invited to. Got it?"

"OK. Thanks. See you."

The rain had stopped and the world seemed re-made in the clean dusk. All round the courtyard the tall windows of

the ground-floor rooms and corridors were like yellow
pillars supporting an invisible roof of gladness. There was
nobody else in the glistening square, so Louise danced a
few remembered twirls from her ballet lessons, and wished
that she could suddenly see Julie crossing the courtyard
from the other corner so that she could halloo to her and
hear their shouts echoing off the walls like the cries of gulls
among cliffs.

She was not merely happy from relief that the secret
they'd been shielding her from had turned out to be a bit
sad, but not dreadful. Father had been right, she now saw,
when he'd said that she'd really been using that as a screen
for masking other fears and resentments, but now she felt
able to share in the happiness which Mother and Father and
Nonny had created between them. It was like a quiet
fountain of good water—no terrific jets and sparkles, but a
basin from which you could drink as much as you needed
and it would still be full.

She didn't want to spoil this feeling by going back to the
zoo and talking to Albert about the joker, so she made her
way up to her own room and turned on the radio. There
were still twenty minutes before Pilfer would sound the
gong as a signal that those of the Family who weren't on
duty somewhere should now congregate in Mother's private
drawing-room for the ritual Friday sherry which marked the
start of the weekend. It would only be Albert tonight. She
could tell him about the pianos then. There was nothing she
wanted to do except to rejoice in the sudden melting of
tensions, but unconsciously she felt a need to express her
happiness in action. She picked up her brush and began to
slide it in slow, stroking movements down through her long
locks. The radio was burbling its way through a program
of classic comic routines on record. A man stopped imitat-
ing steam trains and an extraordinary American with a voice
like a shovel shifting coke began to sing a sort of song about
his search for the lost chord. Louise moved to see what she
was doing in the mirror. Her hair was in quite decent nick,
with blondish tints of summer still glistening amid the
near-mouse. The threatened pimple by the corner of her
nose had decided to recede, thank heavens. Granny's right,

she thought—I'll never know. There's no such thing as a pretty Princess. Ugly Princesses are dignified and pretty Princesses are beautiful with nothing in between. The hair-brushing helped to prolong her purring mood—she was even half aware that the physical act was a distant way of sharing the pleasure that Mother and Father and Nonny had in each other's bodies. Then, perhaps faintly alarmed by this awareness, she began to mime her mockery of her own potential beauty, throwing herself into fashion-model poses while she brushed and brushed as though she never need stop. "They said Mozart was mad," snarled the radio, "they said Beethoven was mad, they said Louie was mad. Who's Louie? My uncle Louie—he *was* mad." She laughed aloud.

She was standing sideways on to the mirror with her head bent over to let her hair hang down, but twisted so that she could see the effect. If you'd tilted the room through ninety degrees she'd have been looking straight up into the mirror, laughing. There was no wide-brimmed hat, no corner of picnic-cloth, but the laugh died and the rhythm of brushing stopped in mid-stroke. Frightened, she tried to recapture the pose and glance but the ghost was gone. Still she was certain it had been there, just as it had been in the photograph of Nonny that Father had shown her. Not the ghost of any one person but something that haunted between them. A likeness. A family face.

◆ 8 ◆

IN SOME WAYS the stifling calm of the Yorks' house,
Purling Park, was a good place to spend that weekend.
Old Cousin Ted doddered and muttered all day round his
croquet lawn. Occasionally Aunt Tim, mountaineering over
her rockery, would look up and wave a friendly trowel at
him, and if he noticed the signal he would wave a friendly
mallet back, but that was quite a lively conversation by York
standards. Some fool (Aunt Eloise Kent, probably) had once
told poor Cousin Jack that he was doomed to marry Louise,
and although he'd left Eton at the end of last half and was
waiting to go into the army, he still blushed whenever he
looked at her. It was lucky none of his five elder sisters was
there, or they would have reproved him each time.

Louise felt that nothing could change, no progress could
be made, in that valley of sleepers, so she allowed the hours
to drift past without thinking about what had happened to
her. She went for two long rides with Jack, and took it into
her head to be specially friendly and forthcoming; it was
almost as though she felt she would never see him again.
And she did her homework with particular care and neat-
ness, because now it was nobody's business but her own.

But perhaps the lull made Monday at school worse than it
might have been. Boring Geog, boring Math, boring Hist,
boring PE. A headache. Jerry in love with a girl in the
Fourth Year. Julie, who'd normally have noticed there was

something wrong and been nice about it, too busy teasing Jerry with hints that the frightful, posturing, busty mascaraed blonde he'd picked on was only pretending to be interested in a boy two years younger than herself because she wanted to be able to tell people that she went around with Princess Louise. Sulks. McGivan at the gate. Vile little dusty wind blowing up Church Street. Knot of tourists outside antique-shop—nudges, stares, cameras, public face...

Not anymore, thought Louise, lengthening her stride. I'm out of that now. I'm ordinary. I'll tackle Father tonight—no, hell, he's in Durham—tomorrow. Another foul day to live through, and then I'll be out of it. At least it gives me time to think. *Why can't I think?*

The trouble was she couldn't imagine any kind of life other than the one she knew. It was quite easy to think of going away and living in one ordinary house with only five or six rooms in it and no servants, and having to make her own bed and all that. But she couldn't put people into the house. She couldn't imagine Nonny becoming Mother—no, Mummy—and leaving... leaving Aunt Bella? Ugh! Anyway, she won't come—but they can't make me stay. They can't, they can't!

"Will Your Highness be coming in front?"

McGivan was holding the door of the Triumph. For some reason he'd not left it at Granny's but parked it near the Embassies, where she'd met the red-headed man. At least it wasn't so far to walk.

"I'll go in the back, please. I've got a headache."

"Aye, it's the weather, nae doot."

She didn't smile at him as she climbed in. McGivan at best was a very moderate driver, with a tendency to move the car in a series of swoops and brakings, and today he wanted to talk, turning his head from the road as he did so.

"Her Majesty's back from Finland," he said.

"Good. Is she all right?"

"Not a care in the world, and Miss Fellowes looking ever sae bonny with her."

No need to answer that, but McGivan's snuffle implied that she should have.

"Ye'll all be taegither again the morn," he said. "It's

grand to see a family so fond of each ither. It makes
working for ye a real pleasure.''

"I'm glad it does," said Louise. "But I'm sorry, Mr.
McGivan, I can't talk. My head's very bad. Could you get
me home as soon as you can?''

Snuffle. A wild swoop and a violent halt at the Albert
Hall lights. Louise hardly noticed. I can't go, she thought,
because there's nowhere to go, and I can't stay either. How
could they do this to me? I thought I loved them. I thought
they loved me. How could they? Suddenly she remembered
Father, kneeling on the Palace grass, unnecessarily easing
soil round the roots of a rhododendron for the sake of his
own internal honor, when all the time it was a lie, all the
time he was pretending to like a bush for which he didn't
care two hoots, and which Mother actually hated. And it's
the same with me. When he talked to me on Friday he only
used the word "Mother" once, not counting when he was
talking about Granny. "It was the early days of the pill and
your mother got her sums wrong." Otherwise he called
them Bella and Nonny all the time. I bet if I could
remember every word he said there wouldn't be a single lie
it it—except that it was all one lie. I'm not going to live
with it, I'm not. They can't make me.

For the rest of the drive this single phrase battered round
and round inside her skull. No other ideas emerged. Mother
and Father and Nonny became just "they" and she was
numb to their feelings and reactions. On the pavements, in
buses, in other cars, the GBP drifted past, unreal, but ugly
and demanding. You've got nothing on me now, she thought.
Not anymore. You can't make me either.

Sentries in scarlet came to the salute. The Triumph slid
under the arch. Tacket, the porter, opened the door. Public
face for the last time, ever.

"Thank you, Mr. McGivan. Thank you, Mr. Tacket."

Neither of them seemed to hear. Had she said it at all?
She ran across the hall and up the stairs, praying to meet no
one. Her speed became a kind of flight, a panic rush through
the nightmare ordinariness of the Palace, a yearning to
escape from the servants, the carpets, the ghosts of dead
Kings. Only her own room was a refuge—hers, Louise's,

the place where she became real and not a gadget invented for other people's convenience. She was panting hard by the time she reached the middle corridor but she raced along it, flung open her door, dashed in, slammed the door behind her and stood shuddering, safe in her known lair.

It was odd that Sukie hadn't made the bed, but somehow it made the room more personal than ever. When Louise bent to pick her yellow nightie from the floor only half of it came. Carefully she picked up the other half and discovered that it had been ripped in two, from top to bottom. And the bed *had* been made, but then someone had pulled it to bits.

She stood still for several seconds, afraid to turn, knowing that whoever or whatever it was crouched beside the door. At last she forced herself round.

In scarlet letters sprayed from an aerosol can the word marched across the wall. They had torn down her Led Zeppelin poster to make room for it. BASTARD. And a neat scarlet X.

Although she felt very cold she was steady now and able to walk round the room and look for further outrages. The word was on her mirror, in lipstick. *The Two Towers* lay on the floor; she flipped through the pages and found the word twice, scrawled right across the type with a red felt pen. She stood and looked round. It might be anywhere.

Slowly she crossed to the door, took the key from the inside, went out and locked the door behind her. Durdy. She had walked several paces before she saw that it wouldn't be fair on Durdy because she couldn't do anything. She felt her teeth clench as she thought of Father—it was his look-out, wasn't it? But he was in Durham and not back for hours. Mother had an opera, one of the sort that start at six, she'd be dressing, and it wasn't *her* fault. That wouldn't be fair either. Nonny—Mummy—it was her look-out too.

Louise turned and marched firmly back the way she had come, past her mined room, down two flights of the other stairs and along the lower corridor. At the fifth door she heard the fantastically rapid rattle of a typewriter, which meant that Janice, Nonny's own secretary, was finishing off the day's letters. She went into the sixth without knocking.

Nonny was sitting in the middle of the floor with her eyes

shut, concentrating. She didn't concentrate on anything in particular, she used to say, because she didn't know how. She just sat still and concentrated twice a day because it was good for her skin.

"Nonny," said Louise. She couldn't say the other word.

Nonny looked up, not frowning—that was hard to imagine—but not welcoming. She stared for an instant before swinging nimbly to her feet.

"What's up, Lulu? Are you all right? I've never seen you look like that."

"Can you come to my room, please?"

"Will it take long?"

"I don't know. Yes."

"I'll just explain to Janice. She has this thing about catching the post, but there's nothing that can't wait."

Louise led her up the stairs in silence. At her own door she suddenly backed out into the corridor and peered right and left on the off chance of catching a glimpse of someone skulking to enjoy the effect of his nastiness. Nonny stood waiting as though this performance, and the locked door, were normal protocol. Louise suddenly felt that she ought to warn her, but couldn't speak. She led her in and shut the door behind her. Nonny stared round.

"Oh dear," she said.

Her softness, her acceptance of the obscenity, her distance from the pain of it, broke Louise's control.

"It's true. Isn't it?" she said harshly.

"Oh dear," sighed Nonny. "What a way to have all this out. I'm sorry, darling—I truly am. I'd never have been a good mother anyway. Oh dear, what can I say? I do love you, and I was very happy when you were born...I'm making a mess of this. Lulu darling, do you mind if I go and fetch Bella?"

"She'll be dressing," said Louise in the same drab, rejecting voice. "She's got an opera. Ambassadors and people."

"She'll come. You'll stay here, Lulu, won't you? Promise. Don't look at the mess—read a book or something."

"They're written in," said Louise, but Nonny was gone.

She couldn't sit down. The defilement seemed to infect

the room—the bed, the chairs, everything. She went to the mirror to start cleaning the lipstick away but was caught by her own reflection, paler than usual, large eyed, but calm as a crusader's wife on a tomb. That's the Nonny in me, she thought despairingly. Better not touch the lipstick anyway. She began to search systematically for other places where the word was written. It was like Sir Sam's trousers—a series of booby-traps waiting to show up. The joker had been tidy where it suited him—it was only because Sukie didn't approve of Princesses wearing colored panties, and so always put white ones on the top, that Louise went through the drawer and found a pair with an aerosol B on their fork, half way down the pile. The logic of the search had begun to steady her, but this shook her like a fresh gust on a night of storm. She understood the violence behind the scrawl, the symbolic rape, and was still standing in a sort of shuddering trance by the shut drawer when Mother came in, magnificent in a long flame-colored dress with a black velvet train sweeping cloak-like from the shoulders. Mother glanced at the word on the wall. For a moment her face whitened and hardened and then she was sweeping across the room with her arms held out and down in that remembered gesture of appeal. Louise rushed to meet her, to be drawn by those cold arms into the private sphere of love, to melt into marvellous, painless sobs.

"Oh my darling," whispered Mother. "Oh my darling."

Somewhere around midnight the door of Mother's bedroom opened and Father came in. He put on his pop-eyed surprise-and-outrage face.

"Why aren't you at the opera?" he said. "I had to go to Durham to get out of it."

"I had a stomach chill," said Mother. "I had not had huone for three years, so it huas high time."

"You'll have something else tomorrow if you and Nonny have drunk a whole bottle of my best champagne between you. I hope you've left some for me. Good God! There's another in the bucket!"

"Hue have been hauiting for you to come and open it. There is a clean glass on my dressing-table."

Louise could see him thinking as he fiddled with the wires and popped the cork. He grunted and poured himself a drink.

"What's up?" he said in a slightly altered voice. "Somebody's birthday?"

"That's right," said Louise. "I'm having two birthdays a year from now on. I don't see why you should be the only person to have an official birthday as well as an unofficial one. And I want presents on both of them."

"Right," he said, going round with the bottle to fill the other glasses. "Health and happiness, Lulu darling. I wish Durdy was here. How did you find out? Was it something I said? I thought I'd been pretty canny."

"It was the photograph. I was brushing my hair when suddenly I saw who it was like."

"Mm. We're going to have to think about that. Who did you tackle first? You know, I'd have expected you to wait and tackle me. Not that . . ."

"Something else happened," said Louise.

"I huill tell you later, Vick."

"No, it's all right now. I can manage. Champagne's useful stuff, isn't it. I'm going to have it on all my birthdays. It was like this . . ."

Father listened, frowning. Louise in the mild daze of drink listened to her tongue telling the story, even explaining the nastiness of it, without having to re-create herself as the being at the center of the shock. It was like a nightmare remembered on waking, apart from the reason why its foolish details were so frightening. She left out her own misery and sense of betrayal. That was over now.

"I see," said Father. "You seem to have kept your head, Lulu. Well done. Now, we have two separate problems—the joker and the likeness. They may be linked, because the joker may have found out about Lulu's birth by spotting the likeness, though it isn't very strong . . ."

"But it's *very* strong sometimes, Vick," said Mother.

"Let's show him," said Nonny, eagerly.

Mother laughed and picked up the hairbrush. While she worked on Nonny's hair Louise slipped into one of the pink chequered blouses and white skirts which lay on the bed,

then sat to let her own hair be put into a pony-tail while
Nonny dressed in the other set. Standing in front of the long
mirror they slid their arms round each other's waists and
grinned inanely with heads bent to one side and legs in the
pose of a comedy routine duo.

"I say I say I say," said Louise, "your public face isn't
as good as mine, darling."

"It doesn't have to be, darling. Shall we do a command
performance? Come on, Vick—command us to perform."

"I went to Durham to get out of the opera and now I
come back to this," grumbled Father. "OK, let's get it
over."

"You lead, I'll try to follow," said Nonny.

Father trumpeted the theme from The Infernal Can-can.
Mother clapped the rhythm. Nonny and Louise pranced.
Nonny was extraordinarily easy to dance with; she made it
seem as though she were actually wired into your own
nervous system, so that the impulse that twitched your limb
twitched hers at the same moment. It was a bit shaming that
she could high-kick several inches further than Louise. The
dance was very tiring, especially when Mother and Father
began to speed the rhythm. Louise got in a tangle and
brought Nonny tumbling on top of her. Father filled the
glasses again.

"Humph," he said. "That's enough. Don't ring us, we'll
ring you. Mmmm . . . sorry to introduce a sour note, but
we'd better get back to business. Of course I'm delighted
that you've managed to sort things out between you so that
Lulu can accept the pretty shabby way we've treated her . . ."

"That huas my fault," said Mother. "It huas all my
idea."

"I don't see why I shouldn't take some of the blame,"
complained Nonny. "She's my daughter, isn't she?"

"All right, all right," snapped Father. "We've all be-
haved equally badly, but now we've got to decide what to do
about it. The point is that pretending Lulu was Bella's
daughter is the only big lie I've told in my life, and I don't
think we can afford to let it come out. This is partly for
Lulu's sake: I know we think of her as every bit as much
our legitimate daughter as Bert is our legitimate son, but

we'll never put that over with the GBP. If we let the truth out, Lulu will become twice as much a peep-show as she is already, without any of the defences that she's got at the moment. And Nonny would have a pretty bad time of it, too. That's one thing. The other seems to me even more serious. I've inherited a monarchy and I've done my best to keep it going so that I can hand it on to Bert. I think it's worthwhile. I think the GBP like us, and in their funny way need us. But these are pretty hard times, with a million unemployed and all that. We can fend off the Willie Hamiltons of the world till the cows come home. If we have to we can also cut down on our expenses almost indefinitely, and we'd still be pretty well respected. But the one thing we can't afford to do is let the GBP find out that we've been lying to them about Lulu. She's extremely popular with them, and that makes it worse. It's funny, but I suspect that the one thing that would really shake them would not be my having a mistress and an illegitimate daughter, but Bella conniving, aiding and abetting. Anyway, there it is. Personally I'd go to any lengths to stop the truth coming out. It's absolutely essential that nobody should know..."

"But people do know, Vick," said Nonny. "There's dear Tim Belcher for a start..."

"You can count him out," said Father. "I'd stake my life on that. Also all the others who've always known. Derek Oliphant—he was the obstetrician, Lulu; the Stuarts at Allt-na-giubhsaich—they got things ready and lent us the baby-clothes—they're OK—you know what they're like if anyone asks the most harmless question about us. Your mother, Nonny..."

"Poor darling," sighed Nonny. "She was far too ashamed of me to tell a soul. She took me to a ghastly hydro near Oban, Lulu, and made a great parade of my husband being in South Africa. You won't remember her. Anyway, she never knew it was Vick's baby."

"And my poor Inez is dead too," said Mother.

"Your maid who died in the plane crash?" asked Louise.

"Oh, how she adored the intrigue of it," said Mother. "Do you remember, Vick, huen..."

"I remember a damned sight too much," said Father.

"But that's the lot, Lulu. We decided from the start that we'd talk, think and behave all the time, even among ourselves, as though you were Bella's daughter. For instance, we've never told Albert."

"But somebody else does know," said Nonny. "Look what happened to Lulu's room."

"Yes," said Father. "I've got an idea about that. I think I might be able to sort that out. But if Lulu's going to start growing more and more like Nonny . . ."

"I'd like that," said Louise.

"Tais-toi," said Mother, sharply enough to break for an instant the gold haze of content in which Louise had been floating along.

"It's all very well your sitting around swigging fizz and dressing up identical," said Father, "but we've got to take the thing seriously now."

"Huat do you think hue've been doing?" demanded Mother. "Hue spend two hours repainting Lulu's room, and then hue come up here to huork out how they can be made to look different. You don't expect us to do that until hue are sure how they look the same?"

"Will you mind if I dye, Vick?" said Nonny.

"Eh? Oh, dye with a Y. No, of course not. What color?"

"A sort of reddy brown. Bouffant. Lulu can stay lank. I'm going to wear a bit more make-up, all-overish, and she's going to concentrate on her eyes. And I'm going in for tighter skirts so that I don't lope so much. It's indecent at my age, anyway. It'll work, Vick. Do you want a demo?"

"Not necessary. You gave me a bit of a shock about dying, that's all. I'm sure you'll make it work—I'm long past any amazement at the sheer flexibility of the female mould. It only seems a week since every other girl you saw was a Bardot, and then it was a Fonda, and now it's . . . what's that hussy's name?"

"I like that," said Louise. "All we're doing is what you did with McGivan."

"Time you were in bed, Lulu," said Father abruptly. "One moment, though . . . Durdy. I was talking to her about all this the night before I went north, and she's been fretting about what you'd feel when you found out. Nip up as soon

as you can—tomorrow after school will do—and tell her it's
OK.''

"Lovely. I'll have tea with her. Don't forget, Mother,
I'll need a note saying I couldn't do my homework.''

"I huill think of a reason, darling.''

"Great. Well, goodnight, parents all.''

Feeling like an eight-year-old, Louise kissed the three of
them and swayed hazily back to her paint-smelling room.

◆ 9 ◆

Louise hadn't meant to worry Durdy by telling her about the rape of her bedroom, but Durdy got it out of her. She was impossible to lie to. Louise thought that she was like a pool among pine-trees, dark and still, miles from the nearest house, a pool where a kelpie lived. If you bathed in the pool and told the kelpie your troubles it would take them away. But it was no use telling it only part of your troubles, just as it was no use only dipping a foot in the pool. You had to undress and trust your whole self to that stillness among the black, hospital-smelling pines. When she'd finished, she felt that she had somehow made a ritual acceptance of the new situation. She was Nonny's daughter and Father's, but Mother was still Mother and she could join hands with them and dance in the ring of love.

She'd had a curious day, almost exactly like yesterday but completely different. Jerry's love-sickness had been funny, his new girl absurd and a bit pathetic, Julie really amusing; even the headache—the mild buzz of a champagne hangover, like radio interference—had been something to clutch and cherish, a continual nudging reminder of the previous evening, of Mother bustling about behind the two chairs with brush and comb, prattling in a mixture of five languages like a hairdresser gone mad with ingratiation, of dancing with Nonny, of Father pouring out champagne to drink her health on her unofficial birthday.

"The only thing that still bothers me is the joker," she said. "I mean he knows, doesn't he? What's he going to do next? He's not just going to stop there, not when he's got something like that to play with."

"Then we'll have to stop him."

"But we don't know who he is! Father said he'd got an idea, but . . ."

"Then leave it all to your Father, and don't trouble trouble till trouble troubles you."

"It's troubling me already."

"Who did I hear saying just how happy she was? Some people don't know their own minds, it seems."

"Oh, Durdy, that's mean. I was only . . ."

Sniff.

Louise nudged the rocking-horse to and fro a couple of times. If Durdy didn't want to talk about the joker, it wasn't fair to make her.

"You've no idea how miserable I was yesterday," she said. "I was longing to get out of the whole princessing business, and I couldn't see how. Have any of the others wanted that, Durdy?"

"Lord have mercy, why, all of them, one time or another. No, I'm a liar. My first Louise—she was seven when I came to the Family—I don't think she ever wanted anything except to do what was expected of her."

"A princessing machine. How did she end up?"

"Why, she was your great-aunt, the Queen of Romania. Dearie me, yes."

"The one who refused to shake hands with the Kaiser?"

"She shook hands with me, though."

"I bet she kissed you too."

"No, never."

"Poor thing. I wonder whether anybody ever kissed the Kaiser. I suppose his wife had to—it must have been difficult without getting his moustache in your eye—I expect there were times when one of the ladies of the court suddenly started wearing an eye-patch and then everybody knew . . . Durdy, tell me honestly, weren't you a bit shocked when Father told you he was going to set up with Mother and Nonny together?"

"What I thought was my own affair."

"You can't come that with me anymore, Durdy. I know all about you—sneaking off to Scotland to aid and abet in the production of illegitimate babies and sitting purring in the window-seat when the deed was done."

"I'll trouble you not to talk till you know what you're talking about, Miss. Her Majesty had a private arrangement with Miss Fellowes to whisper the promises while Her Majesty was saying them aloud. She explained it to me herself, and all about having that nasty modern service."

"Yes, Father told me about that. I bet God knows the difference between a singular 'you' and a plural 'you' even if the Archbishop doesn't. And I bet Nonny kept her fingers crossed too. Oh, I'm happy!"

Rock.

"Happy!"

Rock.

"Happy! . . . Isn't it funny how some people can do that? It doesn't matter if they look a bit cold and stiff. Even poor Cousin Jack isn't shy with Mother . . . and if you think of some of the other Queens—Victoria making people miserable and Mary scaring the living daylights out of everybody!"

"Those that live in glass houses shouldn't throw stones."

"But aren't I right?"

"Queen Victoria was very gentle with children, and sweet, and they loved her as soon as they were used to her. And Queen Alexandra made her children happy, though people will tell you she was stupid, and of course she was always late for everything, and then she became so deaf . . ."

"She didn't manage to keep King Edward happy, did she?"

Sniff.

"Oh, Durdy, honestly! I'm not a baby anymore! Did you meet Edward often?"

"Only just the once, darling."

"What did he say? What did he do?"

"He smelt my breath to see if I'd been drinking."

"Durdy! You?"

"No, not me. But it is a great temptation to some poor women."

"What was he like? Was he terribly attractive?"

Rock, rock in the long stillness. Only the tock of the cuckoo-clock and the grumble of the rockers, a pigeon cooing in the garden and beyond it the endless surf of traffic. Louise began to worry. Usually Durdy gave you warning that she was getting tired so that she didn't drop off in the middle of a conversation. The rockers gradually stilled.

"I wasn't asleep," squeaked Durdy suddenly. "Only remembering . . . things were so different then. I was a servant, you see, and servants knew their place. His Majesty had the family looks, of course, very like His present Majesty, especially about the eyes—only he was older and fatter and he wore that beard . . . but *attractive*? You see, darling, that's what I mean about being a servant—I'd have had to have been a rich lady to tell you that . . . No, when he came to the nursery that night I thought he was more like a hunter . . . only he wasn't hunting me, not me . . ."

Silence again. Louise had never heard Durdy talking quite like this before, her thin old voice so close to whispering that it was difficult to hear what she said. It was almost as though she was talking to herself about something private to her.

"He preferred his ladies of course," whispered Durdy. "They could talk to him and make him laugh. But if he'd wanted one of us it wouldn't have been much help running away. He'd have hunted you down, and then you'd have been like a bird, waiting for the snake to swallow you. A wee bird in the heather."

"I'm glad Father's not like that," said Louise. "It would spoil everything . . . everything!"

She'd meant to speak lightly, but something in Durdy's manner infected her into an explosion of vehemence that was almost like a shout of pain.

"No need to tell the whole world," said Durdy in her normal tones.

"I'm sorry. But it does matter. It really does. Don't you see? The whole thing only works because he isn't like that . . . oh, Durdy, I'm sorry . . . I really don't come here to shout at you about how I want the Family to behave . . ."

"It's not your fault, darling, only I'm a bit tired today."

"You've got a bone in your leg."

"Not any longer . . . no bones . . ."

With a snicker and a fizz the cuckoo-clock started to chant six.

"Help!" said Louise. "That must be fast! I've got a whole pile of homework! Where's Kinunu? She ought to have brought you your green pill ages ago! Don't buzz for her—I'll tell her on my way out."

Durdy was murmuring to herself now, something about a kitten, and children. Louise bent to listen until she realized that it was like listening at a door. Carefully she kissed the stretched, textureless cheek and tiptoed away, alarmed by the sudden retreat of life away from the surface of the old face. Perhaps it was because the green pill was late . . .

The Night Nursery was empty, the monitor still switched off.

"Kinunu!" she called sharply. "Kinunu!"

"I come," answered a voice from the bedroom. "Thorry. I come."

But it was nearly half a minute before the door opened and Kinunu came bouncing out, very flushed, blinking, smiling her teasing smile, but with her nurse's cap on all skew-wiff.

"Thleep," she said. "Thorry, thorry. Oh, late. Oh, thorry."

"Miss Durdon's very tired, Kinunu. I'm worried about her. Oughtn't she to have had her green pill?"

"Pilly. Yethyeth."

"You'll check everything, won't you? I'm worried. If anything's wrong you'll send for the King or for Doctor Simm."

"Yethyeth," said Kinunu, bouncing impatiently away and into the Day Nursery.

Louise hesitated, uncertain whether Kinunu had understood what she'd said and whether she'd check the dials properly. She was just moving to turn the monitor on (though as it took a couple of minutes to warm up she still wouldn't be sure) when she heard Kinunu's voice coming from the bedroom.

"Lo, mithmith."

Of course, the bedroom monitor must be on—that'd be better. She tiptoed through the open door.

McGivan was sitting on the bed, motionless, with his trousers half on. He glanced at her out of the corner of his eye and looked away. His hand rose to twirl the spike of his moustache. Then he appeared to remember his status in the Palace and rose to attention, emitting as he did so one of his richest and most repellent snuffles. His trousers collapsed round his ankles.

"I . . . I . . . ," said Louise, turning quickly away.

"Yourr Highness," whispered McGivan, urgently.

She stopped but couldn't look round.

"Ye wunna tell a body?" he pleaded.

"It's nothing to do with me."

"Yon lassie was sae gey inseestent . . ."

"It's none of my business, Mr. McGivan. I won't tell anybody."

Louise managed to walk quite calmly out of the nursery suite and along the Upper West Corridor, but on the stairs she got the giggles, so violent a fit of them that she was teetering on the edge of hysteria. McGivan had been so appallingly McGivanish, just like one of Albert's take-offs of him, with his snuffle and his joke-Scotch accent and his trousers round his ankles. It was a pity she'd never be able to tell anybody. Vaguely Louise was aware that there was another reason for the force of the fit that shook her: in the past few days she had been seeing glimpses of the great hinterland of human sexuality, not as hitherto in her life as a sort of imagined Narnia-world, part fairy-land and part moral-problem, but as a real country full of richnesses—like her three parents' lives—and dangers—like the ravage in her bedroom and Durdy's unsettling, unDurdylike talk about the snake and the bird. And now she had seen that another part of this reality took the form of bedroom farce. Yes, it was like that too.

Homework went badly. It wasn't difficult, but even while she was reeling off a dozen potty French sentences her thoughts kept wandering between word and word so that sometimes she'd sit for a whole minute thinking about McGivan with his trousers round his ankles, or Nonny's

new hairstyle, or a strange misty vision of a fatter version of
Father smelling little Miss Durdon's breath to see if she was
drunk. She'd just about finished the French when Sir Sam
came into the Library and when she looked up did his little
bob of respect.

"Aha," he said. "I thought I'd find you here. You can
save my legs a trudge. Have you been up in the Nurseries,
and if so was HM there?"

"No, he wasn't, I'm afraid. Is something the matter?"

"I wish Miss Durdon would let me put a telephone up
there. No, no. Just Her Majesty's Reception for these South
American Cultural wallahs this evening. Home Office have
been on the blower with a story about a Venezuelan terror
squad being in the country and of course we've checked the
whole place out—do that anyway, these days. First I just
thought HM ought to know, then I got worried because I
couldn't trace him. He won't answer his beeper, either . . ."

Then he's on the loo, thought Louise. He always switches
it off for that. Poor Father. Poor us. Life's hell when he's
constipated. She smiled a sorry-I-can't-help smile and watched
Sir Sam fade silverly away. Just as the door closed she heard
the sound of voices, his and Father's, Father very abrupt,
lending more weight to the constipation theory. You'd have
thought a doctor would be able to control that, but of course
Father has to be different . . .

She glanced at the clock. Just before half past six. A
ten-minute French homework must have taken her about
twenty—still, it felt like twice that. And supper wouldn't be
till nine, because of this dreary reception. She might be able
to finish her English essay. Come on, Lulu, get it over.

The essay should have been almost as potty as the French,
because it was about the difference between fantasy and
realism and that meant you could waffle on about Tolkien till
you'd done your three sides. But just as she was settling her
thoughts in order Louise remembered Julie's last words that
afternoon—"You're all right, duckie, you can write about
the difference between real and fantasy princesses." It was a
temptation, though Louise knew that Mother would never
let it through. She allowed herself another dip into useless
musings, like those dips back into indulgent drowsing which

one can't help having when one is supposed to be getting up. Story Princesses sit on thrones and wear crowns, and lovers fight duels over a smile from them. Real Princesses do homework and worry about spots. I used to be a real Princess, but now I'm a story one . . . d'you know, in some ways it's going to make it easier, because I'll be able to keep things really separate. The story Princess can put on a show while the real me . . . the real who? I haven't even got a real name . . . oh yes I have, because illegits take the mother's name, don't they . . . May Victoria Isabella Louise Catarina Alice Fellowes, that's me . . . pity they're all such foul names except Isabella and Louise . . . I might call myself Kate, perhaps . . . OK, Kate, get on with your homework.

Kate was an idle hussy. Quite quickly Louise lost patience with her and let the story Princess take over. The story Princess in her best writing wrote quickly down all the things which she knew Mrs. Handishaw would like, paying special attention to what Jerry called the good 'n' evil scene. In Tolkien good is all misty and evil is something over there, in that dirty old mountain, and the best thing to do about it is to whop off a few more orcs' heads. But in the real world good and evil are all mixed together, for instance . . . she stopped writing and thought of instances. Even really good people had things which were wrong with them: Mother could be almost mad in her hate of her few ancient enemies, and Durdy had been a complete bitch to most of her nurses until Kinunu showed up . . . and evil, is anybody *evil*? The image of a single letter scribbled on a pair of clean panties flipped into her mind . . . rubbish! That's not evil. That's just sick. She put on a public face (intelligent attention) and let the story Princess finish the essay off. A minus. Julie will be furious, but how can she expect anything except Bs if she keeps treading on all Mrs. Handishaw's sacred toes?

Shutting the book, she saw that it was still only just after half past seven. Well done, story Princess! You have your uses; now, what would you like for a reward? Why, to sit on a throne, of course. Trouble is, there's only one pair of thrones in the Palace, and that's in the ball-room where Mother's cultural dagoes are whooping it up. Yes, but the curtain will be drawn across the dais and you can get round through the robing-room—and, actually, it might be quite useful to hear how Mother makes a speech in Spanish. At least that's what you can tell people if they find you lurking around on the dais. Lucky you're wearing a dress.Pity it's not a long one, and there ought to be a tiara at least. Louise half closed her eyes and tried to imagine the bitter twinkle of diamonds in her straight mousy hair. Public face, sweet and gracious but capable of stern command. Have to practice stern command. Practice on McGivan? Better start with the dogs.

She strolled out into the corridor still wearing her public face in case she bumped into a strayed Bolivian poetess. The Library lay round the corner from the run of State Rooms along the West Front; the wide corridor was busy with footmen, and the last guests still arriving, looking very much more as though they were used to this sort of thing than English people usually did in the Palace. It would be fun for Mother to be able to speak Spanish all evening and then complain at supper about the agony of listening to South American accents.

Louise put on a proper smile for Pilfer as he stalked towards her, stooped and dismal, looking like the minister of some furiously narrow-minded sect who has been visiting the fleshpots for the sole purpose of going back to his chapel and blasting their wickedness from his pulpit. Probably, she thought, he was just disappointed at once again having failed to catch Mr. Lambert using Private Apartment silver for a State Apartment do.

The hum of talk was not like that of real parties; it was quite loud, but missed out most of the shriller tones of chat. At the door of the ball-room Pilfer's enemy, Mr. Lambert, took a deep breath and raised an eyebrow at her.

"No, I'm not coming in," she whispered. "I just wandered along for a glimpse of the bright lights."

He nodded, then bent his head to listen to a fat little man with a vast, curling beard. When he straightened he let the breath go in the stately bellow which was his stock-in-trade.

"His Excellency Senor Jose Grando Y Batet!"

Under his raised chin Louise could see that the blue

velvet curtains were indeed drawn across the far end of the room, almost like stage curtains. She strolled on against the current of guests and as though it were the normal thing to do slipped into the little robing-room which Father always called the vestry. She shut the door before she turned on the lights. Both the cupboards that held the robes were locked. Honestly, no long dress, no tiara, not even any velvet and ermine! Well, as Mrs. Handishaw was always crooning, imagination is a marvellous gift. In imagination Louise robed herself in grandeur—much quicker than the real thing. She turned off the light, opened the door to the dais and slipped through.

It was very nearly dark behind the curtains, which were also thick enough to fuzz the hundred-voiced mutter of cultural back-chat, making the sculptors and dancers and administrators and so on all sound a bit tiddly. Louise moved slowly forward. Story Princesses don't grope, even in the dark. She felt with her feet for the two steps to the dais and went up them at a stately pace, judging her course so well that the front edge of Mother's throne brushed her knee exactly when she was expecting it. She settled down onto the slightly prickling velvet with her back and neck held as straight as if she had been Queen Mary. She was deep in a fantasy of quelling an incursion of rebellious peasants into her own throne-room when Mr. Lambert's bellow broke through, only the first few syllables drowned by the dying chit-chat.

". . . and Gentlemen, pray silence for the Patron of the Anglo-Hispanic Cultural League, Her Majesty Queen Isabella, Lady of the Most Noble Order of the Garter, of the Royal Order of Victoria and Albert, Dame Grand Cross of the Royal Victorian Order, and Grand Master of the Order of the British Empiyaaah!"

Rapidly Louise re-peopled her throne-room with a glittering throng of courtiers, soldiers, delegations from loyal cities and ambassadors from exotic islands.

"Our much-loved subjects," she murmured, stretching out to touch the hand of the imagined consort at her side.

His hand was real.

With a thundering bounce of the heart Louise jerked

away, almost out of the throne, opening her eyes to peer through the gloom; by now she could see the shape sitting there, a little hunched but wholly familiar. From beyond the curtains Mother's clear voice began its welcome.

"Father," whispered Louise, already more frightened than amazed.

He appeared not to notice, but to be listening intently to the speech. Shakily she rose and touched his shoulder, then shook it. His head tilted slowly, at first as though he were falling asleep but coming at last to an angle which could not be true.

◆ 10 ◆

MUTTERS AND WHISPERS. A choked-back fit of coughing, some way off. Out of dark mists a white light, harsher than sunrise. Screw eyes shut.

"Stand a bit over, Bella, and you'll keep that spot out of her eyes. She's coming round."

Father's voice. His face close in the clearing mists. Mother black against the whiteness. Sir Sam's trousers.

"I thought . . . I'm all right . . . I thought you were . . ."

"Wasn't me. You've only fainted. She'll be OK, Bella. Bert, d'you feel up to putting in an appearance back there—last thing we want's a panic. Sam, get them to send a stretcher, will you, then get on to the Yard?"

"I'm all right. I don't need a stretcher."

"Lie still, Lulu."

"I'm all right, I tell you!"

With a wriggling twist Louise jerked to her knees, almost blacking out again as she did so. She stared round. The curtains were still closed but the glare flooded from spotlights overhead, fierce and shadowless. At its center Father sat slumped on his throne still, with his head at that inhuman skew. She flung round to see who'd been speaking to her.

"Take it easy, Lulu," said Father, kneeling beside her. "It's poor McGivan. Don't look again. Only somebody's

120

been fooling around with his moustache. You'd do much better to lie down again till the stretcher comes.''

"No."

"OK. Well, take it easy. Hold my arm. There. Good girl.''

Louise leaned on him as she stood, shaking her head to clear the last of the mists.

"I'm all right,'' she said, though the floor still seemed to slither a little under her feet. "I'm so sorry. I spoilt your speech, Mother. I . . . I couldn't help it. What . . . happened to McGivan?''

"Don't know, yet. Ah, here's the stretcher . . .''

"I can walk. I really can. Please. If somebody . . . Bert or Nonny . . .''

(You couldn't ask for Mother. She'd have to go back to the guests and put on a show.)

"Sure? Well, OK. No, don't go, Durnley. Will you stay here with McGivan and see that nobody touches anything? Snape, will you find the Prince in the ball-room and ask him to come back here? Bella, you stay with Lulu till Bert comes. We're going to have to tell the guests that they'll have to stay till the police take over, at least. It'll look better if we're both out there together—provided you feel up to it, that is.''

"Of course,'' said Mother. "You huill tell Nonny that Lulu is all right, Vick?''

He grunted and slid between the curtains.

Mother looked more sad than frightened. She bent to whisper so that Durnley, the stretcherman, couldn't hear.

"Hue couldn't both come,'' she whispered.

Louise nodded. Of course, they were on show, and Mother had to be the only mother. She clasped her slim, chill hand and squeezed it to show that she understood and wasn't judging Nonny for not being there. In a very few moments Albert came back through the curtains. Louise put her arm round his shoulders and let herself be led away through the robing-room, wearing her public face, serious, for use at funerals. As they passed the main entrance to the ball-room they heard Lambert's mellow bellow.

"Your Excellencies, your Grace, my . . .''

"That's all right, Lambert," interrupted Father's voice. "Ladies and Gentlemen, first let me assure you that nobody is in any danger at all. But I'm extremely sorry to say..."

The words faded out of hearing. The corridor seemed full of servants, each making a crude pretense, while Louise and Albert went by, to have some duty that brought them there. They didn't find themselves alone till they were on the stairs.

"Bert, was he dead?" whispered Louise.

"Fraid so," said Albert. "I mean Father checked on you, looked at him for a couple of seconds, made a no-go face and came back to you."

"How did you find us?"

He stared at her.

"Jesus, Lulu, when everybody's listening to a speech and then they hear this scream..."

"Scream? Me?"

Now, vaguely, she remembered something wrenching at her throat, but not any noise.

"My first thought was that the joker had struck again," he said. "Putting a tape of *Bride of Dracula* up there, timed to go off during the speeches."

"Bert, I saw him!"

"I know you did, poor kid. Don't think about it."

"No, I don't mean that. I saw him earlier, up in the Nurseries. He'd been... talking to Kinunu."

"Oh. OK, I'll tell Father. I suppose it might be important. Get it clear in your mind, Lulu, but don't worry about it. You must have had the hell of a shock. I did too, though I'd only just seen Father go through the curtains. McGivan did look damned like him, for once."

"Bert! Do you remember what Nonny said?"

"No. About McGivan?"

"Yes. After Father'd first shown him to us. Mother said he'd never be mistaken for Father, and then Nonny said he might do for a lying-in-state."

Without any warning she found herself crying. All along the Middle Corridor the slow sobs came, not wrenching or painful but not easing either. Only a couple of hours ago McGivan had been deep in his snuffling ecstasies in Kinunu's arms; only a couple of hours ago he'd been standing by Kinunu's bed with his trousers round his ankles, as full of shame as a dog caught rolling in a cow-pat, but alive, alive. The suddenness of the change filled Louise with darkness. Not really having liked him made it no better. You could cope with somebody dying, even if you loved them, provided they were ready for it . . .

"Bert!"

"We're nearly there, kid. Take it easy."

"I forgot. Tell Father that Durdy wasn't very well, I thought. I asked Kinunu to send for Doctor Simm if there was anything wrong, but I'm not sure she understood."

"OK. If Father can't make it I'll go up and check, soon as I can. Here you are. Sure you'll be all right? Would you like me to tell Pilfer to bring your supper up here?"

"Oh, yes please. Thank you, Bert. I'm all right now. Don't forget to tell Father about Durdy."

He'd done his best, but it was merciful to be alone, so much so that it took a definite act of will not to lock the door. When Louise went to her bathroom to wash her face she found that apart from a streak of her new anti-Nonny eye-shadow she mightn't have been crying at all. Angrily she wiped away the smear, scrubbing at it as if she was trying to remove the unreal, skin-deep calm as well. If ever she wanted to show grief she would have to act it, and even then there would be no real connection between the desolation inside and the grimaces on the surface. Oh, hell!

She went back to her room and crouched by the bookshelves, looking for something to fill her mind and stop her thinking about McGivan. McGivan and Kinunu, making love. Kinunu giggling and whispering "Yethyeth" and teasing, and McGivan snuffling like a badger digging into an ants' nest. How extraordinary people were. You'd never have guessed that McGivan would have got that far with her. Perhaps Kinunu had simply teased him into it. And all the while the blue square of the monitor had stared down at the bed and the room had been full of the voices of Durdy and Louise, talking next door.

Louise actually had her hand on *The Two Towers* when

the idea came to her. She froze, then slowly dragged the
book clear. McGivan had heard every word. He had heard
about her own birth. Father had talked to Durdy about it
before then. He knew. He knew about Father's struggles on
the loo, too. And of course he knew about Fatty Toad and
Sir Sam's trousers. McGivan had been the joker. And
somebody had killed him because of that.

She leafed through the book in her hand to the chapter
called "The Voice of Saruman." "Behold, I am not Gandalf
the Grey, whom you betrayed. I am Gandalf the White, who
has returned from death." BASTARD!

He'd even have known that this was her favorite book,
because she often talked to Durdy about it. She stared at the
red scrawl, unshaken. She hadn't destroyed the book because it was a present from Albert. Could they prove it was
McGivan's writing? A scrawl, probably left-handed, with a
coarse felt pen?

A knock at the door. Pilfer, very grave with the supper
tray, not saying a word but managing to lay out the cloth and
cutlery in a hushed and sympathetic manner. (Albert said
Pilfer's father must have been an undertaker. That was why
Pilfer wore black gloves, Albert said—his father had got a
reduction on the price of mourners' gloves by buying them
in quantity, and Pilfer had inherited several gross.) Louise
thanked Pilfer and sat down to eat, surprised by her sudden
hunger. Poor McGivan. Poor, dotty McGivan. At least he
must have had some fun out of his jokes. And Kinunu.

She'd finished the soup and was half way through one of
a pair of chops, dressed with a brandy-and-cream sauce,
when Father's head poked round the door.

"How are you feeling? Nothing wrong with your appe-
tite, at least."

He always grumbled like that when a member of the
Family was tactless enough to fall sick.

"I'm all right. But listen, Father . . ."

The head poking round the jamb made a sharp frown, but
cleared as the door opened wide. A stranger followed Father
into the room, a softly handsome slim man, about Father's
age but with a full crop of black hair, slicked hard to either
side of the parting. He had that look of almost machine-

made politeness which Louise was so used to in diplomats, top civil servants and Palace officials—except that Sir Sam would probably have taken him aside and very very tactfully given him the name of a better tailor.

"This is Detective Superintendent d'Arcy," said Father. "My daughter. Lulu, what's this about your having seen McGivan in the Nurseries?"

"That's right. I'd been talking to Durdy..."

"That's my old nurse, Superintendent. She's bedridden."

"...and when I came out he was outside, er, I mean in the Night Nursery. He'd been talking with Kinunu."

"And that's my nurse's nurse. Yes, Lulu, what time was this?"

"Just after six."

"Sure of that?" said Father.

"Six!" said the Superintendent at the same moment.

"Yes, the cuckoo-clock had just struck."

"You can't rely on that," said Father. "It's never been the same since old Haakon swore he could make it tick less noisily. Did you check the time any other way?"

"Er...no, I don't think so. Next time I looked at a clock was when I was doing my homework. It was about half past six. I remember I thought my French hadn't taken me as long as I thought it had. Oh! You met Sir Sam outside the Library just then. He'd been in to look for you."

"That's right, Superintendent," said Father. "It must have been about half past six."

"But the clock in the Nursery is not reliable, er, Sir?"

"I'm going up there now. I'll look at it. Lulu, Bert said you thought Durdy was off color."

"She seemed so tired and wandery. I wasn't sure Kinunu would check her properly. That's all."

"Right. I'll nip up there now. That is provided you don't want me to stay, Superintendent."

He nodded and was going before Mr. d'Arcy could clear his throat.

"Please sit down," said Louise. "D'you mind if I finish my supper?"

The second chop was congealing and the sauce had

become a slobbery goo, but she thought that having to pause to eat might help her think without seeming to think. Mr. d'Arcy got out a notebook and stared at it. Louise chewed a tiny corner of chop and waited. Suddenly he looked up.

"Now, Your Highness," he said. "This won't take long. It's not frightening. I've a daughter just your age, and I wouldn't have her frightened for the world."

His voice was deferential, but like his suit it wasn't quite right—a bit too much here, a bit too little there. Uncomfortable for him.

"It's all right, I'm not frightened," said Louise, also not getting it right, not because of the remains of chop in her mouth but because she was suddenly very frightened indeed. If McGivan had been killed because he was the joker, then all the jokes would come out, including the rape of her own room, and the reason for it.

"Did somebody kill him?" she whispered.

"It looks that way, Your Highness. At the moment we're working on the theory that he stumbled on a terrorist group who were planning to disrupt the reception. They killed him and then ran off. There's a lot of work to be done on how they got in and out, of course. But the first essential is to establish the movements of the deceased. That's why I was surprised when you said you had seen him at six this evening. His Majesty had made a rough estimate of time of death a good half hour earlier than that. Of course His Majesty is not a pathologist, and we'll have to wait for our own doctor's report. At the other end of the time-scale, Sergeant Theale checked the, er, robing-room and the thrones at approximately twenty past five and saw nothing. So the question of the exact time when you saw the deceased is most important. However, I think we had better start by your telling me how you found the body, and we'll leave what happened in the Nursery until His Majesty returns and tells us whether the clock is right. Are you sure you feel up to this, Your Highness?"

Deliberately Louise had been niggling a scrap of meat from the bone while he spoke, to hide the altered tension in her mind. Sir Sam's Venezuelan terrorists! That was frightening, but in quite a different way, a way she could cope with. She put on a public face and turned towards him.

"It's all right," she said, "ask anything you want."

Even at a grisly moment like this the story Princess had her uses. Louise could see how she bowled Mr. d'Arcy over as she answered each of his careful questions. He took detailed notes, which gave her plenty of time to think. The robing-room. Its locked cupboards. Its lights off. The door to the dais shut. All that.

"Yes, I know," she said earnestly. "I felt pretty stupid sneaking about like that. I wasn't asked to the reception and I wasn't really dressed for it, you see. But I wanted to listen to my Mother's speech. I can talk Spanish, but I've never made a speech in Spanish, and I'm bound to have to one day, so I thought it might be useful. I could have arranged to listen in a more sensible way, but I only thought of it while I was doing my homework, you see?"

"Ah, homework. Now, my daughter Eileen . . . erhump! And at what stage did you see the deceased? It must have been pretty dark behind those curtains."

"Pitch, at first. I felt my way and sat on my Mother's throne. I think I shut my eyes. Then when the speech started I happened to look round . . . No, I stretched out and touched his hand. That came first. Then of course I looked. I suppose my eyes had got used to the dark, but even then I could only just see . . . just see . . ."

"Take it easy. Take it easy. It's all over now."

"I'm all right. I thought it was my Father. I could just see his moustache, you see, and McGivan usually wore his twisted into points . . ."

Mr. d'Arcy turned a grunt into a sigh.

"If I could understand why a terrorist organization should go mucking around with dead men's moustaches I'd be a happier man," he said.

Sitting with his back to the door, he hadn't noticed the face peering round it, identical to the one he was fretting about.

"They thought they'd got me, I daresay," said Father.

The Superintendent jumped, sank back into his chair and

then remembered he was supposed to rise anyway. Louise could see how he longed to swear his surprise away and had to bite the words back.

"Good Lord," he eventually managed to say. "That would account for their disappearance, and the apparent absence of bombs. Good Lord. I should have thought of that. But in that case Sergeant McGivan's moustache . . ."

"No problem," said Father. "He was a Rightful King. Sorry, Superintendent—I mean there are about twenty or so pretenders to my throne and poor McGivan was one of them. He wasn't exactly unbalanced, but leave him alone in the throne room and he'd be quite capable of combing down his moustache and pretending to be me for a bit."

"Good Lord," said Mr. d'Arcy. He relieved his feelings by making a note.

"The Nursery clock's twenty-five minutes fast," said Father, sounding pleased about it.

"Ah, that's more like it," said Mr. d'Arcy. "Glad it wasn't any more."

"What do you mean?" said Father.

"Well, Sir, whoever did this job must have had inside help. Five thirty was the time at which a number of people involved in the reception reported for duty. The Palace security staff, for instance—until five thirty they'd been split up to check the premises, but then they assembled for a briefing on the guests. That was when McGivan's absence was first noticed."

Father looked as though he was going to argue about something, but changed his mind and swung suddenly to Louise.

"Durdy's OK," he said. "A bit fretful—if I believed in telepathy I'd say she'd sensed that something like this was going to happen. I put her to sleep. Have you finished in here, Superintendent?"

"Not yet, Sir. I want to ask Her Royal Highness about her meeting with Sergeant McGivan in the Nursery. Now we've got a better check on the time . . ."

"I'll wait," said Father.

There wasn't much to it once Louise had decided to carry on with the lie she'd half begun. She'd heard the clock strike, thought it was later than it really was, and rushed off to start her homework and tell Kinunu to give Miss Durdon her green pill. McGivan had been talking to Kinunu in the Night Nursery but they'd stopped when she came in. She didn't know how long McGivan had stayed after that. He'd seemed normal—a bit shy perhaps, but he was often like that.

"You'll want to talk to Kinunu next," said Father when Mr. d'Arcy looked up from his notebook.

"I gather there's a language problem, Sir."

"Yes. She's only got a smattering of English. She gets along in Malay, but her own language is a hill dialect. There's a woman who lived out beyond Maidenhead who's come up a couple of times to interpret for us, a retired missionary—could it wait till the morning?"

"I think so, Sir."

"Fine. Of course if Kinunu knows anything you've got to get it out of her, Superintendent, but you'll have to handle her very gently. This is the one place in the country where we really can't afford to seem to be picking on a colored girl."

"I quite understand, Sir," said Mr. d'Arcy a little stiffly.

They began to move towards the door.

"Father," said Louise in a feeble voice. "I'm feeling a bit . . . I mean could you . . ."

He turned and glared at her.

"You'll have to find your own way down, Superintendent," he said. "I'll just check this out—she's had a pretty traumatic evening. If you see Sir Savile tell him I'll be down in ten minutes."

Mr. d'Arcy was half way gone when the thought must have struck him that he was supposed to retire backwards from the Royal presence. He got himself through the door somehow. Father returned to Louise with raised eyebrows.

"D'you really feel ill?" he said. "I'm going to give you a sedative anyway. You *have* had a shock, though no one would know it to look at you."

"I'm all right. I get sudden waves as though I was dropping into a black hole, but they go quite quickly. But listen. It's important. I didn't know what to tell him until I'd talked to you. I didn't find McGivan in the Night Nursery—I found him in Kinunu's bedroom—they'd been making love.''

"Good God!"

"But that isn't the really important thing. They'd had the monitor on in there all the time. McGivan could have heard everything I said to Durdy. And he could have listened before. He could have known about me, you see. That means he must have been the joker!"

"Might have been, not must," said Father.

"So perhaps somebody killed him because of that," said Louise.

"Wait a bit. Let's take one thing at a time. Tell me what really happened in the Night Nursery."

He managed to keep a straight face as he listened but his hand crept towards his moustache. Irritation at his inner amusement made her almost bark the last words at him.

"... so don't you see, he'd have known all about Nonny being my mother, *and* about your obsession with your loo.''

He glared at her, then nodded.

"Yes. OK. I'd had my eye on him before, as a matter of fact. D'you mind telling me why you didn't tell d'Arcy the truth, straight out?"

"I don't know. Honestly I don't. I was a bit ashamed, I suppose ... and I'd promised him I wouldn't ... and I suppose it's almost instinctive not to come out with things like that except when we're among ourselves ... I wanted to ask you first. I could easily tell him if you think I ought to ...''

"Mmm. No doubt about that. You ought to. But I don't want you to. You probably don't realize quite how close Durdy is to death. She might go tomorrow or she might last another six months, but she's teetering on the edge all the time. One of the things that keeps her here is the funny relationship she's struck up with Kinunu. I don't understand it at all, except apparently Kinunu reminds her of somebody she knew before any of us were born. She won't talk about it. Now, if the police start badgering Kinunu about her sex-life there's every chance she'll crack up and have to go, and that would kill Durdy. You see?"

"What do you want me to do?"

"Nothing. Before the police see her I'll try to explain to Kinunu what you've told them. The point is I don't think any of this is relevant. I don't see how it can have anything to do with McGivan's death."

"Perhaps somebody else was in love with her. Perhaps they were jealous of McGivan."

He shook his head.

"But you can't *know*. You didn't know about Kinunu and McGivan, even!"

"I had an inkling. I didn't realize they'd got that far... Look, Lulu, let's leave it for a while, and see how they get on with the Venezuelan line..."

"But if McGivan was the joker!"

"I'm coming to that. We've got to step a bit careful there, too, you see. Your crucial bit of evidence won't do, because it would mean telling d'Arcy about your birth, and I'm not having that. I'll tell him about the frog in my bog—God, that I should see the day!—but that's not so significant. I mean, a number of people could have known I have bother with my bowels without having to listen to Kinunu's monitor... so we'll lay it on the line about the jokes, except the one in this room. I'll say that I was beginning to think McGivan might be the joker—I'll explain that he was the only one of the security staff who wasn't in the clear when the joker rang up about sending my mother those pianos. And we'll leave it at that. OK?"

"I suppose so," said Louise.

He had settled onto the edge of the bed while he was speaking and leaned forward, tense and solemn. Louise was conscious of pent urgency behind his low, hypnotic monotone. She'd been hoping that he would tell her to go straight to Mr. d'Arcy and change her story to the truth, but now she saw that she was stuck with the lie she'd begun. At least he thought she'd done the right thing.

"There's another point," he said. "Apart from d'Arcy I'm not going to tell anyone, not even Bella or Nonny, about McGivan and Kinunu or the possibility of his being the joker. Because we know about it you and I are going to have to watch our step, and lie when the questions come anywhere near the danger areas. I don't want to drag them into the same mess. I don't like it for you and I don't like it for me, but at least we can let them off. Do you agree?''

"Yes. Of course. I suppose if we could *prove* McGivan was the joker . . . I've still got the scribble in my book . . . couldn't a hand-writing expert . . . ?"

She opened the Tolkien and showed him the scrawl across the type. He looked at it for a while, then shook his head.

"It's the same thing all over again," he said. "In fact it's an exact parable of the bind we're in. Don't you see? Suppose we could prove McGivan wrote those letters—so far so good. But the letters make a word, and somebody'd be bound to ask what the word meant."

"I suppose so."

"Let's hope to God these Venezuelans . . ."

"Do you believe in them, Father?"

"I think they're the main chance. No time to thrash all that out now. If McGivan was the joker, that's only the sort of coincidence which really does sometimes happen. Now listen, Lulu, I want to know what the hell you were up to in the throne room."

"I wanted to listen to Mother's speech."

"I don't really buy that," he said after a pause. "Oh, don't be a fool, Lulu. A couple of days ago I told you a lot of my personal secrets because I thought it might make life a bit easier for you. Can't you see that now I'm trying to protect you and a few other people, and to do that I must know as much as I can about what's been going on? I'm on a real tightrope, Lulu. I can't afford any more areas of uncertainty than I must."

"Sorry. It's only that it sound so silly when you say it out loud. I don't even know if I can explain. You remember you told me about Nonny not wanting to be Queen, and you couldn't understand it? I think it's obvious. I feel just the same about princessing. Not all the time, but sometimes. Only of course I'm landed with it, and Nonny wasn't. Well, now I've found out that there's really an official me and an unofficial me I can treat them as two different people . . ."

"You're playing with fire, Lulu. Honestly. That's how psychoses begin. Just think . . . no, we haven't time now. I think we'd better have a long talk about that when the dust's settled a bit. Go on."

"I think it's all right. It's only a *game*, Father. Oh, well, I call the official me the story Princess, and she'd done my homework for me when the unofficial me was acting up rather—I haven't got a name for *her* yet—so I thought I'd give the story Princess a treat by letting her go and sit on Mother's throne and pretend that all you behind the curtain were courtiers and so on. That's all. Honestly, Father! Don't look at me like that. It's really only putting on a show, except that I'm putting it on for myself. I know what I'm doing!"

He sighed.

"All right," he said. "Provided you promise to try and keep it at that level until we've had a chance to thrash the whole thing out. Now, anything else before I go?"

"You said you'd got your eye on McGivan already. What did you mean?"

"It started with that business about the pianos. Because I knew Theale at least was in the clear for that I got him to start eliminating anybody who couldn't have been responsible for that or any of the other jokes. It's surprising how that sort of process cuts the suspects down. There were still about a dozen possibles left, and as I told you McGivan was one of them. Then, do you remember that night when I came back and found you and Nonny hopped to the eyeballs on my best Heidsieck? While I was watching you I started wondering what kind of nut could have done that to someone like you. It wasn't quite in key with the other jokes . . ."

"But it was!"

"Only superficially. It was an outburst. The others were quirks. Now, I said, who would *mind* so much about your being what you are? Who might have a real bee in his bonnet about illegitimacy, and royal blood? When I thought about it I saw that the other jokes might be milder expressions of a grievance at not belonging . . . I mean, either they were aimed at unsettling the private workings of the Family—my bog, our breakfast—or at people who were allowed to play a rather grand part at functions. I think he might have had a practical motive too—you remember how he tried to frame Theale about my Mother's pianos? They've all got the jitters about losing their jobs in the reorganization, so you see the jokes not only gave McGivan something to investigate, and prove his usefulness, but a reason for seeing that it was somebody else who got the sack."

"But it still could have been Sanderson, or anybody, couldn't it?"

"The reorganization part, yes; but the other part no. Practical joking runs in the blood, Lulu. McGivan was my Father's first cousin."

◆ 11 ◆

WHILE LOUISE SANK out of her private wulli-wa of shock into the soft dark of the sedative Father gave her, the Palace Press Office came to life. The Duty Press Officer called Commander Tank, and he summoned the rest of his staff from chess club and night club, from dismal bedsitter or raucous family abode. Cats went unbrushed, children unbathed, neighbors uncuckolded. Commander Tank always tended to treat any contact with the media, unless he had personally arranged it, as an armed invasion; now it was as though Hitler's landing-fleet had been sighted in the Channel and he with his Few were all that stood against it. Of course he was overwhelmed, but he went down fighting, or at least shouting.

At ten o'clock the Press Office issued a statement that the body of a Palace Security Officer had been discovered during the course of a reception for a South American Cultural Mission. The police were working on the theory that in the course of his duties he had discovered a group of South American guerrillas planning to disrupt the reception and that they had killed him and then escaped. A tip-off had been received shortly before the reception, but His Majesty had personally given the orders that it should go ahead as planned.

Even those scanty scraps would have been enough to fill every front page on the British breakfast table; but by

midnight somebody had told somebody that Princess Louise
had found the body. Commander Tank's Few withdrew to
hastily prepared positions, but in less than an hour they
were being blasted from an exposed flank by reporters
wanting to know whether it was true that the dead man was
a double of King Victor, that Princess Louise had found him
sitting in the dark on the King's throne, and that the police
were working on the theory that the assassins had believed
that their victim was the King himself. By dawn they had no
knowledge left to withhold and the Palace switchboard was
flooded with calls from five continents.

That was how it happened that Scotland Yard Traffic
Control came through on Nonny's private phone in the
Breakfast Room to ask whether Princess Louise was going
to school, as serious jams were building up in Church Street
caused by crowds waiting to see her do so.

"Tell them no," snapped Father. "Can't you see, Lulu . . ."

"Oh, all right, all right," said Lulu. "You needn't go on
at me. Honestly. At least it means I can go and see how
Durdy is. I bet you've all forgotten her."

"She's fine," said Father. "I was up there first thing and
she was still asleep. But every dial was right back to
normal."

(Of course. He'd have been to try and tell Kinunu what to
say. Poor Kinunu. Perhaps he'd been the first to tell her
McGivan was dead.)

"Nonny huill ring up the school and get them to send
you some huork to do," said Mother. "And you huill please
not make that face at me, Lulu. You are behaving like a
baby."

"I don't think that's quite fair, darling," said Nonny.
"Everybody feels like that. It's a ripe tomato situation."

Father and Bert grunted agreement. In the family slang a
ripe tomato was anything which caused an unexpected or
undignified jolt in the Royal routine. Once, when Queen
Mary had been visiting an East End soup kitchen, somebody
had thrown a real tomato at her and caught her full on the
toque. She had stalked on, smiling and gracious, as though
the dribble of yellow pips and scarlet juice were part of her
normal coiffure. When a ripe tomato occurred your instinc-

tive reaction was to try to behave with the same inhuman calm. If circumstances permitted, you allowed somebody to wipe up the mess; if they didn't you acted as though the tomato were an impolite fiction.

Nonny was right. McGivan's death was a ripe tomato of the most ghastly kind. Louise had known all along that she wouldn't be allowed to go to school, but she'd woken full of a determination to behave as though this were an ordinary day, and herself an ordinary girl. Going to school was the most ordinary thing she could think of. She was confusedly aware that when somebody is murdered in a house where an ordinary girl lives she probably doesn't go off to school next day, or react to the horror with ripe-tomato behavior; but at the same time she felt that going to school would have been a definitive method of shutting the story Princess away like a doll in a drawer.

As it was, the story Princess stared across the table at her from the front page of the paper Albert was reading—that particular paper had chosen the funeral face.

"Has anybody found how these alleged assassins got in and out?" said Albert suddenly.

"What do you mean 'alleged'?" said Father.

"I think they're a load of codswallop," said Albert. "The joker was planning something and it went wrong."

"Huat sort of something?" said Mother.

"Well, for instance, get Father out of the reception somehow, switch on the spotlights, start the motor which draws the curtain and there, apparently, is Father sitting on his throne. Respectful silence. Nothing happens. Then somebody spots that he's unconscious. Yes, that's it! The joker only meant to lay him out and when he realized he'd killed him he panicked. That's why there was no red cross."

"Have you told Mr. d'Arcy about the joker, Vick?" asked Mother.

"He was polite but not all that excited."

"Well, I think he ought to be gingered up," said Albert.

"So do I," said Mother. "Can't you . . ."

"Oh, for God's sake!" said Father. "It's out of my hands. I've got a tricky relationship with poor d'Arcy."

"But couldn't one of our own people . . ." said Nonny.

"Theale's working on the other jokes already, isn't he?" said Albert.

Father banged down his cup so violently that he spattered the table with coffee. For a moment it looked as though he was going to start one of his breakfast shouts which would certainly have relieved the tension. Usually these explosions were set off by a spark between his public and private selves, and to most of the Family this must have seemed to be just what was happening—a burst of fury because he wanted to behave like a good citizen helping the police in their investigations, and now he was being asked to tell them what and how to investigate. But to Louise there was something else behind his fury and its unwonted suppression. Having decided not to tell the Family that he thought McGivan had probably been the joker, he'd be exasperated by a conversation in which he knew things he'd deliberately kept from Mother and Nonny. That had been a mistake, Louise thought. There wasn't any real reason why he shouldn't have told them about it, or about McGivan and Kinunu. "Spit it out," Durdy would have told him. Only he'd made it seem to matter so much last night...

"Oh, all right!" he said suddenly. "If d'Arcy can spare Theale I'll suggest he does a bit of work on this. And now will everybody please stop screaming at me and let me catch up with the newspapers!"

He didn't get much chance, because Sir Sam, looking very tired but neat and smooth as ever, turned up earlier than usual with a long list of alterations to the next fortnight's Royal engagements. After all, if the assassins had had one go at His Majesty...

As Louise slipped away she heard Mother and Father beginning to react with a classic display of ripe-tomato behavior, niggling at every change and trying to restore the original schedule. Just like me, she thought. They're making things ordinary again.

But nothing was ordinary. McGivan's death was like the first sign of a disease that was going to infect the whole Palace. At breakfast Pilfer had actually spoken without being spoken to, telling Father that one of his ham radio contacts in Honolulu had heard the news and tried to get him to talk to a local reporter. Now Louise found Sukie cleaning her bath with grim energy, muttering "Those dagoes—we'll show 'em!" as though somehow spotless enamel would foil assassins' vileness. Messengers moved down the forbidding corridors at a different pace, half-uncertain, as though the ancient machinery of the Palace routine had at last packed in and everything now had to be learned afresh. Sanderson was on the landing of the Private Stair, checking everybody who passed.

And even in the cloister of the Nurseries the disease had hold. Kinunu was crying. Louise found her loading the washing machine with tears running down her flat smooth cheeks. There was no mockery in her weeping. More than ever Louise wanted to hold her close and comfort her for her dead lover.

"Oh, Kinunu, I'm so sorry," she said, moving towards her as she did so.

But just like a cat being choosey and unpredictable about who it will allow to touch it, Kinunu rejected her.

"Tho thorry," she whispered, then rushed into her bedroom and shut the door.

Damn, that's stupid of me, thought Louise as she finished loading the washing. She put the soap in, switched the machine on and the monitor off, and crept into the old Day Nursery.

"Good morning, Your Highness," said the squeaky voice. "Have you done your business?"

"Oh, Durdy, you are marvellous! I believe you'd say that on the last morning of the world!"

"Perhaps I should. I never let that Kaiser stop any of my children sitting on their pots each and every morning," said Durdy, as though this had been the German Emperor's prime aim in starting a world war.

"I was worried about you last night. I thought I might have made you too tired."

"Worry's a bad master, I always say. I was a little bit tired, darling, and when I'm tired I can't sleep. But His Majesty came up and gave me an injection and I was in dreamland before he'd taken the needle out."

"Did he tell you what's happened?"

"The Lord giveth and the Lord taketh away. It's the end of an old story, darling, and I daresay it's time it was ended. You never know how things will turn out, never."

Louise was about to ask what she meant when she remembered about the other monitor. She went out and found Kinunu in the Night Nursery, ironing, with her back turned. She made no sign as Louise crossed to the bedroom and checked that that set was switched off too. Back in the Day Nursery she settled as usual onto the rocking-horse.

"Did you know that Mr. McGivan was a relation?" she said.

"Oh, yes, darling. His Majesty didn't, not when he brought him down here, but I knew who he was the moment I clapped eyes on him. His granny was a . . . was a poor silly girl I used to know . . . dearie me, yes. But we'll let bygones be bygones, shall we? His Majesty tells me that you found the body."

"Yes. That's right. I wish I minded more, Durdy. It was quite horrible when I thought it was Father, but now . . . well, sometimes I feel as if I was suddenly going down in a lift into a black place, too fast to stop, but mostly it's just something that happened and I can think about it quite easily without getting the shudders. I get a bit browned off when Bella keeps on badgering away about people's alibis . . ."

"He should leave all that to the police."

But the mention of alibis had reminded Louise. She twisted in the saddle and looked at the cuckoo-clock.

"It *is* fast," she said. "I can't have been up here three quarters of an hour already."

"Nonsense!"

"But Durdy it is. It's terribly important, because . . ."

"I know that clock as well as I know my own name. Your Great-grandfather King Victor brought it back for me from Geneva after he'd been to the opening ceremony of the League of Nations, and what a precious waste of time that turned out to be. That clock doesn't gain, it loses. Three minutes a day in summer, and five minutes a day in winter. It's been like that ever since His Majesty King Haakon tried to stop it ticking so loud. He said a loud tick was bad for the nerves. So there!''

"But listen, Durdy. Don't you remember? I was talking to you yesterday evening and you got a bit tired and then the clock struck six, and I suddenly thought I was late with starting my homework and Kinunu was late with bringing you your green pill. You do remember that, don't you?''

"Maybe I do, maybe I don't.''

"Well you'd better make up your mind, because it's important. When I went out I found Mr. McGivan in the Night Nursery. He'd been talking to Kinunu—she's terribly upset this morning, Durdy—you'll have to be specially nice to her—oh, dear, and I'm afraid I made it worse . . .''

"Least said soonest mended. What were you saying about that dratted clock, Your Highness?''

"If you start Highnessing me now, Durdy, I'll burst into tears. The point about the clock is that if it was fast I saw Mr. McGivan at twenty-five to six. If it wasn't fast I didn't see him till six. But it must have been fast, Father says, because if he'd still been alive at six his body would have been warmer and things like that. Don't you remember in all those Agatha Christies you used to read, it's always frightfully important when the murderee was last seen alive?''

Sniff.

"Oh, Durdy, you're hopeless!''

"And why aren't you going to school today, Miss?''

"Because the whole of Kensington is jammed solid with foul photographers waiting to take pictures of the girl who found the body, that's why.''

"It would never have happened in your Great-grandfather's day. That Ray Bellisario! I'd have liked to have heard Queen Mary speak to him!''

Louise smiled. Durdy detested reporters with a fervor equalled only by Commander Tank, but she pored like a stamp-collector over the end-product of their work. Now she seemed determined to talk about anything else but the murder.

"If you aren't going to school you won't see my friend Master Jerry, then? How is he these days? Is he in love again?''

It was curious that Jerry, the son of a postman, had hit it off instantly with Durdy, whereas Julie had not, despite coming from a Debrettish sort of family. Louise laughed and explained the awfulness of the new girl, and the things that Julie had said about her, and Jerry's blindness. It was an effort to keep the giggling stream of chat flowing, because now, suddenly, she found herself going down in the lift into blackness again. McGivan. Cousin Ian. Rightful King. Snuffler. Dead. The stream dried up. The rockers of the horse grumbled and stilled. Into the silence the cuckoo-clock injected its fluting hiccoughs.

"That clock's fast," said Durdy.

"That's what I told you," said Louise.

"Never could trust the dratted thing," said Durdy.

"Oh, Durdy!"

"I'll trouble you not to take that tone with me, young lady. And what was that you were saying about upsetting my poor little Kinunu?"

"It wasn't me, honestly. She was crying when I came in. I think she was fond of McGivan, you see. I know it sounds funny, but . . ."

"Nothing funny about it that I can see, Miss. You shouldn't laugh at things you don't understand."

"Oh, Durdy, you did get out of bed the wrong side this morning."

"I don't know what you're talking about. Me get out of bed! The idea!"

Louise was bewildered. Almost for the first time in her life, when she came to the Nursery for sanity and comfort, Durdy was refusing to give it to her. It was almost as though she was trying to drive her away.

"I'm sorry," said Louise. "I didn't mean that. I'm afraid I'm making you a bit tired. It was my fault, shooting up here straight after breakfast when you aren't used to it."

"Well, perhaps I am a trifle tired," said Durdy, relenting. "I think I'll have a little nap. Come and have tea with me, darling, and perhaps I'll feel better."

"That'll be lovely. We'll have crumpets. And anyway Nonny's supposed to be ringing up school to get them to give me some work to do, so I suppose I'd better go and see what she's squeezed out of them. Bye, darling. See you."

Miss Durdon had just enough feeling left in her face to sense the touch of lips. She managed a thin smile as she closed her eyes and gathered her soul and mind into a single compact force, a force like the remnants of a professional army after a long battle. The trenches of her body might all have surrendered, but here at the central redoubt the last platoons could still be summoned into a disciplined unit, able to fight and endure. The will sent a message to the last outpost, the two middle fingers of her left hand, which still had enough movement in them to press the buzzer on which they lay. She kept her eyes shut until she heard Kinunu's step close by the bed.

"Yethmith," whispered Kinunu.

"Hold my hand, Kinunu. My good hand. The one by the buzzer. Don't let go."

She could barely sense the pressure of the small fingers, but used her will to construct the feel of the whole hand, a hand like Kitten's, not rough but feeling as though it had an extra layer of skin on it, a nurse's hand. Tear runnels textured Kinunu's smooth cheeks but her face was unreadable. Her dark eyes carried no message.

"You've been very good to me, Kinunu. I've been lucky. A lot of old women lie in bed all day waiting to die. Their nurses can't look after them, because there aren't enough. Nobody ever visits them. But I've been lucky, very lucky. I'm glad you came. Do you understand?"

"Yethmith. Old, old."

She made a strange little gesture with her free hand. On Royal Tours Miss Durdon had sometimes watched Far Eastern dancers who seemed able to make every knuckle of each finger carry a charge of meaning. Kinunu often used the same kind of hand-talk. It was like a foreign language of which Miss Durdon knew not a single word, but could guess certain meanings from the tone. She'd seen this gesture before. It said to her that Kinunu came from a people where the old, however senile, were still respected for their mere age; to them the grey ranks of a British geriatric ward would have been a nightmare impossibility.

"I want to help you, Kinunu. I want to talk to you about Mr. McGivan."

She thought she could see a change, not in the face but somehow behind it. By a pulse of will she forced her two good fingers to move, to make the beginnings of a grip. For all her effort the pressure must have been as faint as a falling petal, but it was enough to make Kinunu look down and stay where she was. She shook her head and began to cry.

"Eee no thay me ee King," she whispered. "Ee no thay me ee King."

By listening to the woes and wonders of generations of children as they struggled through the entanglements on the frontier of speech, Miss Durdon had become almost telepathic in the interpretation of jumbled syllables. She had her own reasons for liking to see Kinunu moving about her room, but was not so lost in that old dream that she didn't know how the girl must have appeared to the other people in the Palace—so small and neat and secret that she was more of a pet than a person. And McGivan had been a pet too, of a quite different sort—like one of those smelly, hairy, useless old dogs for which certain English families seem to have such a strange leaning—a cat and a dog, with nothing else in common than that they were the Palace pets. Miss Durdon had long known that McGivan visited the Nursery whenever he got the chance; she had let Kinunu see that she approved of him—she still owed Kitten that much; but she had seldom talked about him directly, because that would have interrupted the dream.

Now, while Kinunu knelt by the bed with her cap fallen off and her blue-black hair streaming over her ivory arms, pouring out her own language smattered here and there with bits of lisped English, Miss Durdon thought at first that she was weeping only for the loss of the friend of her loneliness. She was not at all surprised to find that McGivan had taken what advantage he could of the relationship.

"Ee thay me ee King," sobbed Kinunu. "Ee want kithkith."

"So you let him kiss you?"

"Ee thilly. Ee want kithkith, but ee fraid. Ee want . . ."

She didn't know the word, but her demonstration caress woke a flush of feeling down Miss Durdon's arm, as though Kitten's ghost were stroking the withered flesh. The pang of memory left Miss Durdon unprepared for Kinunu's collapse forward onto the bed and the fresh torrent of sobs and syllables. She gathered that McGivan's ritual visits for a timid kiss and cuddle had been going on for some time, that he used to tell her that he was the Rightful King of England, and that Kinunu had thought him foolish but amusing. But then something had happened, something which had caused this misery, and it wasn't poor McGivan's murder.

"When, Kinunu? Yesterday?"

"Yethyeth."

"And you took him to your room?"

"Yethyeth. Ee like . . ."

She pointed at the monitor camera and shaped her forefingers and thumbs into the rectangle of a tiny screen.

"Yes. Of course," said Miss Durdon. "He liked to have the camera on and to listen to what we were saying?"

"Yethyeth."

"And that happened yesterday. And then . . ."

"Kithkith a little. I laugh. Ee angry. Ee want . . . I thay ee nono. . . . Ee . . ."

She slid into her own language, waggled her head, stopped speaking and gave a funny little twittering whistle, peering intently at Miss Durdon while she did so. Her hand and arm roved sinuously down the sheet. Her gaze moved to watch it. The twittering stopped. She craned towards it, hopeless, hypnotized. Then she stopped the play and turned back to Miss Durdon, peering for understanding through her silent tears.

"A bird and a snake," whispered somebody's old lips. "A bird and a snake."

"I thay im yethyeth," sobbed Kinunu.

Miss Durdon had seen scores of Royal Visits, and knew that however Europeanized the monarchs might be, with their bowings and smilings from the State Carriages and their well-turned speeches after the Banquets, all sort of foreign customs persisted at the lower levels of their entourages—

the levels which lapped against the fringes of the Nursery.
She knew too that often these strangers considered quaint or
horrible many things that the English took for granted. So it
was no surprise for her to discover, as she disentangled
smatterings, that Kinunu's grief was neither for the death of
her lover nor for her own fall from chastity, but for her
parents' financial loss, in that they would no longer be able
to offer her on the marriage market as a virgin. Somehow
she had got it into her head that McGivan would marry her,
and the King would pay her parents the bride-price because
it was his servant who had seduced her, and that would have
been all right. So now she was weeping not for a lover but a
husband. Her gabble ended in a strange wail.

"Ee no thay me ee King! Ee no thay me ee King!"

"There, there," said Miss Durdon, for about the ten
thousandth time in her life. "The Bible tells us we mustn't
cry over spilt milk, and that's true. There, there, darling.
We'll find you another husband."

She spoke of it as though a husband were something like
a toy cannon or a doll, replaceable at Hamley's. The
important thing was to still the sobs and wails and let herself
think. She was badly shaken, she didn't yet know why.
Something was wrong. A snake and a bird. Kitten. King
McGivan. Bastard. A word never spoken but endlessly
brooded on in the thin-lipped, kirk-ridden household where
the boy had grown up. A mother's boy. He hadn't lied to
Kinunu when he gave himself the title, because he was
Kitten's grandchild, and Kitten didn't lie. What she said
was true, for her, until she changed her mind and said it was
not . . .

"Mithmith."

Miss Durdon opened her eyes and saw Kinunu standing
by the bed, almost her teasing, unreadable self again. Sure
that Miss Durdon was watching her she put a hand on her
slim stomach and made a rounding-out movement.

"Baby come," she said.

It was probably only a question. She'd never managed to
catch the English interrogative lilt.

"There, there, darling. We'll look after you. The King
will find you a husband, and if there's a baby we'll look

after it too. I'll be glad to see a cot in here again before I go."

Kinunu probably only understood half of that but she picked up the tone and smiled.

"I'm tired, my dear," said Miss Durdon. "Stay here if you want to, but I think I'll have a little nap. We'll look after you. There, there. Tired."

In 1952, when His Majesty had still been a bachelor, he had taken Miss Durdon as part of his retinue on his Royal Visit to Ethiopia. There Miss Durdon had seen the whirlpool. It happened on a day when the men were shooting wild goat across a harsh mountainside and the women had gone ahead to meet them at the place chosen for their midday picnic, a canyon where a river dropped suddenly into darkness. This place had given her the horrors—the river driving peacefully for mile after mile between lush-creepered cliffs and then, in a few yards, gone into its smoking hole. Beyond the hole the canyon continued, bare rock now, rust-colored, lifeless. Close under the far cliff, about twenty feet short of the falls, the whirlpool circled. Anything caught in it stayed there for a while, turning and turning, saved from the drop but trapped into this meaningless dance. But not trapped forever. Miss Durdon had watched a dead animal, about the size of a rabbit, a sodden blob of fur, circle for nearly ten minutes and then, just as though the whirlpool had tired of it, edge out into the stretched water of the river and shoot over the edge.

She often thought of the place now. It had lost its nightmare quality and become an image of comfort. The Day Nursery was her whirlpool, in which she circled the weeks away on the edge of darkness. It couldn't last forever. One day, despite all His Majesty could do, she would slip out and away. It would be soon, quite soon. She wouldn't live to see the cot in its proper place to the left of the windows, nor, asleep on the cream-colored cashmere, the minute head of Kinunu's baby, flat-faced, black-haired, but showing for the first few days those heavy Hanover eyelids that might or might not return in middle age. No, she would

never see that. Her time was almost up. Her last baby was
no longer a subject of her kingdom. It had happened inside
a fortnight. It wasn't the same as growing up—Princess
Louise was still a child, still full of childish notions, but her
own idea of herself had found its proper shape. She could
do without Durdy now. Some of them had never achieved
that, but Louise would be all right. My last baby. I can feel
the tug of the current. I'm ready to go.

Miss Durdon's mind drifted, not on the usual purposeful
voyage back to Abergeldie in the snow and Kitten in the
dark, but among misty islands. She had never in her life felt
the faintest prickle of yearning towards any man, though
across the years she had been courted by a score of Palace
retainers. Some might have really wanted her, others felt
that they'd be doing themselves a good turn by hitching on
to such a favorite with the Family, most a bit of both—it
didn't matter. She'd long ago come to the conclusion that
something in her own body—one of those glands His
Majesty was so interested in—hadn't worked properly, and
that was why she was so tiny, and had never grown a proper
bosom, and never wanted a man. Or it might have been the
adventure with Kitten, and her own decision to shut that
side of her nature away. But whatever it was, this was one
area of her long life where memory was no use to her as she
tried to make sense of what Kinunu had told her. What
would make timid Ian McGivan suddenly confident enough
to stop telling the girl that he was King, suddenly strong-
willed enough to become the snake to her bird? It would
have to be something that overcame the old shame of his
father's birth . . . If he'd known about Louise, known what
had happened at the Glas-allt-Shiel, would that be enough?
She tried to make the picture of the scene in Kinunu's room,
but it wouldn't come right; it wasn't McGivan in his
shapeless clothes who had suddenly grown angry and
dominant—it was a stockier man, bearded, older, in evening
dress; a tall hock glass stood on the dresser and a fat cigar
smouldered beside it, already scorching the varnish; and it
wasn't Kinunu whispering and pushing him away with
strangely feeble arms.

No, there was something wrong. The clock, too.

Miss Durdon gave her mind an angry shake to clear away the nonsense pictures, the baby in the cot, the old King in Kitten's arms. It's never gained before, she thought. It only loses. Five minutes a day in summer, three minutes in winter. His Majesty knows that, perfectly well. There's something wrong. I must stay here and put it right. I must do what I can for the Family, as long as they need me. I mustn't go over the edge yet—not yet.

• 12 •

SATURDAY. ANOTHER BLANK DAY. Princess Louise's engagements (a visit to the North Bucks Dairy Show, of all stupid boring things) cancelled. Prince Albert's ditto. But Mother and Father breaking out of Sir Sam's security net to do a swirl through East Anglia—open one research lab, one stretch of Motorway; present new Colors to Royal Norfolks; attend christening of Mother's forty-third godchild (Sandringham farmer's daughter); sleep at Sandringham, attend church there Sunday; review Lowestoft fishing fleet Sunday P.M.; back to Palace Sunday evening. Miss Anona Fellowes one of those in attendance.

"Rather them than me," said Albert. "Did you hear the weather forecast? I missed it, but I'll bet it blows up a hurricane as soon as they're afloat. One thing we can safely predict about my reign—nobody's ever going to call me a Sailor King."

The only good thing about the parents being away was that you could take two hours over breakfast. Pilfer approved of this, too. It was as if the strict routine of Palace life prevented him from showing how good he was at his job—a real butler, he seemed to think, should be able to sound the ritual gong at the proper time, but then—supposing nobody turned up for three quarters of an hour—still being able to produce an absolutely fresh breakfast. Albert was wearing forbidden pajamas and dressing-gown and playing at Sherlock Holmes. The Sunday papers were still full of the murder. Albert wanted to talk about it—Louise didn't.

"I'm going off terrorists," he said.

"Oh."

"I was never very gone on them—I mean, it might have turned out that I was really on their side. Some of the thugs Father entertains!"

"It was a cultural reception."

"You can be a cultural thug. Did you hear about the group who claimed responsibility?"

"No."

"D'Arcy told me. They turned out to be a brother and sister, both over sixty, living in Worcester. Their mother was Venezuelan, OK, but their father was Greek. He didn't tell me what they were doing, living in Worcester. That's not the sort of question d'Arcy asks himself."

"I don't think they ought to be allowed to bring dogs in to sniff for explosives when there aren't any explosives to be sniffed for."

"Quite right. They'll think it's their fault they haven't found anything. Hell, Lulu, what are we going to do?"

"Nothing."

"I've got a new theory."

"Oh?"

"I think McGivan was the joker."

"Oh!"

"I thought that'd make you sit up. Listen, what hasn't happened since the murder?"

"There haven't been any jokes."

"Right. So two possibilities suggest themselves. One: McGivan's death was a joke that went off the rails, which was what I first thought, and since then the joker's been too scared to try again. There's a lot of things wrong with that, though—not just there being no red cross, but I can't see how it was all supposed to work, even if it hadn't gone wrong. But the main thing is that it sort of smells different from the other jokes. Not so funny, more dangerous. I go much more for possibility two: McGivan was the joker and somebody killed him for that very reason. Right?"

"I expect so."

"Now why should anybody kill a practical joker? I mean, say Sir Sam had spotted him for the bloke who scissored his trousers, he'd have blown his top all right, got Father to sack him and so on, but he wouldn't have blotted him right out. OK? Second possibility, to prevent him playing his next joke. I can just about imagine a set-up in which that makes sense, so we can't rule it out, but it's all pretty intangible. Third possibility, which is the one I go for myself: we know the joker had a good line in gathering information about us—I mean, he knew about Father's obsession with the loo, and about how to get a pile of pianos up to Granny's, no questions asked. I don't know how old McGivan got this stuff, but after all he was paid to poke about, wasn't he? Now, suppose in the course of gathering material for practical-joke purposes he'd come across something really hot, something that simply had to be kept quiet—that'd be a motive for rubbing him out, wouldn't it? Wait a bit, Lulu. It might also explain why you found him where you did, kitted up to look like Father. Suppose you were going to murder a practical joker for a reason like that, you might try to disguise his death as another practical joke, thus concealing your motive for doing him in. Only you make a bit of a mess of it—don't bring your red felt pen along—so there's no red cross. Right? I must say, I think it makes a good deal better sense than anything anyone else has yet come up with."

As if to emphasize his confidence in his own logic Albert tossed a slice of carrot in the air, caught it in his mouth and began his ritual of chewing. Louise stared at him. At first she was only startled by how close he had come to guessing what she and Father already thought to be the truth—and if he could arrive there by logic, so could anyone. Then they'd start asking themselves what it was that McGivan had found out. Then . . .

Suddenly, before the next rush of ideas had even begun to cross her mind, she felt a hideous change take place in her body, as though all her blood had been drained away and replaced by clammy, cold, unmoving slime. Father! He would do anything to prevent the secret getting out—he'd said so himself. When he'd come up to her room with d'Arcy his first questions had been about time—when had she seen McGivan? Had she checked with any other clocks? And then he'd rushed off to see Durdy, given her an injection, and come back saying that the clock was fast. And all those secrets—secrets from d'Arcy, secrets from the Family, secrets that weren't truly important . . . And Durdy! She must have guessed—that or something—because at first she'd said that the clock never gained, then she'd gone all funny and refused to talk about anything to do with the murder, and then she'd said that the clock did gain, and then she'd practically driven Louise away. Durdy was trying to protect Father, because she realized . . .

"You might at least respond with applause to my chain of reasoning," grumbled Albert. "I don't put on these cerebral fireworks to be greeted by blank stares."

"Bert! Can we go somewhere?"

"What do you mean?"

"Anywhere. Away from here. Just for the day. You could drive us in one of the black-windowed cars. Couldn't you ring up the Kents?"

"Aunt Eloise would eat you alive, Lulu, and then tell all her friends what you'd told her, and half of them get retainers from some bloody little tick on a gossip column. Shall I try the Yorks?"

"But don't you want to see . . ."

"Oh, I'm taking Soppy out on the tiles next Thursday, poor kid. It's the Round House—the Gabon Mime Group against Imperialist Explotation of Natural Resources. Not at all her cup of tea."

"Oh, Bert!"

"Actually she'll love it. They just call themselves that to get idiots like me to come along. It'll be a lot of noise and prancing. Stunning drums. And afterwards I'll take her to a proper carnivorous restaurant so she can have my steak as well as hers, and she'll be as happy as a sandboy. D'you like her, Lulu?"

"Yes. And she's a lot cleverer than she looks."

"Right. We live funny lives, don't we? I mean, if we hadn't been landed with all this Soppy and I would be hitch-hiking around Turkey together, finding out how we got along . . . Are you all right, Lulu?"

"Yes, it's only. . ."

"You needn't say it. I'm sorry I went beavering on about the murder like that. I should have realized, only it's so difficult to know what you're thinking—Soppy finds you a bit alarming, you know?"

"Me!"

"Uh-huh. I'll go and ring up the Yorks. It's my bath morning, but I'll skip that. If you'll help me feed my animals we ought to be able to get down there by lunch. Meet you at the zoo in ten minutes. Right?"

"OK. Thank you, Bert."

Louise walked somberly back to her room, thinking about Albert in order to avoid thinking about Father. She had blood back in her veins now, but somewhere between her stomach and her spine lurked the cold slime, contracted into a globule but ready to spread through her body again, like panic through a crowd. Albert was a really kind person. He was obviously very much in love with Soppy, and he'd often said that the Yorks were a wasted asset and that Britain should use them as a diplomatic deterrent, to bore the pants off anybody who tried stonewalling against us. But for Louise's sake he'd suggested enduring that ordeal. And to change the subject, he'd talked about Soppy, which he'd never normally have done. He was clever, too, about getting his eccentric way in a fashion which didn't inconvenience other people. Like taking Soppy to this awful-sounding show which she'd really enjoy. The best example of that was the way he'd persuaded the Regiments of which he was Colonel-in-Chief to let him inspect them without their weapons— he'd persuaded them that it was just another of those rum privileges which the British army so enjoys, such as drinking the Loyal Toast direct from the bottle on Salamanca Day, or wearing radishes in their caps when marching through Portsmouth. Father had once said . . .

Father. The globule of slime stirred as Louise reached her room. She brushed ferociously at her teeth, as if to clean a chill and cloying film from them; but when she moved to her mirror to put on her anti-Nonny eye-shadow the ghost was there, the family face, untroubled. It was horrible to see it looking so calm and pretty when behind it slithered these waves of fear and betrayal. The story Princess. Father.

Suppose you'd just killed somebody. Suppose your mind was full of the shock of it, and fear of being found out, and complicated plans about covering your tracks by changing the times of clocks, and awareness of the need to act innocence and ignorance of some things but not others—would you find the time to warn your daughter that she was playing with fire by acting out a little fantasy that had struck her? He might, thought Louise. He has funny ideas about what matters. Even so this other image of Father—an actual man who had said actual words—became steady in her mind. Perhaps I'm only acting out another fantasy, she thought. Murderer's daughter—stupid little girl. He was the one who'd *liked* McGivan. Even if some of what he'd done didn't make sense.

She began to feel better, and actually ran along the corridor and down the stairs, catching up Albert at the far side of the main courtyard.

"I dunno about the Yorks," he said. "It's Cousin Ted's annual jamboree for the Berkshire Bee-keepers Association. What do you feel about coping with three hundred old buffers with veils down to their knees?"

"I could put on a veil too."

"It won't come to that, I think. The bee-boys don't turn up till three. Aunt Tim'll give us lunch and then we can go for a ride and not bother anyone. Right?"

While he had been talking he'd fished his key-ring out and unlocked the zoo door. He paused with his hand on the handle and looked at her. She nodded. As he opened the door a voice said, "Go get 'em, you two." The mynah swooped chuckling across the room.

"Hey! How did you get out?" said Albert.

His body went rigid. As he swung slowly round Louise saw that the patches of cheek between his eyes and his beard were a strange blue-white.

"What's the matter?" she said.

"Somebody's been in and opened the cages. Christ!"

He darted across the room and dropped to a crouch by

one of the trestle tables which supported the cages. Out of the cave-like darkness flashed a greyish thing with something yellow at the front, a cat with a bird in its mouth, darting for the door. Without thought Louise flipped the door shut. The cat came on, still thinking it could make the closing gap, but realizing too late that it couldn't. In its instant of hesitation Albert was on it, gripping with efficient firmness as it wriggled and spat. The yellow blob—no, it wasn't a bird—dropped to the floor.

"Open the door," said Albert. As she did so he tossed the cat through the opening, even in his shock and anger taking care not to hurt it. At the same moment another cat streaked out of somewhere and into the passage. Louise couldn't see anything in its mouth. She shut the door and turned to see Albert kneeling by the scarlet and gold blob on the floor. It was the lion-maned tamarin, gazing with blank blue eyes at the ceiling, its face drawn into a shrieking grimace.

"Go get 'em, you two," said the mynah again. This time as it swooped down the room it added a wavering cry of pain.

"Is he dead?" said Louise.

"Think so. Hope so, in fact. It's be a sick job putting him down."

"How on earth did the cats get in?"

"They were *put*, Lulu. Didn't you hear the mynah? Oh, damn!"

He picked up the tamarin's body and laid it carefully on his bench. Only now did Louise realize how silent the zoo was. Usually when Albert first came in it was a bedlam of welcoming calls, cackles for food and attention, hoppings and scufflings and mews. Now only the mynah called, answering its own voice with a ghastly cry. Nothing else seemed to breathe.

"Let's see what the damage is," said Albert quietly. "You don't have to stay, Lulu."

"I'm all right. I'd like to help. Oh, Bert, I'm sorry!"

He shrugged. His face was still very white.

"Thanks," he said. "I'll check down the cages. You start on the tanks, working from that end . . . Well, that's a start—this chap's had the sense to hide in his own nest. All right, mate, you're OK now. Nightmare's over. Any sign of Fatty, Lulu? He quite often buries himself under his leaves.''

"I can't see him . . . Yes, I can . . . there's . . . Bert!''

The great Blomberg toad lived in its own dry glass tank, where it spent much of its time either asleep or arranging and rearranging its collection of plane-leaves and fig leaves. They were all piled into one corner this morning, so Louise began to unbuild the mound, leaf by leaf. Soon she came to a patch of mottled skin, glistening in one corner, glistening red. Carefully she picked away another two leaves and saw the gash, just as though a ripe fruit, ready to seed, had split itself open.

"OK, Lulu,'' said Albert, still in the same controlled voice. "I'll take over. The next tank's supposed to have three green whip-snakes and a terrapin in it. The snakes aren't poisonous. If you find anything else nasty, leave it for me. Hello! He's alive! The bastard! Look—no, don't look, but he's just taken one of my scalpels—that must be it on the floor—and slashed two cuts on its back. Christ! D'you know what? He's made a red cross. He's mad. I wonder whether that'll mend, in spite of everything. What's up, Lulu?''

"There's a couple of animals in this tank with the snakes. I think they're kangaroo-rats.''

"That's right. They'll be OK. They live in that third cage. You don't have to grab them. Put a bit of corn on your palm, let 'em see it, then hold your hand flat above their heads and they'll jump up to eat it. See how you get on—I'm going to do what I can for Fatty. Stupid idiot if he thought the whip-snakes would go anywhere near kangaroo-rats. Now, Fatty, how'm I going to get you onto my bench without you falling apart?''

The kangaroo rats did their trick as if they were practicing for a circus. Louise stroked them as she carried them to their cage, more to calm her own horrors than theirs. On her way back to the tanks her eye was caught by a brown blob crouched in a corner where a row of the old King's parallel bars still ran up the wall. It looked like a bit of wrong-colored fluff until a black eye blinked at her. She took a tumbler and a filing-card from the bench and moved carefully towards it.

"Lulu . . ."

"Sh."

The animal crouched till she was almost on it, and then didn't bolt fast enough. She trapped it under the tumbler, slid the card beneath it and carried her catch to Albert.

"*Mus musculus,*" he said. "The common house mouse."

"Common palace mouse, really."

"Not one of mine. Wait a sec—I haven't had mice in here before. It might be evidence. I wish to God Father had persuaded d'Arcy to take the joker more seriously. We ought to have the police in here before I muck around much more—on the other hand I daren't wait for them in case there's more like Fatty, or ones the cats half got."

"How is Fatty?"

"I don't know. I've given him an anesthetic—killed him very likely. But if he comes through that and the wound doesn't get infected I think he might do. Hell, I'll try d'Arcy."

He picked up the telephone and dialled a house number. Louise heard the whine of the engaged tone. After three tries Albert put the handset down with a snap.

"He's keeping all lines permanently open to Caracas, I bet," he said.

"Father said he was going to ask Mr. Theale to see what he could find out about the joker."

"Damned Saturday," said Albert. "There won't be anybody about I can ask to go and find Theale. I daren't leave Fatty."

"I'll go. I suppose I'd better ring up Aunt Tim and tell her we're not coming."

"D'you mind? Sorry, Lulu . . . Fatty's going to have the hell of a scar if he does heal. He'll look like a mobile hot cross bun."

Aunt Tim was a marvellous old dear. She was clearly glad not to have to cope with runaway Princesses on top of three hundred bee-keepers, but managed to sound disappointed. Sergeant Theale was working with three other policemen in the outer office of the suite which had been assigned to the police. Louise explained what had happened in the zoo. He shook his head.

"I'd like to come, Ma'am," he said. "I think it could be important. But I don't know as I could persuade Superintendent d'Arcy. He's run out of leads, you see, and now we're cross-checking all the guests at the reception, to see that none of them was an impostor."

"Bloody waste of time, if you ask me," said one of the other policemen. "Inside job if ever I bloody saw one."

He looked up from the list in front of him, remembered who Louise was and blushed like a rose.

"Do you think the Superintendent could see me for a few minutes?" asked Louise, smiling at him, public face (for reassuring subjects who have committed gaffes).

"He's pretty busy, Ma'am. I'll ask."

In the inner office Louise sensed a different sort of frustration. It took the story Princess, distressed and serious but quite coherent, to persuade Mr. d'Arcy even to listen.

"What d'you think, Jack?" he said to the officer at the other desk.

"Better have it checked out, sir. Two things: it sounds a bit violent, which the other jokes His Majesty told us about didn't; I'm not saying that means it's got anything to do with the murder, but it does make more of a pattern. Chappie plays a series of practical jokes—he's a bit unbalanced anyway—does his nut—kills McGivan, then this. And I suppose you've got to reckon on what His Majesty might say to you if he was here."

He might have been more tactful, but it did the trick. For an instant Mr. d'Arcy looked furious, then he nodded and smiled bleakly at Louise. The other officer fetched Theale, who stood to attention in front of Mr. d'Arcy's desk.

"Her Royal Highness has told me about the incident in the zoo, sir," he said.

"Well, nip along there and check it out. How are you going to tackle it?"

"I'll do a thorough search of the zoo, sir, though if it's the same chappie as before he'll have worn gloves and left no traces, except what he meant to leave. But it being

Saturday makes a difference, sir. A lot of the Palace staff goes off, Friday night; we have a different staff weekends. I've made a chart of the other incidents, sir, but because they all occurred weekdays there was a lot of staff I couldn't eliminate. With a bit of luck this incident should bring it down to not more than half a dozen, and I can concentrate on them."

"All right," said Mr. d'Arcy. "Only don't take longer about it than you have to."

"I think you're making a mistake, sir," said the other officer. "OK, suppose these jokes are a red herring, they've still got to be cleared up or they'll go on messing around with our main investigation. In fact it sounds to me as though this chappie was sufficiently unbalanced to start deliberately trying to muck around with us."

"All right all right!" said Mr. d'Arcy. "You look into it, Theale. See what you come up with. Report back to me if you need help. Don't waste time, but do a thorough job."

"Very good, sir."

Albert was at his work-bench, very carefully weaving strips of tape across the wounds on Fatty's back. The toad looked like one of those parcels which often arrived at the Palace—a loyal gift of a Lancashire black pudding, say, wrapped with more fervor than skill, delayed in the post and now bulging or oozing from a dozen seams.

"Won't be a sec," he said.

"Go get 'em, you two," said the mynah, swirling overhead.

Louise had never seen a man as startled as Sergeant Theale. For a moment he had the look of someone shot in the back in a Mafia film.

"It's all right," she said. "It's only the mynah."

"I wish to God he was better at voices," said Albert. "My guess is he's picked that up from whoever put the cats in here. Good of you to come, Sergeant. I gather you couldn't interest the Superintendent."

"He's a bit tied up at the moment, Sir."

Louise saw Albert suppress a little flare of temper with just the same quick smile that Father would have used.

"Fine," he said. "The point is that I don't want to touch anything till you've seen it and I don't want to hang around doing nothing while my animals die. That's the scalpel he used to slash the toad with, I think. I haven't touched it."

"Right, Sir, I'll get on that at once. I suppose there's no question of the cats having got in by mistake."

"Just possible. But I don't see them bringing a mouse with them, slashing poor Fatty, opening cages and teaching the mynah a new sentence."

The mynah, delighted by the stir it felt it was causing, chuckled to itself as it tried to perch on the central light.

"George the Third ought never to have occurred," it said. "One can only wonder at so grotesque a blunder."

"You see," said Albert. "That's supposed to be my voice. Not very close, I hope."

"Pity, Sir. That would have been really useful. Now, can you give me any sort of estimate of when the incident might have occurred?"

"Early this morning, I think. It was all OK when I locked up at ten last night . . ."

"The zoo's kept locked, Sir?"

"Of course."

"Who has access to keys?"

"I keep one on my ring. There's a spare for the family to use if they want to come down—hangs on the key-board in the lobby outside the breakfast-room. Jack Jakowski looks after the animals when I'm not here so he has one. I'm pretty certain he keeps it on his key-ring."

"I'll look into that, Sir. The one in the Private Apartments sounds the most accessible. Now, about the time . . ."

"Well, it wouldn't have been safe to try anything in the dark because the animals would have been bound to kick up a racket. But they always shout a bit around dawn—I daresay you've heard 'em—so that'd have been a possible time. Much after that and there'd have been people about. I don't know how fast Blomberg toads bleed, but at a guess I'd say Fatty was knifed not less than four or more than eight hours ago."

"Then that ties in," said Theale.

(Dawn, thought Louise. The parents left at seven thirty.

Father. Could he be mad? Were they wrong about McGivan being the joker? Could McGivan have told somebody else what he'd found out? Or if McGivan knew nothing, Father could still have thought . . .)

That feeling, like cold slime, was beginning to stir again when a yellow creature skipped chattering across the floor and hid under the work-bench.

"See if you can catch him, Lulu," said Albert. "He bites, but he's tough as old boots, so you can be rough with him if you have to."

Louise spent the morning on hands and knees because in the course of capturing the yellow biter—it turned out to be a squirrel from Java, and to have neither fear nor manners— she unearthed a hysterical family of long-eared jerboas which scuttled and gibbered and cowered in impossible corners. There were several more bodies, some half-eaten, including the remains of another house mouse. The cats appeared to have gone berserk, like a fox in a hen-run, striking out at anything that moved in a frenzy of blood-lust. Albert worked steadily and dispassionately, examining the maimed animals as they came to light and usually putting them to sleep without even a sigh. Sometimes he was able to patch a wound or set a limb.

Sergeant Theale too worked methodically, powdering for finger-prints and taking photographs of the results. He seemed excited by a thread of black cotton caught on a splinter by one of the latches.

"Bloke wore gloves," he said. "Not rubber but cloth— I've got a place where you can see the weave. Now, if this comes off one of them gloves . . ."

"Perhaps he nicked a pair of Pilfer's," said Albert. "He's got drawersful."

"That's one possibility, Sir," said Theale, in the tone of somebody who is thinking things out as he speaks. "There's something else ties in—from what His Majesty told me, and there's points here which support it, like knowing where you kept the spare key, whoever's been playing these tricks is pretty intimate with things in the Private Apartments."

"I'd begun to think it was McGivan," said Albert. "But he couldn't have done this, could he?"

"No, Sir."

Just before lunch Mr. d'Arcy and one of the sergeants from his outer office turned up.

"Found anything, Theale?" he said.

"Yes, sir. We've made a bit of progress and come to certain conclusions. With your permission I'd like to spend the afternoon interviewing staff."

"Show me."

Sergeant Theale took him on a conducted tour. He stared at the toad parcel, and then at the dead tamarin lying farther along the bench.

"Jesus Christ!" he whispered. "Jesus Ho ——."

He must have seen much more horrible things in his life, but the extraordinary appeal of the tamarin, even in death, cracked the smooth shell of Palace officialdom he'd been growing. Then he pulled himself up and spoke in a different voice.

"You've got a nut case here, Theale," he said authoritatively, just as though nobody had thought of the idea before.

"Yes, sir."

"I think we're going to have to take this seriously, whether it's got anything to do with McGivan's death or not."

"I think it has, sir. I think it's part of the series."

D'Arcy's reply was cut short by a cry from the other sergeant. Louise had just managed to dislodge a bright blue lizard from under a radiator, and as it flashed across the floor the sergeant thoughtlessly brought his foot down like a man trying to stop a rolling coin. The lizard gave a wrench and darted on, leaving three inches of tail twitching violently beneath the leather sole. The sergeant—a young man in a flash blue suit, very well endowed with teeth—started to grin with embarrassment, but at the same time his face turned to a whitish green, and Louise thought he was going to faint like Pilfer.

"That wasn't very clever," said Albert in a restrained voice. "Never mind—you haven't done much harm. It's an escape mechanism. They do it quite often, and a new tail grows."

He picked the jerking tail up and tossed it into a waste

paper basket, where it continued to thrash against the metal side.

"All right," said Mr. d'Arcy. "We'll put a forensic team in here this afternoon. You've done well, Theale. I'll second a couple of officers to you for the afternoon and you can see how you get on with eliminating members of the staff."

"Very good, sir."

"Excuse me, Superintendent," said Albert. "I'm sure my father would insist on the Family being included in the elimination process. It really wouldn't look good to leave us out."

"If you wish, Sir," said Mr. d'Arcy coldly.

"Yes please."

After lunch Louise decided that she'd be in the way in the zoo, with a whole forensic team mucking around. She settled down to break the back of the extra homework which the school had sent for her, and managed to keep Father and McGivan out of her mind until the sergeant who'd trodden on the lizard knocked on the Library door. His name was Bannerman, and he took Louise through the whole series of "incidents," making ticks and crosses according to whether she could or could not have been responsible for any of them.

"Waste of time, really," he said when he'd finished. "We kept you to the end, seeing you're in the clear for the first two. And the pianos, of course. That's number five. You're about average. Funny how it works out—you don't get anybody who's in the clear for the whole lot, then there's a couple for all but one, a few twos, a lot of threes, fours and fives, and then you're back in the low numbers— half a dozen who could have done all but two, and four who could have done all but one."

"There ought to be at least one person who could have done the whole lot," said Louise.

He looked at her, hesitating and running the butt of his pen along his fabulous teeth like a boy running a stick along railings. The story Princess smiled back at him and found, as she had guessed, that detective-sergeants do not keep secrets from story Princesses.

"Just a couple so far," he said. "A Mr. Pilfer..."

"Oh, it couldn't be him!"

"You never can tell, this sort of thing, Ma'am."

"Well . . . who else?"

"We haven't been able to question her about this morning's incident, but there's a Miss Fellowes."

"It couldn't be her, either."

The story Princess's voice came out quite calm and even. Behind the screen Louise's mind said Nonny! That would explain about Father! He knows! He's trying to protect her. Nonny going mad. She never wanted to be Queen. She still hates the Royalty scene, but she can't show what she feels because she doesn't know how. Like me, like me.

Sergeant Bannerman looked up from making a few more marks on his chart.

"We ought to get him next time, whoever it is," he said.

Next time! There mustn't be a next time.

◆ 13 ◆

Next time Louise saw what happened.

She had managed to insist on going back to school on Monday, compromising by allowing herself to be driven right up to the gates. The extraordinary thing was that quite a lot of the GBP had turned out to see her arrive and a few had even cheered in a subdued and sympathetic way, as if she'd just recovered from a serious operation. School itself had been a bit like the horrible first weeks of her first term, with people glancing at her and away all the time, as though she'd been a strange but repulsive kind of goldfish. But Julie had been really nice, and Jerry was recovering from being let down by his new girl. So it was better than another day in the Palace.

She didn't usually visit Durdy on Mondays, but when she'd done her homework there was still forty minutes till the supper gong; supper was going to be edgy; she decided to go and see Durdy after all—though it wouldn't be fair to worry her with the nightmare suspicions that kept creeping in and out of Louise's mind, at least she'd be amused to hear the gossip about Jerry.

"Julie keeps telling me we've got to find him somebody really nice," she said, nudging the rocking-horse to and fro. "I don't see how. The trouble with Jerry is he's so precocious, and he's a baby at the same time. Most of the other

boys in my year are still really interested in football and
things, and only make an occasional play for a girl because
they think it's time they did so, but Jerry really likes girls.
What's more he likes them at least two years older than he
is, all bust and smothered with make-up and loud-voiced
and *thick*. One after another. You can spot a Jerry-type girl
at a hundred yards. And he's got a good line to start with—a
sort of junior Paul Newman—so the girl doesn't see what a
baby he is and he's in his seventh heaven for a week which
is perfectly ghastly for Julie and me. And then something
turns up with its own motor-scooter, and wearing one of
those moustaches, and the girl drops Jerry flat. He never
learns, never. So then he's miserable, which is a bit better
than when he's moony but not much. Julie says we're lucky
to have known him because all men are like that underneath
so he's an object-lesson, sort of. But I don't see how they
can be or the human race would have died out long ago.
What's the answer, Durdy?''

"I don't know much about men, Your Highness. In my
experience they cry for the moon and when they get it they
find they don't want it.''

Louise had done all the talking, prattling away mostly to
occupy her own mind. She knew Durdy was tired, but this
weary bitterness was new.

"Don't Highness me, Durdy darling, or I'll start Durdoning
you and you won't like that one bit. What's up? What's the
matter? What do you mean by pretending not to know
anything about men? Half your babies must have turned into
men, roughly. Look, there's Father, and Bert, and Uncle
Bill. They're all right, aren't they? I mean it's not their fault
if . . .''

Sniff. An upsettingly feeble signal, like the growl of a
dying dog. Louise longed to cry, not just for the dog, or
Durdy, dying, but for the island of love and happiness which
she'd inhabited a week ago and now would never find
again. She let the rumble of the rockers still. The clock
whirred. Its little door opened and the wooden bird began its
idiotic call. Eight! She leapt from the horse.

"Drat that clock,'' squeaked Durdy in her proper voice.
"It's fast again.''

"Thank heavens! How fast? Oh, you've got the Mickey Mouse going. Is that right?"

"*Of* course."

"Twenty minutes fast! Still five minutes to the gong. Durdy, that clock's gone mad. Why did you tell me it never gained, it only lost?"

"Didn't hear is own brother to Won't listen, Your Highness."

"But Durdy, you said. . . ."

"I daresay I said it never *used* to gain. That's not the same as doesn't gain now, is it, Miss?"

"But twenty minutes in a day!"

"You can't count on anything these days. Dearie me, no. You can't count on anything."

After the sudden spurt of proper Durdy-talk the old voice lost its energy between sentence and sentence.

"Oh, Durdy, you do sound tired. Shall I ask Father to come and look at you after supper?"

"His Majesty was here an hour ago. Perhaps I am a wee bit tired, darling. Give Durdy a little kiss and then goodnight."

That was the wrong way round. Durdy was supposed to say that when she tucked *you* in for the night. Again Louise felt the frustrated pressure of tears dammed somewhere behind her eyes as she bent to kiss the chilly cheek. She completed the ritual in its proper fashion, though still the wrong way round.

"Goodnight, sweet repose. Lie on your back and not on your nose."

Durdy didn't even smile.

Louise raced down the stairs and swung herself round the half-landing to take the last flight. As she did so Pilfer marched across her line of sight along the corridor below. He didn't seem to notice her as he stalked past, silent as one of the Palace ghosts, his pale and hollow-cheeked head stiff at the top of his black attire. Albert was right—he did look as if he were attending a death; even his gloves were black. Pilfer! Whoever had opened the cages in the zoo had worn cotton gloves and left a thread of black by one of the locks! It *couldn't* be Pilfer, but . . .

Normally Louise would have waited on the half-landing

until the gong sounded. It wasn't exactly a rule, because it was one of those things you knew without having to be told, but you didn't start making for the dining-room until Pilfer had sounded the gong. If you happened to be in the lobby when he appeared, you pretended to have some tiny mission to complete elsewhere, so that you could go and come back. It was as if striking the gong was a ritual central to Pilfer's craft, a summons to the Royal Family to gather for a meal which he would then serve in due order. It would detract from the ritual if the Family was already there, slavering in the lobby, while the deep round note swam along the corridors to tell them grub was up.

But this evening Louise felt she wanted to see Pilfer strike the gong. She felt that the way he did it would tell her, somehow, something about him, about whether he was the kind of man who could at one moment be so formal and unbending and at another savagely attack Albert's harmless pets. So she came quietly on down the stairs and turned the corner at the bottom. That was how she happened to witness the next "incident."

The gong, Mother said, was the ugliest object in the whole Palace, and the competition was stiff. It was a trophy of the Burma Wars, almost four feet across, hung from a frame of black wood carved with grimacing heroes and demons. It stood in the lobby which was really just a widening in the main corridor outside the dining-room and breakfast-room. It only made its noise if you knew the knack—if you biffed it at random you just got a thuddy sound out of it. You had to catch it a real wallop almost at the rim, and then keep the resonances going with little patting strokes. The dull, hammer-beaten bronze had one bright patch where Pilfer used to wallop it. Now Louise saw him pick the stick off its hook, give his cuff an absurd little flick as if to make sure it wouldn't impede the stroke and swing.

In the instant before the lights went out she saw Pilfer lifted off the floor, suddenly unshaped, like a rook at the moment of impact with a car's windscreen. Then the blast reached her and she was hurtling backwards. She felt the buffet all down her side as she banged into the carpet and

sprawled draggingly along the skirting-board. What had hit
her came as noise, one deep bellowing thud, like thunder
slap over the Palace. When it was gone there was a shrill
high whine but no other noise. She scrambled to her knees
and pressed her palms to her ears to shut it out, but the
whine went on. The lights behind her were still working,
and she saw yellow fog billowing down towards her from
the lobby. She dropped to her hands and crawled forwards,
now only able to see about a foot through the choking dust.
Into that visible space a chunk of plaster dropped and
exploded without a sound on the carpet. She crawled on
over its crumbs. There ought to be people shouting, she
thought, and alarm-bells, and running feet, but she could
hear no noise except the unvarying whine.

She found Pilfer by feel. He was lying face down against
the door of the dining-room. She reached up for the handle
but couldn't shift the door. She realized that she'd been
holding her breath for some time against the fumes and
wouldn't be able to much longer. Desperately she got to her
feet and shoved at the door, which opened wrenchingly,
biting into the dining-room carpet. The lights were on in the
dining-room. She stepped to one side of the door, took two
deep breaths, crouched and worked her way back to where
the yellow fog was now streaming in. Pilfer's body had been
partly supported by the door and had now slumped a little
further into the room. She linked her hands under an armpit
and hauled at him until she collapsed choking in the stinging
fumes. Between spasms she saw a black sleeve close by her
head. There was no hand at the end of it, but something that
gleamed and seemed to be jumping about like a small
trapped frog. At its third or fourth wriggle she saw that this
live thing was a pulse of blood from the smashed wrist.
Even in the convulsions of choking she knew what to do
because Father had always insisted that the Family's Christmas charades should contain gruesome accidents which had
to be realistically treated. She had no chance of getting
Pilfer's jacket off without help so she felt for the elbow joint
with her right hand and dug her thumb into the softness of it
while she bent the forearm back with her other hand.
Pilfer's flesh beneath the black broadcloth felt squishy and

boneless and the choking made it difficult for her to keep a steady grip. She was trying to twist herself round to a better position without letting go of the joint when she was picked bodily up from the floor and carried across the room.

"Pilfer!" she yelled. "He's bleeding to death!"

She felt the movement of words in her throat and a vague vibration of sound, but all she actually heard was the piercing whine in her skull. Whoever was carrying her halted, twisted her over and laid her neatly down on the yellow chaise-longue against the far wall. He turned to open the windows. It was Theale.

She shouted to him again about Pilfer and saw his lips move. The fog wasn't so bad now, but she still couldn't see across the room. She rolled herself off the chaise-longue and crawled back towards the door, but it was shut, with Pilfer right inside the room and Father kneeling by his body holding the arm just as she had done. Pilfer's face was all mottled meat. Father saw her and spoke.

"I can't hear you," she said. "I've gone deaf. I can hold the artery while you get a tourniquet ready."

He nodded and let her take the appalling arm. Because she was no longer trying to cope all by herself she felt a sudden wave of revulsion, but she forced it down and let Father guide her thumb to the right spot. He shouted over her shoulder at Theale, disappeared from her line of sight, came back at once with the carving-knife from the sideboard and slashed through the sleeve at the shoulder. She was just getting ready to alter her grip so that he could free the cloth from the elbow when a man's hand moved to take over from hers. She stood dizzily up. The room was still hazed with smoke, but no worse than it often was when Nonny contrived to burn her toast. Nonny was there now, and Mother was coming through the door. Nonny put an arm round her shoulder and led her out into the lobby. Two men seemed to be fighting, but it was only Sergeant Bannerman trying to prevent one of the Palace firemen from covering the whole area with foam. A man came rushing along the corridor with a big Calor lamp.

"Nonny, I'm deaf."

Louise felt her mother's arm tighten round her shoulders.

She began to laugh, and laugh still more because she couldn't hear the sound of her own shrieking.

In the middle of a tumbled dream the story Princess stepped down onto the platform. She was wearing an achingly heavy crown and a nurse's overall with nothing underneath. The wind kept snatching at the overall, which wasn't properly buttoned, so with one hand the Princess had to hold it down while in the other she carried the Proclamation she was going to read in a language she didn't know. All the time she had to smile and smile while the people cheered. She could hear them cheering. Even in the confusion of dream the return of sound was enough to wake Louise.

The whine was there, but far fainter, and a heavier noise was fading away. Her neck hurt. She was in her own room, which seemed to be bathed in a strange mild glow as though the moon had got inside it. She shifted and saw a hospital nurse sitting in her armchair and reading a magazine by the light of a shaded lamp.

"Nurse."

She could hear her own whisper through the whine. The nurse looked up.

"Say something, please, Nurse."

The nurse was a spruce middle-aged Englishwoman, who gave Louise an understanding smile but shook her head.

"I think I can hear things now," explained Louise. "Wasn't that an aeroplane?"

"Just now, Your Highness? Yes, I think one did go over."

The voice sounded furry, though Louise could see from the movement of the nurse's lips that she was speaking with extra care.

"Great!" she whispered. "I'm not going to be completely deaf, like Alexandra. How's Mr. Pilfer?"

Still with the same mechanical smile—her version of public face—the nurse rose, crossed the room and felt Louise's pulse.

"You go back to sleep my dear," she said. "You oughtn't to be awake at all, the size of the sedative they gave you. You shut your eyes and stop fretting. That's right."

It was true that a treacly heaviness seemed to be sucking Louise back into the bog of sleep. She listened to the whine of another jet going over. It wasn't quite right—too dull—but it was noise. She smiled until she remembered how the nurse had avoided answering the question about Pilfer, but she was too sleepy to open her eyes and ask again.

"It wasn't your fault, Lulu," said Father. "You did bloody well . . ."

"If only Theale hadn't dragged me clear! I was quite all right."

"He thought he was rescuing you. I daresay I'd have done the same if I'd got there first. But I can't have been more than a few seconds behind him, and I thought poor Pilfer was a goner the moment I saw him. It wasn't just his arm, darling. He had bits of gong all through him. Try not to think about it. Now, listen, Lulu—d'Arcy wants to see you. Are you up to that?"

"Yes, of course, provided he doesn't whisper. You're a bit woolly still, and this whining noise hasn't quite gone, but it's better. Will it go right away?"

"Sir James was pretty optimistic, and he wouldn't lie to me. My own guess, Lulu, is that it'll clear right up, but you may get it back sometimes when you're very tired or under tension."

"I don't want to be deaf and boring—I really don't."

"You'll be all right. Now, do you want me to stay while you talk to d'Arcy?"

"Aren't you supposed to be shaking hands with all those American lawyers?"

"I've cancelled everything. It's up to you, Lulu."

"Then stay. If he clams up you can ask him questions. He'll have to tell you."

Only after she'd spoken did Louise remember that Father might have quite different reasons for wanting to stay—to hear what she told Mr. d'Arcy.

In fact the Superintendent was very forthcoming. He sat by Louise's bed, taking his endless notes, while she described how she'd come down the stairs and seen Pilfer going past at the bottom.

"Was he carrying anything, Ma'am?" said d'Arcy—who had clearly been getting used to the conventions in the last few days. Even his suit seemed a better fit.

"No. I don't think so. I certainly didn't see anything in the hand nearest me. Then I came on down the stairs and when I reached the corner he was just getting ready to biff the gong."

"One moment. Would he have had time to do anything to the gong before you saw him again?"

"I don't think so. He was hovering in front of it, and then he gave his sleeve a hitch and bashed it, forehand, as though he thought he was Jimmy Connors."

"Are you saying that he seemed to you to hesitate and then to hit the gong harder than usual?"

"You had to hit it pretty hard to make it work at all."

"Superintendent, are you implying that Pilfer might have seen something wrong with the gong?"

"That's not exactly the position, Sir. You remember I reported to you on your return to London that as a result of an incident in Prince Albert's menagerie I had decided to include the series of practical jokes in my investigations? And that, on the assumption that the whole series was the work of one person, it had been possible to eliminate all the potential perpetrators except Miss Fellowes and Mr. Pilfer?"

A savage-sounding grunt from Father. Louise looked at him. She thought of Nonny's strong arm around her shoulders, holding her steady through the bucking spasms of hysterics. If you were mad, you could be loving and ordinary at one moment, and murderous the next, and perhaps not even know yourself what you had done. Nonny was strong enough to kill McGivan, but she could never have made a bomb. But somebody trying to protect Nonny . . .

"We respected your wishes, Sir," said Mr. d'Arcy, "and pursued our investigations along other lines. But as a result of this latest incident I ordered a search of Mr. Pilfer's room, and the following articles were discovered."

He flipped back several pages in his notebook and began to read.

"One manual on bomb construction; one ditto on unarmed combat; one aerosol can of red paint; several pairs of black cotton gloves, one with a thread pulled which appears to match a thread found on one of the opened cages in the menagerie; a large tin can, pierced with breathing-holes and containing a quantity of what appear to be mouse-droppings; a quantity of electrical tools and apparatus suitable for the construction of a bomb..."

"I know about that. He was a radio ham."

"Yes, Sir. And finally an empty package to which one of our dogs, trained to detect explosives by smell, reacted very strongly."

"Good God!" said Father. "Pilfer! No question of anybody having planted the things there, I suppose."

"I think not, Sir. I understand that the deceased was touchy about people meddling with his radio apparatus and kept his room securely locked."

"Good God!" said Father again. "Of course he did. How does your theory work, Superintendent?"

"I think we have to assume, Sir, that we are dealing with a mind becoming steadily more and more unbalanced. I think the progression of incidents shows this—the first three more or less harmless, then the damage to property in the shape of Sir Savile Tendence's trousers, then an attempt to ruin Sergeant Theale's career, then the clearly unbalanced cruelty to the animals in the menagerie."

"You've left out McGivan," said Louise. (And the other, she thought.)

"I'll return to that later, Ma'am. Now, as I told you, our process of elimination had reduced the suspects to Pilfer and the extremely unlikely person of Miss Fellowes. Let us suppose that Pilfer learnt of this fact—I've never known a place like this for rumors, Sir. The Yard's bad enough, but here! If you'll excuse me saying so..."

"We did tend to say things in front of him pretty freely," said Father. "I don't think we'd have discussed that, but..."

"He might have worked it out from our not talking about it," said Louise.

"Exactly," said Mr. d'Arcy. "I don't think anyone really knows how the mind of a madman functions, but I think it's reasonable to suppose that he realized that the game was up and decided to go out with, well, a bang. We found a piece of card in his jacket pocket with a red cross on it, and another of the objects in his room was a felt pen of the right shade. I understand he normally wore gloves when on duty."

"I can't believe it," said Louise.

"Let's think," said Father. "Your idea is that this was a final practical joke, meant to make us all go on suspecting each other? But he must have known that the kit would be found in his room. Surely he'd have disposed of that first."

"Perhaps he felt he hadn't time before we got on to him," said Mr. d'Arcy. "Or having set the bomb he may have decided to get it over—otherwise he'd have had to sleep on it, which even for a madman . . ."

"Quite," said Father. "Or he might have wanted us to find out in the end, so that we'd know who'd been fooling us. Yes, I see it makes a sort of sense, but I still don't believe it."

"If you'd seen some of the suicides I've seen, sir. The things they get up to. There's some of them whose one idea seems to be to go out in a way which'll get them into *The Guinness Book of Records*, it doesn't matter how messy or painful. I assure you this isn't all that out of the ordinary, Sir."

"That's not what I meant. I've known Pilfer all my life—much better than you'd realize. He taught me wireless. I spent a whole evening with him, calling up distant pals, only a month ago. There must have been somebody else."

"I assure you, Sir, that everybody else has already been eliminated from the series of jokes. We've put in some very thorough work on that in the last few days. And have you asked yourself how the red cross got into his jacket pocket? Her Royal Highness was on the scene within a very few seconds of his death. Are you suggesting that somebody slipped it into his pocket while he was alive?"

"No, but . . ."

"I assure you, Sir, that I haven't got a closed mind. I'll check and re-check the evidence. I'll go very thoroughly into the possibility of all that gear being planted in Pilfer's room. All I'm saying is that as of now this appears to be the most likely solution.''

"All right. What about poor McGivan?''

"Well, Sir, I still don't go along with McGivan's death as fully part of the series. We've drawn a complete blank so far in our investigation of terrorist groups, and in the matter of entry and exit from the Palace—but you'll understand that all that's a very complicated matter to check. I understand that Pilfer was younger and stronger than he looked, and the unarmed combat manual suggests he might have been able to kill McGivan. But there was no red cross left. So it's possible that Pilfer was interrupted in the process of setting up a joke—by Her Royal Highness, maybe—or alternatively that he simply found the body and fixed it like that.''

"Hang on,'' said Father. "Pilfer wouldn't have been on duty at the reception. He was our personal family servant.''

"He was seen in the vicinity not long before the body was found, Sir.''

"I know about that,'' said Louise. "I saw him too. He'd got a bee in his bonnet about Mr. Lambert nicking Family silver for official binges. He used to hover about and count the spoons.''

"If you saw him,'' said Father, "that was quite a bit after McGivan died.''

"By the way,'' said d'Arcy, "we've had the pathologist's full report now, Sir. You'll remember we had it checked because of the apparent discrepancy over possible time of death? Well, it appears the original report was a bit inflexible, and the symptoms are now thought to be consistent with death at approximately twenty to six—that's to say immediately after McGivan was seen by Her Royal Highness and the nurse Kinunu. When I say consistent, I mean not inconsistent. Without other evidence the time of death would have been put some twenty minutes earlier.''

"You mustn't go too much on the cuckoo-clock,'' said Louise. "It was wildly fast yesterday.''

"Was it, by God?'' said Father.

There was something odd about his tone. Louise glanced at him. She could read nothing in his face, but for a moment the old nightmares stirred. Don't be stupid, she told herself. It was poor old Pilfer, and now everything's going to be all right. Mr. d'Arcy didn't seem to have noticed the oddness and went on checking his notes.

"Well, that's about it," he said. "The immediate point is that the Princess thinks there was not enough time for Pilfer to have attached a bomb to the gong immediately before hitting it. Therefore he must have arranged it earlier, when there'd be fewer people about it. It would take at least two minutes, in the opinion of our explosives chaps."

"He'd have had the place to himself from about eleven on, apart from the other servants," said Father. "The whole Family were eating for England—I mean we had lunch engagements."

"Good," said Mr. d'Arcy, snapping his notebook shut. "At least it's a working theory."

He would have made a good courtier. In the short time he'd been in the Palace he'd learnt the curious shorthand of inflection and expression which meant that he was now ready to leave if His Majesty would be so gracious as to grant permission. Father grunted. D'Arcy rose. His little nod as he reached the door was an exact replica of Sir Sam's mini-bow.

Father shook his head as the door closed.

"Not quite out of the wood yet, Lulu," he said. "Sure about that clock?"

"Yes. Durdy was rather rambly, but when it struck eight she pulled herself together and cursed it."

He shook his head again, frowning.

"Father," said Lulu. "When Pilfer saw the toad on your ham-dish, that was a real faint, wasn't it?"

"Yes. That's what I mean about not being out of the wood. McGivan was the joker all right . . . but listen, suppose Pilfer worked it out—he might even have done that from the toad, somehow—and tackled McGivan and then suppose that they started to work as a team, pooling their information . . . and then McGivan finds out about you and Nonny and tells Pilfer and Pilfer kills him . . ."

"Why?"

"Depends how mad you think Pilfer was. If not very mad, because he realized that the knowledge could be used to squeeze a great deal of money out of us, or to sell to the media. I'd have paid up without a murmur, Lulu. If very mad, out of loyalty, because he didn't want the secret to come out. I'd rather it was the second. I liked old Pilfer. He was very good to me when I was a kid. Sorry. Yes. OK, then killing McGivan unhinges him a bit more—he starts setting the body up as a joke, then panics, but hovers about. You saw him, and thought it was for the spoons. Then he does the zoo. At least that explains the savage attack on Bert's toad—the way he fainted that breakfast shows he had a thing about toads—and of course he'd have known where Bert kept the keys. And then he decides to do himself in. He does it with the gong, because he had a thing about it. I don't know. . . What do you think?''

"I don't know either. It sounds a bit wishy in places. I hope it's true. Are you going to tell Mr. d'Arcy?''

"I don't see the point. It doesn't make any real difference, and I never managed to persuade them that McGivan was the original joker; if I brought it up again it'd take us nearer a lot of things we don't want known. Let's let sleeping dogs lie, eh?''

And lying dogs sleep, Albert used to add. When Father had taken her pulse and temperature and asked a few medical questions, brusquer even than his usual bedside manner with the Family, Louise lay back on the pillows. In the silence the whine in her ears seemed worse, but she closed her eyes and waited.

She woke somewhere in the middle of the afternoon, to judge by sunlight on her window-frame. Mother was sitting in the arm-chair, wearing her specs and working at the tiny-stitched embroidery which she believed to be the only proper occupation for the idle hands of Queens.

"Don't huake up, darling,'' she said.

"I've done it now. Are you all right, Mother? Was anybody else hurt?''

"Nobody, thank heavens, and Vick says your ears huill soon be huell. If I huere a Catholic I huould light a hundred candles in thanks to Holy Mary.''

"Why don't you do it anyway? I'd like that. You could do it in secret. Nobody would ever know.''

"God and the saints huould know. And there are too many secrets already."

Looking at her properly, Louise saw that she was paler even than usual, and her eyes were sunk into dark sockets.

"Darling Mother," she said. "It's all over now. It's going to be all right. It's not going to be the same as it was, but it's going to be a new all right. There's nothing to worry about."

Mother smiled at her, a tired and unmeaning movement of lips. Louise sank back on the pillows and shut her eyes again. It's not all right, she thought. Something else is wrong. Something to do with Father. Something I mustn't know about. Oh, God.

• 14 •

I N THE HUSH of Wednesday morning Miss Durdon lay and
listened to the wireless—the old, brown, domed box from
which she'd once heard the boy-King's voice coming
clipped and firm as he made his first Christmas broadcast to
his people in 1938. A year later she'd heard the same child
speaking to an Empire at war, and almost a year after that to
him saying, in words which he had for the first time insisted
on writing for himself, that though Hitler's armies seemed
poised for an invasion, he had persuaded his advisers to let
him stay with his people in England.

In Miss Durdon's mind the box seemed to vibrate with an
unheard duet—Churchill's thick, furry, melodramatic bass
interlacing with King Victor's no-nonsense tenor. The box
had had three new sets of innards since those days, but to
Miss Durdon it was still the same wireless, just as Vick was
still King Victor II in spite of his baldness and his bad temper
and his doctoring.

This morning there was a flavor of wartime in the an-
nouncer's voice. For months it had been like that as the
economic crisis lurched on, and every new fall in the pound
had to be greeted with a darkest-days note, such as had
announced the sinking of HMS *King Victor* by the *Scharnhorst*
or the surrender of Singapore. And, just as in wartime, any
heartening little gobbet of good news or story of British
courage was given its special rift-in-the-clouds resonance:

"In a bulletin issued from Buckingham Palace this morning, and signed by the Otorhinolarynogologist Royal, Sir James Corker, it is announced that the hearing of Her Royal Highness Princess Louise continues to improve and is unlikely to be permanently damaged. No further bulletins will be issued. It will be remembered that apart from the dead man Her Royal Highness was closest to the explosion that occurred on Monday evening in the Private Apartments of the Palace. She was found by rescuers attempting to stem the flow of blood from the man's arm. In recognition of her bravery the President of the Royal Humane Society, HRH the Duchess of Kent, has suggested . . ."

That Eloise, thought Miss Durdon. Trust her to stick her oar in. Bad as the Dowager Princess, she is.

After the News came the *Today* program. Miss Durdon had already forced her good hand to press the buzzer when a voice said, "And now, with an account of American reactions to the tragedy in Buckingham Palace, here is Sir Alastair Cooke."

The door opened and Kinunu came prancing in.

"No, don't switch it off," squeaked Miss Durdon. "I want to listen. Just do the clock."

"Yethmith."

Miss Durdon approved of Sir Alastair. This morning he talked about the American love-hate of British Royalty, and some of the absurd things that were said and done on old King Victor's visit to the States in 1936, and then picked his way delicately back to a tone of grave sympathy. Meanwhile Miss Durdon watched Kinunu cross the room, check and wind the Mickey Mouse clock, pull the chain that wound up the weights of the cuckoo clock and finally move its big hand ten minutes forward. Then she came round the bed and waited by the wireless for the voices to change.

"Yes, turn it off now, thank you," said Miss Durdon. "Kinunu, my dear, I feel a little cold this morning."

That was only a way of putting it. Miss Durdon could no longer feel the drop in body temperature. Memory could construct for her the icy draughts of Abergeldie, and the rubbery shivers of her own skin under a flannel nightdress with the inner warmth fighting outwards against the chill, and the feel of two bodies clinging close as if their love was a hearth for them to cluster to; but nowadays all she knew of cold was that the blood seemed to run thin in a tired brain.

Kinunu had already checked the console of instruments by the bedside, as she did first thing each morning, but now she went round the bed again and frowned down at the dials, comparing each with the chart His Majesty had drawn above.

"OK. All OK," she whispered.

Then it will be soon, thought Miss Durdon. Perhaps it will be today. I feel cold when I'm not cold. That's a sign. I'm going over the edge at last. I mustn't tell Vick. I'll try and live long enough for another crumpet tea. I'll die with butter on my lips.

"Make me a little warmer," she squeaked.

Gingerly Kinunu slid a lever an eighth of an inch up its groove.

"I talked to His Majesty last night," said Miss Durdon. "I told him he's got to find you a husband. He's got such a lot of worries now, poor man, but he said he'd try."

"Yethmith. Marry pleethman, pleathe."

"A policeman!"

"Yethmith."

"Policemen don't grow on trees, you know," said Miss Durdon sharply.

Kinunu's frown was beginning to deepen with worry when there was a firm rap at the door.

"See who that is, my dear," said Miss Durdon, glad of the chance to collect her old wits and explain—as she must have done ten thousand times to other greedy infants—that Father Christmas could not gratify all conceivable wishes, even in a Palace. A man's voice muttered at the door. Kinunu turned.

"Pleathemith. Pleethman," she said.

"We'll talk about that later," snapped Miss Durdon. "Who's there?"

"Pleathemith. Pleethman. Thee you."

Cunning little wretch, thought Miss Durdon. She's already found herself another follower, and she'd had him out

there, listening to that dratted monitor; she'd have brought
the subject up herself if I hadn't.

"All right, I'll see him if you want me to. You'd better
wait outside."

The man who came in wasn't in uniform. He had a doggy
look, not McGivan's boring-old-housedog air, but the bright-
eyed sharpness of a hunt terrier, or a good ratter. He was
younger than McGivan, and ten times more of a man.
Kinunu wouldn't tease *him*, thought Miss Durdon.

"I don't know you," she said. "What's your name?"

"I'm Sergeant Theale, Miss," he said.

"Oh, you're one of *our* people?"

"That's right, Miss. Only I've not had the honor to visit
the Nurseries before. All right if I check this clock now?"

The question caught Miss Durdon so much off balance
that he had crossed to the far wall and put the black
Gladstone bag he was carrying down on the high chair
before she'd collected her wits.

"You leave that clock alone, young man," she said. "It's
not been the same since King Haakon went meddling with it,
and I don't want it getting any worse."

"Orders, I'm afraid, Miss," he said.

He pulled a stop-watch out of his pocket and set it going.
He seemed to be counting the swings of the pendulum. The
tick of the clock came and went, sometimes seeming to be
inside her head and sometimes far away, beyond the barred
windows, as though the cuckoo was hovering with it out
over the gardens. She felt herself sliding down the slope of a
shallow wave and then gradually floating up to the crest of
consciousness again. When she was fully herself the clock
was back on the wall with the man still counting its ticks.
Miss Durdon felt what she called "hot," but there was no
knowing whether the buzzing in her mind, like the beginnings of a fever, was caused by Kinunu setting the lever too
high or the panic of watching the man check the cuckoo-
clock or was something to do with the slide out of the
whirlpool and over the edge. I can't go yet, she thought. I
must do something.

"Excuse me, Mr. Theale," she squeaked. "That dratted

girl's set my bed too hot. Be so kind as to move the switch down for me, save me calling her in with my buzzer.''

He stayed where he was for a few more ticks, stopped his watch and made a couple of notes in a notebook. At last he turned and crossed to the console, which he stared down at, smiling slightly.

"Like the flight deck of a jumbo," he said. "I'm Miss Durdon. Fly me to San Francisco."

"I don't know what you're talking about," said Miss Durdon in the tone she used for boys whose independence she approved of but whose impertinence had to be kept in check. "It's the third lever along. There's a chart above shows how it ought to be. And don't you be pert about my friend there—that machine's the better half of me, these days. It does my heating and my breathing and Lord knows what. If it stopped working I'd be dead in half an hour."

Out of the corner of her eye she could see him using the butt of his pencil to move the lever down to its proper setting.

"Lot to go wrong there," he said.

"Lot to go wrong with all of us, young man."

"And they've given you a buzzer too?"

"Under the bedclothes by my left hand, where my two good fingers are."

She wanted to keep him talking, to prevent him going back to the clock. But he wasn't to be put off.

"Your clock's running a bit slow, far as I can see," he said.

"Or your stop-watch is fast, young man."

"No, it's spot on. I do a bit of hurdling and I need it for training, so I have it checked, regular. I make it your clock's losing two or three minutes a day. Funny it's being fast while it's running slow."

"It has its ups and downs," snapped Miss Durdon, no longer indulgent.

He nodded and returned to stare at it, then opened his case and took out an aerosol can with which he carefully sprayed the clock face, producing a fine grey film all over it, like mildew.

"Stop that," said Miss Durdon. "Stop that at once, or I'll know the reason why."

He paid no attention but stood on tiptoe to peer at the clock through a pocket magnifying glass.

"Somebody's been dusting, I see," he said. "It's not often you get 'em conscientious enough to dust the clocks. But here's a nice print. Now, that's a small finger—would that be Princess Louise's, Miss Durdon?"

"I don't know what you're talking about, and I'll trouble you to clean the mess off my clock this very instant."

He stood gazing at the clock a moment longer and then, to Miss Durdon's great surprise, he took a duster out of his bag and cleaned the whole surface. She watched him spray the clock again and photograph it with a neat little camera. Finally he cleaned it up for the second time. When he turned to the bed he was smiling.

"Good thing to get everything dusted pretty regular," he said. "Now, I'll tell you something, old lady. You see that pendulum wagging to and fro? Suppose somebody wanted that clock to go fast, there's a little screw under the weight there, and they'd only have to take a couple of turns on it, shortening the pendulum, you see, and it'd begin to swing faster. Perhaps they might take it into their heads to rub a bit of dust into the thread under the screw, make it look as though it's been like that a long time—you follow me?"

"I still don't know what you're talking about."

"No, of course not, old lady. You've seen a lot of 'em come and go, but never seen anything like this, I dare say. Perhaps you'll explain to Princess Louise next time she comes up . . . it won't matter if she touches it again, or that nurse of yours . . . you can't tell from a fingerprint whether somebody's been putting it forward a-purpose, or putting it back because it'd got fast of its own accord . . . I only went through all that palaver to show you I'm on your side, see?"

Miss Durdon had needed all her will-power to pay attention to what he was saying, because she'd just felt herself beginning to slide into another of the wave-like dips of consciousness, but she forced herself to understand.

"That's very kind," she squeaked.

"Trouble is," he said, "I can't bring anyone else in on it.

I've got to look after things by myself, because you can't expect the others to see things our way. They might, they might not—you can't take the risk. My problem is I'm working in the dark, and there's always a danger I'll make things worse. That's why I worked it so it was me they sent up to check the clock, because I wanted to have a word with you. For instance, I'd be able to move a lot freer if I knew why HRH took it into her head to say she'd seen McGivan up here when she hadn't, and then to go messing around with that clock."

"I don't know what you're talking about."

"Ah, come off it. I'm sure as I'm sure my name's Desmond Theale that she hasn't been doing anything wrong— and even if she had I'd stand by her. That's what I've been trying to tell you, old lady. But if whatever she's been up to is important enough for her to muck up a murder investigation— and she's a sensible little thing—she wouldn't be doing that for a lark—then I've got to know what it is, so as I don't go putting my big feet in it, see? The only other thing is for me to chuck up trying to help and go and tell the Superintendent about the clock being mucked around with."

He had a funny way of speaking, with a rising lilt as though even the last threat weren't a serious one. Miss Durdon lay and looked at him. He was outside her experience, she realized, not just because of what he'd done, but because he was a complete loner. She wondered whether he'd ever had any family at all.

"Well?" he said.

"You killed poor Ian McGivan," she said.

I'm getting deaf again, Louise kept thinking, but it was only the horrid silence of breakfast. Usually there'd be quarrels over the papers, and Mother reading out bits of recipes and Father grousing about his Ministers saying "refute" when they meant "repudiate" and Nonny trying to get advice on what horses she should back; but on Wednesday morning the loudest sound in the room was the crunch of Albert's carrots, and it was that steady rhythm that told Louise that her ears were almost well again. Mrs. Mercury, the housekeeper, did Pilfer's work, stealing in and out and looking as though she'd been crying all night, though she and Pilfer had been ancient enemies. Mother looked tired and old, and had moved her place so that she sat between Nonny and Albert; she and Nonny were breaking all custom by muttering their way through Mother's schedule for the day, long before Sir Sam was due to appear. Nonny was her unreadable self; only once, when Father looked up from his paper, began to say something and stopped in mid-sentence, Louise thought she glimpsed another Nonny, the one you never saw, tense as a tennis-player waiting for a serve. Father himself was in a state Louise had never seen; it looked as though he were furious about something but couldn't get his temper to catch fire. Mostly he hid behind his paper, eating his food with one hand. When Louise caught Albert's eye she could see that he was as mystified as she was. She ate her breakfast quickly, as though she were getting ready for school, and managed to slip out of the room unnoticed. I can't stand any more of that, she thought. I'll go and see Durdy and make her tell me the truth about that clock. Then I'll know where I am.

The sense of deafness came back as she walked along the corridors and climbed the stairs. All the usual mutters of the Palace getting ready for the day were there, but muffled and tentative, as though even the Hoovers vacuuming the miles of carpet were conscious that their next stroke might set off a booby-trap. Louise opened the door to the Nursery suite without any of the old sense of coming to a haven.

Kinunu was leaning against the jamb of the door into her bedroom gazing up at the inner monitor screen, but she turned to Louise with a grin of happy wickedness and beckoned to her to come and see.

"What's up, Kinunu?"

"Pleathemith, pleethman. Mithmith tell ee marry Kinunu."

"No!"

"Yethmith."

Louise hesitated. She'd been gearing herself up to tackle Durdy alone and didn't want to have to put on a public face and make conversation till the man went away. She could hear the murmur of his voice, and as she crossed the room its direction changed, coming now from the monitor in

Kinunu's bedroom. He stopped talking before she reached the bedroom door.

The monitor was trained on Durdy's bed. You could see only a corner of the console, but its dials were wired to an identical display by Kinunu's bed so that even in the middle of the night she could check them without disturbing Durdy. On the other side of the screen Louise could see the arm and shoulder of a man's jacket. Durdy was looking up at him. There was a long pause. Then the familiar voice squeaked out.

"You killed poor Ian McGivan."

"How do you make that out?" said the man.

It was unmistakably Theale.

"If you knew he wasn't here when the Princess said he was, then you knew when he died. And I'm told it was you that checked the thrones for bombs. You said he wasn't there then, but *you* knew he was."

Theale bent down, still mostly out of sight, and seemed to make a small adjustment to Durdy's bed-clothes.

"That's right," he said. "And I'd do it again."

"Poor Ian. He never did you any harm."

"Didn't he just?" said Theale. "Didn't he just? Trying to fix me with those stupid jokes of his. Bloody little erk."

"I knew all along there were two of you," squeaked Durdy.

"What do you mean?"

"There was a lot more to poor Ian than met the eye. Those jokes of his—just like some of my babies. You wanted to belt them but you couldn't help laughing. But not after you killed him . . ."

"Didn't mean to."

"That's what they always say. Oh, Durdy, I didn't know it would break."

"That's right. How did you know?"

Theale sounded surprised and a bit less cocky. For the first time Louise could see his head as he moved round the foot of the bed and up the other side. Suddenly she felt that he was going to do something to Durdy and started to move towards the Day Nursery door, but Durdy's answer was so placid that she turned back. Theale was standing in front of the console now, with only his other arm visible.

"Go on," said Durdy. "Tell me."

"Go on," said Miss Durdon. "Tell me."

There was nothing she could do. He had twitched the buzzer a couple of inches beyond her reach, and all the will in the world couldn't make the fingers stretch down to it. He had used the butt of his pencil to move the temperature lever down to the very bottom of its groove. He was sending her over the edge—he couldn't know that she was going anyway. The troughs between the waves were getting deeper, and each time she felt the downward slither begin it needed more will-power to force her consciousness to stay aware. I'll go soon, she thought. But I'd like to know how Kitten's story ended. Ian was all that was left of Kitten, and I'd like to know how he died.

"What do you mean?" said Theale.

"It wasn't your fault, was it? You want to tell somebody it wasn't your fault."

"That's right. Silly little erk, and useless with it. It got on my wick, the way he was somehow in with the Royals, and the rest of us wasn't. I'd had my eye on him since that business with the pianos, because I knew he could do voices. I was just waiting to catch him. That night we had to check the ball-room and apartments double thorough, because of a rumor about some terrorists, and that's how I found him sitting on HM's throne in the dark, with his moustache combed down like HM's, grinning to himself like an ape. I'd switched on the spots when I came in, and for a couple of secs I thought it was HM himself—but of course you couldn't really mistake him, so I saw who it really was pretty well at once. Now I've got him, I thought. Setting up another of his jokes. He didn't even look round, though he must have noticed the spots come on. 'What the hell are you up to, McGivan?' I said. 'Don't you use that tone of voice to me, Theale,' he says. No accent, mind you. Might have been HM speaking. 'Come off it,' I said. 'I know it's you who's been playing these stupid tricks around the place, and first thing tomorrow morning I'm putting in a report.'

'Oh, no, you're not, Theale,' he said. 'No harm your knowing I did play one or two jokes on the Family—I thought if they were cutting down on staff it'd do us a bit of good if there was plenty going on to investigate . . . ' 'And you tried to frame me for it,' I told him, 'so if anybody got the chop it wasn't you.' 'Well, maybe,' he said. 'You'd have done the same thing if you'd had the wits. But that's all over now. They can't get rid of me anymore, not knowing what I know, and you can't either, Theale. I think I'll have you posted,' he says. 'We're spending too much on security staff. There's got to be cuts, hasn't there?' It was that 'we' that did it, old lady. He was just sitting there, grinning at me, legs crossed, pulling at the corner of his moustache the way HM does. He was even beginning to look a bit like HM after all, in spite of everything. And when he said 'we' like that I hit him. I don't know what came over me, but it was one step forward, chop, and there he was with his neck broke. That's how it happened.''

"'Course it was,'' said Miss Durdon. "It's always the one who starts the trouble that ends up in tears. I could have told you that.''

"You should have told *him* that, old lady. So there I was. I didn't panic, not really, but I didn't have time to think things out, not then. If I had I'd have left a red cross somewhere, but that only came to me later. I propped him up, made it look as if he was still alive, because I thought anyone who came on him might think it was HM sitting there and let him be. Give me a bit more time, you see. I'd left my fingerprints on the doors and switches, so I had to say I'd been there, but I nipped off and joined up with the other security staff and prayed the body wouldn't be found till the cleaners came in the morning. How was I to know that HRH would go sneaking around like that? I was dead scared for a couple of hours, but then I found I'd got an alibi. I couldn't believe it. First of all HRH gave me an alibi when all those pianos were sent to Kensington Palace, and that got me out of one mess, and now she'd given me another. I want to ask you about that in a minute, but I'll finish telling you what happened first off. The Yard turned up, you see, and started on this terrorist caper, and I thought it was all going to quiet down. Then, because I was working alongside them, I began to see that some of them were beginning to think it was a nonsense, and they'd bring the Superintendent round to that in the end. Now, of course I didn't want it coming out that McGivan had been the joker, because everybody knew how the joker had tried to fix me, and I didn't think my alibi would hold up once they really got to work on it. So the thing was to carry on with the jokes. You're right about that, old lady. It's not my line. Funny how hard it was to think up a couple of jokes.''

"I don't think it's funny," said Miss Durdon. "As soon as they told me about the zoo I knew it wasn't poor Ian."

"I had my worst moment of the lot there," said Theale. "HRH fetched me along, and as soon as I was through the door that bloody bird said 'Go get 'em, you two.' Just what I'd said to the cats. I thought the Prince had spotted me and fetched me along to see how I reacted. You could have heard my jaw drop in Scotland. But they didn't seem to pay much notice, so I carried on as if nothing had happened. I'd picked Saturday morning because I'd got my eye on Pilfer already. He was another one got on my wick. You see, it wasn't enough having the jokes going on, I had to end them in a way which tidied it all up, so nobody'd ask any more questions. So I thought I'll frame Pilfer for them and then I'll suicide him. Being security, of course, I'd got a spare key to his room—same with the zoo—so I could plant all the evidence, but I had to fix it so it'd look as though he thought he was going to get copped any day, and that meant eliminating everyone else, see? Anyway, it all worked a treat, and I was down at the bottom of the stairs waiting for the bomb to go off so I could rush up and find Pilfer dead and shove a card with a red cross in his pocket—but what do I find if it isn't HRH in the middle of the smoke, deaf as a post, trying to save the old bugger's life? When all we needed was to have him dead and everybody could settle down to a bit of peace and quiet at last?''

His voice rose to a questioning lilt. It caught Miss Durdon's attention as she floated up out of a deeper trough, in which his voice had been only a hazy sound, a buzzing in her ears. He had killed McGivan. He had killed Pilfer. He was a bad boy. A dangerous bad boy.

"How are you feeling, old lady?" he said.

"As well as can be expected, young man."

"Glad to hear that, because there's a couple of things I want to ask you."

"Ask isn't the same as get," she snapped.

"We'll see. McGivan knew something, didn't he? Something important enough to make him feel that he could do what he liked and the Royals wouldn't be able to touch him? What was it, old lady?"

"Those that ask no questions will be told no lies."

"And another thing—or perhaps it's the same thing. What did HRH mean by saying she'd seen McGivan up here when she hadn't, and saying it was six o'clock, and then, when HM tells her McGivan must have died before that, the two of 'em mucking around with the clock there? I've got it into my head that what McGivan knew was something to do with HRH. What is it, old lady? You know, don't you?"

Miss Durdon felt her lips tighten. The blood in her brain seemed weak as water. She was very "cold." It would be a good moment to go now, before he could ask her any more questions.

"Ah, come on," he said. "If it's something big enough I won't need to do you in, because HM will have to look after me. I was thinking last night how he'd fancy me as a son-in-law one day. Show what a democratic age we live in . . ."

Bee-bip. Bee-bip. Bee-bip. Bee-bip.

The sharp note of the warning-signal forced itself through the misty chill in Miss Durdon's mind.

"What's that?" snapped the bad boy.

"That's my friend, telling me I'm cold," she whispered.

McGivan could never pretend to be Father. But the opposite wasn't true. Father loved charades. They were spit images. You looked at the moustache. You heard the snuffle. So you saw McGivan. He'd been more McGivanish than ever. Because he'd been Father.

Bee-bip. Bee-bip. Bee-bip. Bee-bip.

The sharp note of the warning-signal forced itself through the swirling images in Louise's mind. She had no idea how long she had stood here, only half hearing the buzz of Theale's talk, full of the sickness of knowledge. She remembered writing a note for Kinunu to take to Father, telling him to come at once. Yes, Kinunu was gone.

"What's that?" snapped Sergeant Theale.

"That my friend, telling me I'm cold," whispered Durdy.

"You answer my questions, old lady, and I'll warm you up again, quick as winking. I've got to know, in case they get on to me after all."

Louise dragged her gaze from the monitor to look at the dials by Kinunu's bed. On the third one along the needle was right down into the red segment, and the orange light beneath it was winking off and on in time with the signal. Louise put on her public face, ran to the door of the Day Nursery and walked in without knocking. Theale stopped whatever he was saying in mid-sentence.

"Hello, Durdy," said Louise. "Good morning, Mr. Theale. Did you have a good night, darling?"

"Quite good, thank you," said Durdy. "But I'm talking to Mr. Theale just now, Your Highness."

"All right, I'll push off and come back," said Louise. "I'll just give you a kiss, shall I?"

She walked round the foot of the bed as though she were still too deaf to hear the acid whine of the warning-signal. Theale was between her and the console but she came forward like somebody who was used to people standing out of her way, and at the last instant he did so. There was no need to say anything. Durdy would recognize the public face and know that she knew. As she bent for the kiss Louise put out her left hand to balance herself and slid the lever up its groove. The signal stopped.

"I'm not going to school," she said. "I'll come back in half an hour."

"All right, Your Highness," said Durdy. Her voice was faint and drowsy, but the sentinel will still stood to its post.

"You mustn't let her get tired, Mr. Theale," said Louise, straightening up.

He didn't answer. She turned and saw that he had moved

away from the bed and was taking something out of a black Gladstone bag that stood on the old high chair by the cuckoo-clock. He walked with quick steps to the door. For an unbelievable second she thought he was going to make a run for it, but he simply opened the door, looked out into the Night Nursery, closed and locked the door and turned back. The thing he had taken from his bag was a pistol.

"Where's that nurse?" he said.

"I sent her to get help," said Louise.

Theale paused, looking at her with his quick, intelligent stare. Louise looked back at him, confident in the mask of her public face.

"Stand where you are," he said. "Check you got that lever right. OK? Now don't move. I'm going to open the windows. I want to be able to hear if anybody tries anything fancy from the roof."

Louise watched him haul the sashes down. He climbed on to the little desk where she'd learnt to write her letters and peered briefly out over the bars at the three-story drop, then jumped back into the room. He still looked as though he thought what was happening was somehow amusing.

"Who did you tell her to find?" he said.

"I gave her a note. I told her to find my Father."

"He'll do. How long have we got?"

"I don't know. I really don't, Mr. Theale."

(It was just before nine. Father would be on his way to the loo. It would depend whether Kinunu had found him first.)

"Right," he said. "Now, I want to know something, and you'd better give me a straight answer. Just before you barged in I was asking the old lady what the hell you'd been playing at up here, saying you'd seen McGivan when you hadn't, and then fooling around with that clock. You can tell me just as well as she can."

"It's all my fault," whispered Louise. "Everything's all my fault."

"Why don't you tell me about it?"

"No."

"Come on, Your Highness, don't be a fool. I've only got

to muck about with those instruments and the old lady will be dead. You don't want that, do you?"

"Don't tell him," whispered Durdy. "I'll be gone soon, no matter what."

Louise shook her head. After the clarity of action, of knowing what to do, the mists had come back into her mind. Nothing mattered. It was all her fault for being born.

Theale took a step round the bed towards the console, but before she could move there was a bang and rattle from the door.

"You there, Lulu?" called Father's voice. "What the hell's going on?"

Theale sprinted back towards the door and raised his pistol.

"Stand clear," he called.

There was a sharp, fierce crack which brought the deafness-whine back into Louise's ears. Theale's next words had a furry sound through it.

"Listen to me," he called to the door. "I have Princess Louise in here, as a hostage. Anybody tries to come through that door and she's for it. I want to talk to the King."

"I'm here, you bloody fool," said Father's voice. "Are you all right, Lulu?"

"Yes," said Louise. "Durdy's not too good. He's been mucking around with her temperature."

"Quiet, everybody," shouted Theale. He seemed to have forgotten about the monitors. "I want everybody out of that other room except the King and that nurse."

Pause.

"I'll stay, but not the nurse," said Father.

"You heard what I said."

"I'm not giving you any more hostages and that's flat," snapped Father. "Can't you see it, man? I haven't the right."

"Come off it. You can do what you bloody well want. Now you'll do what I say or I'll put a bullet through the Princess's knee-cap."

Pause.

"I tell you I haven't the right," said Father. "I'll be a hostage, but not the nurse."

"No good. I'm going to count up to ten."

"I'm not going to change my mind. Sorry, Lulu."

"I'm glad," said Louise. Her voice came out tremorless, but that was the story Princess standing between her and the gunman. The real Louise cringed from the burst of agony and the life-time of hobbling.

"One," said Theale.

"D'you really want to saddle yourself with a badly wounded hostage?" called Father. "Think it out, man. She won't be able to walk."

He sounded merely irritable at Theale's lack of forethought. Theale shook his head and stopped counting.

"I'm alone in this room now," called Father. "Tell me what you want."

"Give me time. I'll have to think it out. You stay there, but don't come back at me for twenty minutes. Princess, move away from that bed and go and stand over by that wall. That's right."

He looked round the room, nodded, put his pistol down on the Heal gate-leg table, drew up a chair, sat down and began to make notes in his police notebook. The silence deepened. No sound at all came from beyond the door. The whine from the pistol-shot dwindled and vanished. Suddenly, close by Louise's shoulder, the cuckoo-clock whirred, clicked and started on its banal call.

She turned and stared at it. This is why I'm here, she thought. I came to tackle Durdy, and now I know. Nothing will ever be all right again. I don't care whether I live or die.

The bird was still leaping in and out of its idiotic little door when she reached up, lifted the clock off its hooks and with a single sweeping movement flung it through the open window.

Theale shouted.

She took three running steps, put a foot on her little old desk and swung herself up and over the sash, calling good-bye to Durdy as she did so. She was already reaching down for the bars above the sill when she heard the clock hitting the terrace far below.

* * *

The waves were steeper now and closer together. It was as though the meddling with Miss Durdon's temperature had started an up-and-down oscillation which couldn't now be stopped. There was no change in her perception of her own body; that remained as it had been for the last six years, a hazy blur of feeling, like the image of a bright window that stays on the retina after the eyes have looked away; it was a fading ghost that refused to fade. But her mind, her inner self, felt the pull towards darkness. I'm going, she would say, this time I'm going, and all down the slithering slope the darkness would deepen. But then the curve of fall would soften, level and begin to float her upwards with no more speed or effort than the downward swoop, and then she would swim into daylight, still alive in her own Nursery, with Louise standing by the cuckoo clock and that dangerous big boy sitting at the table and a smell like fireworks in the air. Then, before she could summon her will together to take command, she would be swooping down again towards the darkness.

She was conscious all the time, but conscious without being aware. In one of the troughs she heard a loud bang, and Vick shouting, but she didn't remember she'd heard them till she floated to the next peak and smelt the gunpowder-smell. That boy's been shooting at things, she thought. In my Nursery, too. I'll show him who's master here. But then she was slipping again towards the dark. A few waves later she was floating up towards the unwelcome light when she heard the cuckoo-clock begin its call. Then there was a shout and a movement.

"Good-bye, Durdy darling," called Louise.

"Good-bye, Your Highness," whispered her lips. "Have a lovely journey and sit with your back to the engine."

And then she was at another peak, knowing she'd said something which didn't belong, and the big boy was running across the room with his gun in his hand.

"If you come any nearer I'll drop," shouted Louise.

Louise was clinging to the bars outside the window, kneeling on the sill. Her face was twisted and hurt, hurt, Vicky's hurt face, the Nursery at Windsor with its coal fire lighting Vicky's face as she told the slow, wrenching story of trust betrayed. It must be Vicky—my last baby could never show hurt like that . . .

Sliding down towards the next pit, Miss Durdon could not feel the tear-drops that trickled across her parched temples.

Voices, shouts, anger, her own lips saying that somebody must have got out of bed the wrong side that morning, Vicky's hand round the locket, the ringlet of hair given her by the mean little boor she loved, the crack as the glass burst on the coals, all fading, fading into the bleak now.

"Don't be a fool, Lulu. Come in at once. That's an order."

"Tell him it's nothing to do with him."

A strange voice, sour and quiet, but it came from Louise clinging like a monkey outside the windows. You mustn't give in when they're like that, you mustn't promise to take them to the zoo, but you must let them feel that you haven't trampled them flat. The dangerous big boy was trying— didn't think he had it in him to speak so gentle.

"Now come on in, Your Highness. I promise you won't get hurt, not if everyone's sensible."

"I don't care whether I live or die, I tell you!"

More waves—silent now, mostly—the deeps deeper and the climbs more slow—almost into darkness, almost over the real edge, at the peaks the sharpness of knowledge hazed, the edges of dusk closing in.

"Take it away! I don't want it! Take it away or I'll jump before you're ready!"

That must be Louise. Her voice had the tone of things ending, but not calmly like Miss Durdon's end. Harsh, miserable, wounded.

"Can't you do something, old lady? She's going to jump."

Who whispered that? Do something. Do something. Do something. Down the long slope the words stayed with her, a whispering echo, muttering round her through the black valley and up the slow floating towards this last brightness. Do something, or Louise will fall. My last baby. Do the one thing left. The garrison of the redoubt lay inert, sprawled across their weapons, but as Miss Durdon came back for a few final seconds to the world where they had fought so

long their ghosts rose hovering and stood to their posts. She
heard her own voice squeak out with perfect firmness.

"I can't die, Your Highness. I want to die but I can't.
Come and help me die, please, darling."

The sill projected a sharp two inches beyond the bars.
Kneeling hurt, and the bars came at points where it was
difficult to grip them firmly and still be absolutely ready to
let go. And it was hard to see clearly into the room because
of the kinky reflections from the double layer of glass, the
cedar tree and the sky and the lime that had the swing on it.
The clearest place was through the reflection of Louise's
own face, kinky and double-edged, the face of a stranger, a
face in the Hall of Mirrors, a monster. It had three eyes and
its mouth was a wide, wavering gash, but it was Louise—
not the story Princess, not the public face, but herself,
visible at last.

At first she stared through the reflection trying to see what
Theale was up to. The panting of the quick effort of
climbing out died away. He stood facing her with his back
to the bed, his gun half raised. If he hadn't been there,
staring at her, she might have let go and finished everything
at once. Her mouth was full of a taste like vomit and the
muscles of her cheeks screwed themselves into aching
knots. Her eye was caught by the reflection, the grief-
monster, herself. Behind it Theale raised his gun and came a
pace nearer. She took a hand off the bars.

"I'll drop," she said.

He stopped but the black hole of the gun still pointed at
her.

"Don't be a fool," he said.

"You don't understand," she said. "Nothing matters anymore. Nothing."

She saw the gun lowered. He shrugged, turned, went
back to the door and started talking to Father.

"Don't be a fool, Lulu. Come in at once. That's an
order."

It was impossible to answer his shout, but she got words
out of her mouth telling Theale to tell Father not to inter-
fere. Theale said something and she told him the exact

truth. She wasn't anybody's hostage because she didn't mind if she lived or died.

Something rattled to her left. A sash slid up—it must be Kinunu's window. Father leaned out, pleading and commanding. She refused to look at him or hear him. She stared at her reflection in the panes, shutting everything else out of her mind. Everything else was lies. The happiness was lies, the love was lies, the strolling by the lake with arms round waists, the careful, honorable explanations, all lies. All putting on a show. A show to the GBP, a show to the Family, a show to themselves. People should understand that you have it in you to make them suffer. It doesn't matter who you hurt, how much you hurt them, provided you can still put on a show. I say I say I say, your public face isn't as good as mine. It doesn't have to be.

Her sobs contorted the grief-monster.

"Lulu. Lulu, darling. Listen to me."

She dared not turn her head and see that pale face craning from Kinunu's window.

"Go away, Mother. Go away, please. I love you, but please go away. You're making it worse. Please."

Mother tried again, several times, but it was best not to answer. That would only hurt everybody all over again. Perhaps it would be best to let go at once, but Theale was still in there with Durdy. He had to be beaten first. Durdy wasn't lies.

When her knees hurt she shifted them without noticing. Pictures began to nudge into her mind, like bits of dream— Kinunu with her cap skew-whiff . . . Father leaning back in his chair like a lazy tom-cat . . . you'll get all the cuddles you want . . . I was a pretty randy young man . . . Mother turning from her desk, straight-backed, with arms held slightly out as though she were raising them for her crucifixion . . . a snuffling little bald man with his trousers round his ankles . . . Nonny hauling herself laughing from the mud behind a Land Rover . . . McGivan's head toppling forward to an angle that couldn't be true . . . Pilfer's face like mottled meat . . . her yellow nightie ripped from end to end . . .

Something nicked her awareness, something outside the

room, a movement or sound, she didn't know which. She looked to left and right, and then down. Men were coming along the terrace. They wore fire helmets. Some of them carried a canvas sausage. Her mind made the leap to a picture of them spread below like a flower, straining the canvas circle between them to catch her. She shouted furiously down, waved an arm to show she meant it, almost fell . . . And even when she clutched back at the bar she felt none of the prickle of vertigo on her palms. That shows I really don't care, all through, she thought. My body's ready as well as my mind. I'll get it over.

She peered through the grief-monster for a final glimpse of Durdy and saw Theale bending over the bed. What was he doing to her? Did he know that he could still get at Louise through Durdy? Down below the firemen had halted— she could afford to wait a little longer and see what he was doing. The late September sun, clear and strong, seemed to distill the morning into silence.

"I can't die, Your Highness," squeaked Durdy, with that old, familiar touch of petulance as though she'd been complaining about her inability to twist the screw-top off a bottle of cough-mixture. "I want to die, but I can't. Come and help me, please, darling."

Unwilled, Louise's left hand rose from the bars and gripped the top of the sash. She saw Theale had turned to watch her.

"Go to the other side of the room, Mr. Theale," she said. "Right round the table. Go on. I'll count five, and if you don't go, I'll drop. I really will. One . . ."

He shrugged and turned away. He was beaten.

Now it became difficult to move without the fear of the drop. There was sweat on her palms and her right leg was numb where the pressure of the sill had closed off a nerve-circuit. She worked her way tremblingly upright and stood flexing her ankles to get the feeling back—she'd need to be able to dash for the window if Theale tried anything. He was standing right over at the far corner of the room with his gun half raised. His bright-terrier look was puzzled now. She worked her way onto the desk, letting him see that she could always get back out of the window before he could reach her. She took the three paces to the bedside with her eyes still on him.

"Don't die, Durdy darling," she whispered.

"Over the edge. Going now. Let me go. My last baby. Let me go—oh, Kitten, let me go."

"Oh, Durdy, I love you, but you must go if you want to. Oh, Durdy, there's only you . . ."

Forgetting all about Theale, Louise crouched by the bed and slid her left arm under Durdy's shoulders. The body seemed as light as that of a dead bird picked up, fluffed and frozen, starved with midwinter.

"I mun choose," breathed Durdy. "You've bin tearing me in two. I mun steay wi' my girls, and I cawn't teake you wi' me. I mun be their Durdy, always there. Doan't cry, Kittten . . ."

Louise was crying in smooth, easy sobs, sobs not wrenched from her but as natural as singing. She craned forward to kiss the mottled old cheeks and didn't start or look up when the room filled with a crash, a warning shout, the crack of a gun and the yells of men. Somebody touched her shoulder. She shrugged the hand away. Through the blur of tears she saw it come down, move the bedclothes aside and feel for the pulse of Durdy's "good" hand, whose arm lay along the sheet as thin as the shank of a heron. She kissed the dry forehead again and gently lowered Durdy back onto her pillows.

"She's gone," said Father quietly.

The strangeness of his voice made Louise look up. Her tears distorted his face, but when she wiped her eyes on the sheet she saw that the real face was twisted with grief, like her own face reflected in the window. Tears ran down either side of the nose and hung in droplets from the corners and fringe of the moustache. He was looking down at Durdy.

Staring at him, at this real person, Louise rose groggily to her feet. She found Mother close beside her, pale and tearless, so she reached out an arm to hold her close to her. Several men were standing around at the other end of the room, and one kneeling by Theale's body where it lay face down between the table and the dolls' shelf.

"Shot himself clean as a whistle," said somebody. "Neat little bastard to the very end."

◆ 15 ◆

MISS DURDON'S MEMORIAL service was held in St.
George's, Windsor, and everybody came, about a
third of them incognito—the Norways and the Swedens
and the Denmarks and the Belgiums and the Netherlands
and the poor deposed Greeces and all Mother's Spanish
cousins (forgetting for the day their feud about who should
have succeeded old Franco) and a charming Japanese Prince
(representing the enemy, so to speak) and dozens of deposeds
and exes, not to mention all the other cousins, innumerable
Mecklenberg-Baden-Hesses and similar many-barrelled Ger-
mans, kissing and crying, besides all the home-growns—the
Yorks and Clarences and Kents and so on, plus the usual
swarm of Mountbattens, and quite a lot more who weren't
really related at all but had, as it were, sent ambassadors to
Durdy's Kingdom—children to stay for Balmoral holidays—
Marlboroughs and Norfolks and such—a mighty ingathering,
a Royal mafia, a sceptered wake. Everybody revelled in the
event, their enjoyment spiced by the knowledge that it was a
very proper thing to be doing and perhaps the last time
they'd get the chance.

But only the Family went to Durdy's funeral, the service
in Balmoral kirk and the burial in the grounds of Abergeldie
Castle. Father, supposing he'd wanted it, would never have
dreamed of asking the owners of Abergeldie whether they
would allow him to be buried in their garden; but he had no

hesitation in insisting that they should let his old nanny have
the resting-place of her choice. Nobody knew why she'd
chosen it. Edward VII when Prince of Wales had merely
rented the Castle so that he could be within range of his
mother but out of the immediate draughts and disapprovals
of Balmoral. But chosen it she had, taking Father ten years
ago to show him the spot.

So they buried her there on a drenching October morning,
with streamlets runnelling off the stacked turves beside the
grave and falling in continuous lines from the rib-points of
the umbrellas. The minister had a bad cough. Louise saw
Father looking at him, clearly wondering whether he ought
to prescribe something. It was a dismal little ceremony, but
it felt right. Durdy was going to have a memorial tablet in
the kirk, but here there would be smooth lawn, smooth
snow in winter, under which she would lie as secret as the
secret of why she wanted to be buried here at all. Louise
thought it was something to do with Kitten. You couldn't
call a young man Kitten, and tell him not to cry; and it
wasn't the voice in which Durdy ever spoke to children. No
one would ever know. But I shan't carry my secret to the
grave, Louise thought. I'm not as strong as she was.

On the plane south everybody was tired and silent. Father
read despatches and Albert a zoology text-book while Mother
and Nonny played one of their endless games of six-pack
bezique. Louise looked out of the window at the last light
fading pinkly from the cloud-banks below. When it was
dark, somewhere over Manchester, she got up and crossed
to Father's chair.

"I want to talk to you," she whispered.

He nodded, rose and led her farther forward to the
compartment off the main saloon which he used as an office
for work on longer flights. Two chairs, a bleak desk, the
radio telephone extension. They sat down and he looked at
her with a question on his face.

"I'm not going to get over it," she said. "I can cope
with it, but I can't go back to what it was like before."

"Sorry about that. That was a good time."

"Yes."

"What do you want me to say, more than that I'm sorry?"

"I don't know. What did you say to Mother?"

"How did you know I'd told her?"

"The day after Pilfer... she was sitting in my room. I knew something else had happened. I didn't know what till I heard Durdy telling Theale that he'd killed McGivan, so it wasn't McGivan I saw."

"All right. Yes. I told Bella just what happened. You want me to tell you?"

"Will it be any use?"

"Perhaps—if you think I'd gone up there, dressed up as McGivan, so as to get a chance of screwing Kinunu. Is that what you thought, Lulu?"

"Yes."

"Well, you're wrong, my girl. Bella trusted me better than that. I suppose I'll have to go through it all again ... look, I was pretty well certain that McGivan was the joker, but I wanted to be dead sure. I'd made the same guess as you about him listening to the monitor. It was going to be tricky enough tackling him about what he knew without having to cope with not being quite certain whether he did know it. So I chose a point when I thought he'd be helping with the security check before the reception, waxed my moustache and trotted up to see Kinunu. You'll remember I asked you to go and have tea with Durdy. My idea was that McGivan had simply persuaded Kinunu to let him turn on the monitor in the Night Nursery and see what we were talking about, and I wanted to check how she reacted when I tried it. But I'd hardly put my face round the door before she was all over me, tugging me into her bedroom as though she couldn't wait for an instant. That's when I should have put a stop to things—then—soon as they started. But I didn't want to let on I wasn't McGivan and I did want to check about the monitor. Besides that, I was ... well ... inquisitive. McGivan of all people! I won't pretend, Lulu, that the sex urge wasn't there too, but at my age ... after all, I spent a lot of my early manhood fending off women who threw themselves at me ... it still happens quite a bit ... you'd be surprised ..."

"Go on."

"I don't want to be unfair to the girl. She was very good to Durdy. But it was a bit outside my experience. One moment I was sitting on the edge of the bed and she was switching that monitor on for me—so far, so good, I thought—and the next she was all over me, tumbling together, all our clothes on, she didn't even give me a chance to kick my shoes off, with me thinking of McGivanish things to say to get me out of this, and then, just as suddenly, she'd maneuvered me to the edge of the bed, given a quick wriggle and heaved me off. That was fine by me. I got up, ready to go, when I saw her lying there, giggling and looking sideways at me. I saw it was a game, a game she always played. She never let McGivan get anywhere with her, and never would. She'd spotted that he'd never quite have the confidence . . . he had the most frightful mother, my grandfather's half-sister . . ."

"I don't see what that's got to do with it."

Father shrugged.

"A bit," he said. "And quite a bit with what he did to your room. In fact I'd bet that if Kinunu hadn't been leading him up the garden path and then slamming the door in his face, he wouldn't have exploded like that. Still . . . I won't pretend I thought about any of that at the time. All I thought about was old McGivan, never being given a chance by anyone, everybody's butt—oh, I know it was all my fault bringing him down to London in the first place—but here he was, and this cunning little bint . . . I blew my top. I'll teach her, I thought. I suppose I also thought that if I got her over the first hurdle then she might let McGivan have what he wanted and that'd make him easier to cope with . . . No, that's only a rationalization. I was pretty blind with fury for old McGivan . . ."

"So you raped her?"

Father stared, looking for an instant as though he was going to yell at her. Then he smiled and pulled at his mustache.

"You saw her, Lulu. Did she look like a girl who'd just been raped?"

"No, I suppose not."

"So I should bloody well think. The trouble with you, Lulu, is that you've become so grown-up of a sudden that one forgets that there are areas in which you haven't the experience to evolve an adult judgment. Look at it this way—what good would I be doing old McGivan if she hadn't enjoyed herself? Make her more of a tease, if anything. I suppose a text-book would say something like I aroused her sexual urge sufficiently to overcome a superficial neurosis . . . You want me to go into details?"

"No."

"Well, that's what happened. Bloody good thing you didn't start shouting half way through."

"What do you mean?"

"Well, you can imagine I'd rather forgotten the original object of the expedition while all this was going on, but the monitor was there with you and Durdy burbling away about something, and I was just about coming up for air when I noticed Durdy was sounding a bit odd. She was telling you about some man—Edward the Seventh I think it must have been—and how women reacted to him."

"That's right. She said she didn't know whether he was attractive. She said you'd have to be 'a rich lady' to know that. She thought that with servants he was more like a hunter. And then she said something very unDurdyish about a wee bird in the heather."

"Yes, I heard that. It made me feel a bit rum, I can tell you, but not half as bad as when you yelled out you were glad I wasn't like that and it would spoil everything."

"I'd forgotten. I was right, wasn't I?"

"Everything, Lulu?"

"No, I suppose not. No, not everything."

"Is what I've told you any use to you?"

"I don't know yet. I expect so. Yes. That foul clock . . ."

"I made a mess of that. I didn't realize how critical McGivan's time of death was going to be—I just put it forward as far as I dared—I'd made a guess at his body temperature. The first pathologist's report said he'd been dead longer, but there were a couple of discrepancies in it and they had it all rechecked—do you remember d'Arcy talking about that?—so I thought I could afford to hang on and see. Perhaps I was over-influenced by what I'd heard you saying about spoiling everything. Meanwhile Durdy guessed what had happened and got Kinunu to keep fiddling the clock, which only made it harder to back out of the mess. While there was still a good chance that McGivan had been killed by terrorists I didn't think the time of death would be absolutely critical. But the mayhem in Bert's zoo shook me up . . . and then Pilfer . . . it took me a day or so to realize that in spite of the evidence I couldn't swallow the idea of Pilfer going off the rails like that. And then there was the fact that d'Arcy was the hell of a chap to persuade to look at things any other way than his own . . . But that very morning when Kinunu brought me your SOS from the Nursery I'd made up my mind that as soon as I'd sat on my bog I'd go and tell d'Arcy that it wasn't McGivan you'd seen up there."

He stopped at the sound of a light tap on the door, just audible through the engine-boom. At Father's call Captain Tabard's head poked into the office.

"Message from Heathrow, Your Majesty. We're landing in about ten minutes, and apparently there's quite a crowd waiting for you."

"Oh Lord. How big?"

"About half what the Osmonds had last time they flew in. I saw that. Even half of it's a lot of people."

"Hell," said Father. "Can't divert, I suppose—not fair on the poor sods, anyway. Thanks, Captain. Will you tell Her Majesty?"

"Will do, Sir."

The head withdrew. Father stretched and sighed.

"Well, I think that's all I can usefully tell you," he said. "We'll just have to try to build things up, best we can."

"There's something else," said Louise. "You don't have to do this at once, and you'll have to get Nonny to agree—and Mother too, I suppose—but as soon as you can manage it I want people to know that I'm a bastard."

He had started to get up, but dropped back into his chair and stared at her, very tense.

"We've only got ten minutes," he said at last.

"I know. We can talk about it properly later. I don't want

to hurt anybody. I've found I still love you—all three of you. But don't you see, if we hadn't had to keep it secret none of this would have happened? I suppose McGivan would have played his jokes, but they wouldn't have done any harm. But now he's dead, and Pilfer's dead, and Theale, and you went and made love to Kinunu, all because we thought we had to go on lying about me. I want to stop being a lie—provided Nonny agrees, I mean. That's important."

"I'm glad you think so. But she's not the only one, Lulu. For instance, have you thought about Derek Oliphant?"

"Who's he?"

"The obstetrician who went along with us in pretending that Bella was pregnant when she wasn't. I had to put a lot of pressure on him about that. He'd be ruined if it came out."

"If it was wrong in the first place he needn't have agreed."

"But don't you see, Lulu, I picked him *because* I thought he would give in to pressure? And he's only an example: the effects would be far wider than you can imagine. Put it this way—supposing it would involve my abdication, would you still insist on the truth coming out?"

"No. No, of course not. Would it?"

"About fifty-fifty, I'd say."

"Oh . . . there isn't time, now . . . look, if you'll promise to see if you can find a way of doing it . . . it doesn't have to be at once . . . by my eighteenth birthday, for instance. But the other thing is I want to stop princessing and start living more like Nonny—I know I can't get out of everything, but . . . look, even if I've got to go on being a lie, I don't have to live like a lie all the time, do I? I won't let you down, but do you see . . . ?"

"I see very well, darling. It's my argument with Nonny all over again. But I'm glad you think her feelings are important. She doesn't show them, but that doesn't mean she doesn't have them. You ought to know that if anyone."

"Because I'm a bit like her doesn't meant I'm like her all through. I'm myself."

"Of course you are. But listen. I told her about me and Kinunu . . ."

"I expect she thought it was funny," said Louise sourly.

"She laughed. But there are laughs and laughs. It was Nonny who made me tell Bella."

"Oh. I meant . . ."

He snorted and rose as the jet-boom changed its note. They went back into the saloon, settled into arm-chairs, swung them to face aft and worked the cunning seat-belts that locked them in that position for the landing. Do I believe him? thought Louise. Half and half. I bet he didn't say anything that wasn't true. But I bet he enjoyed himself with Kinunu. And I bet there's been things like that before—in fact I can remember Mother having that sad old face once when I was quite small. And he'd get away without her knowing most times. It's my fault, my minding so much. I wanted them to be a Paradise Island, but they're people. I expect Mother's done things she's ashamed of, by being careless or blind or angry. She can be almost mad when she's angry. I'll hurt people too, I expect, quite often. Granny's right about that. I must have hurt them horribly when I was hanging out on the window-sill, making up my mind to drop, thinking only about me and how I felt. I was even sort of glad I was hurting them. That's horrible . . . I was trying to make story Parents out of them, and when they spoilt the story . . .

She yawned with the pressure-change. The plane bumped, once, and she let the deceleration down the runway sink her into the upholstery while she listened to the strangely satisfying well-that's-over note of the reversed jets. I wonder if Nonny's been faithful to him all the time, either, she thought. Mother has, of course. I mightn't even be his daughter . . . No, that's nonsense, that's starting another sort of story. They love me. He loves me. That isn't half-and-half. I love them too—not Paradise Island, but people . . . and I'm free now. He'll find a way of letting me go. I think Nonny might be glad to stop the lie, too—it must have been a frightful strain on her, sometimes. And when Mother sees it's right . . . And I'll never need to remind him that I've seen him standing to attention by Kinunu's bed, with his trousers round his ankles, snuffling . . .

As the plane swung to its bay Father twisted to peer through the rain-streaked window.

"I'll never understand the GBP," he said. "Not if I live till I'm as old as Durdy. Here we are, an expensive luxury, time of crisis, pound at two dollars—we let the Family get itself into a godawful mess, mostly my fault—bombs and murders and other unbecoming mayhem—and then more by luck than judgment we get ourselves out again, and they turn up in thousands to cheer us as if we'd just flown in from winning a war single-handed. God, it's absolutely pissing down. At least somebody's managed to find the steps this time. No thank you, Turner, we'll have to do without brollies and brave the elements—there's a lot of them on the roof up there and they won't see a thing otherwise. Will you go first, darling? I'll come slap behind you. Leave a bit of a gap, Lulu—you're the one they want to see—sure you can face that?—then Bert. OK, Turner, tell them to open up."

The rain was streaks of diamond under the floodlights and made a rattly drumming on the metal of wings and fuselage. A big jet was taking off, but both sounds were drowned by the crash of cheers as Mother stepped out into the rain. When Father followed her the noise screwed itself up a pitch. Louise saw Nonny smugly getting her umbrella ready to open. She squeezed her hand, got a squeeze back, put on her public face—the one for use at funerals—and walked to the door. The white, lit faces were banked shingle, the rain was spume, the cheers were roaring surf. She paused at the top step, as though waiting for Albert. Flashlights sparkled like fireworks at a Royal birth. As she came down the steps she thought, I hope Durdy's watching. This is just her cup of tea.

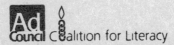